D1425922

# DEAN CLOSE SCHOOL

## LIBRARY

This book must be returned by the latest date stamped below

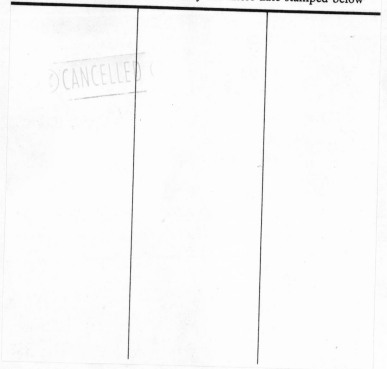

CANCELLED

# Dress in Eighteenth-Century England

*To*
*A. B. and E. B.*

# Dress in Eighteenth-Century England

Anne Buck

B. T. Batsford Ltd   London

First published 1979
© Anne Buck 1979

Filmset by Keyspools Ltd, Golborne, Lancs
Printed by The Anchor Press Ltd, Tiptree, Essex,
for the Publishers B. T. Batsford Ltd,
4 Fitzhardinge Street, London W1H 0AH

ISBN 0 7134 0415 9

# Contents

Acknowledgments                                                    6

*Introduction*                                                     9
The Evidence

*I  Crown and Court*                                              13

*II  People of Fashion*                                           25
Full Dress, The Influence of France, Masquerade, Fashion
at Home, Fashion Out-of-Doors, Mourning

*III  The Gentry*                                                 64
The Country, The City, Spas and Watering Places

*IV  Servants*                                                   103

*V  The Common People*                                           120
Farming People and the Country Towns,
Labourers and Small Tradesmen,
The Northern Counties, Wales, The Poor

*VI  Buying and Making Clothes*                                  156
Shopping in Europe, London Shops,
Wigs and Hairdressing, Provincial Shopping,
Travelling Salesmen, Markets and Fairs, Second-
hand Clothes, Making Clothes

*VII  Fabrics and Wearers*                                       186

*VIII  Dress and Society*                                        201

*Notes*                                                          211

*Glossary*                                                       225

*Bibliography*                                                   229

*Index*                                                          233

# *Acknowledgments*

I have been fortunate in the many opportunities I have had to study and discuss eighteenth-century dress with colleagues in museums. From them and others, who have shed light on particular aspects of it from their own special studies, I have gathered knowledge and ideas, consciously and unconsciously, over so many years, that it is not now possible to make individual acknowledgment of all the help that I have received. I hope all will accept this collective acknowledgment of my debt.

For help while I was actually preparing this book I should like to thank Mrs Vanda Foster, Keeper of the Gallery of English Costume, Manchester; Miss Kay Staniland of the Museum of London; Miss Penelope Byrde of the Costume Research Centre, Bath; Miss Patricia Bell, Bedfordshire County Archivist and her predecessor, Miss Joyce Godber; Miss Natalie Rothstein, Deputy Keeper of Textiles, Victoria and Albert Museum, for her help with eighteenth-century textiles; and Miss Evelyn Vigeon of Salford Museum for the reference from Samuel Bamford's *Tawk o' Searth Lankeshur*.

For permission to quote from archives deposited at the Bedfordshire County Record Office I am most grateful to Lady Lucas (Wrest Park Papers); Mrs C. Manning (Williamson Letters) and Mr R. and Mr N. Bagshawe (Diary of John Blundell). The passage from *Ann Cook and Friend*, edited by Regula Burnet, is quoted by permission of the Oxford University Press.

Finally I thank my niece, Mrs Elizabeth Bentley for her interest and patience in typing the manuscript, my brother and sister-in-law for reading it and Miss Ruth M. Taylor of Batsfords for her careful guidance of its progress from manuscript to book.

## Acknowledgments for Illustrations

Figs 31 and 69 are reproduced by Gracious Permission of Her Majesty the Queen.

For permission to reproduce other illustrations I am indebted to:

Ashmolean Museum, Oxford, 68, 72;
Bedfordshire County Record Office, 40, 73, 84;
City Museums and Art Gallery, Birmingham, 81;
Bowood Collection, 32;
The British Library, Col. pl. 3, 33, 53, 56, 77, 88;
Buckinghamshire County Museum, Aylesbury, 24, 25;
Trustees of the Cadland Settled Estate, 65;

Courtauld Institute, University of London (photograph), 90;

The Earl of Mar and Kellie, K. T. and the Scottish National Portrait Gallery, 26;

Fitzwilliam Museum, Cambridge, 5, 43, 45, 58;

Glasgow Museums and Art Galleries, 35;

University Art Collections, Glasgow, 12;

The Greater London Council as Administrators of Marble Hill House, Twickenham, 16;

The Trustees, The Cecil Higgins Art Gallery, Bedford, 22, 64, 89;

The Executors of Miss Olive Lloyd-Baker, and the National Portrait Gallery, Col. pl. 2;

Lady Lucas, and the Bedfordshire County Record Office, 66;

Gallery of English Costume, Manchester City Art Galleries, 3, 4, 9, 14, 15, 17, 18, 21, 27, 36, 38, 67, 76, 82, 83, 85, 86;

Museum of English Rural Life, University of Reading, 71;

The Trustees, The National Gallery, London, 8, 28;

National Museum of Wales, 78;

National Museum of Wales (Welsh Folk Museum), 2;

National Portrait Gallery, 1, 10, 20, 30, 34, 47, 49, 50, 61;

Norfolk Museums Service (Norwich Castle Museum), 19;

The Royal Bank of Scotland Ltd., and the Paul Mellon Centre for Studies in British Art (photograph), 46;

Southampton Art Gallery, 37;

The Tate Gallery, London, 6, 11, 55, 57, 59, 62, 63, 70;

Temple Newsam House, Leeds City Art Galleries, 29, 87;

Tyne and Wear County Council Museum Service, Laing Art Gallery, Newcastle, 79;

Victoria and Albert Museum, Crown Copyright, Col. pls. 1 and 4, 23, 39, 41, 42, 44, 51, 60, 74, 75, 80, 91;

Walker Art Gallery, Liverpool, 7, 13, 54;

Whitworth Art Gallery, University of Manchester, 52;

The Estate of the late Mr R. G. Wrightson and Norfolk Museums Service, Norwich Castle Museum, 48.

# Introduction

Clothes satisfy the basic physical needs of the human body for protection, warmth and comfort, but as far back and as widely as we can trace, no sooner have these needs been satisfied than clothes become a means of personal and social expression. New threads enter the basic fabric of use and weave into it an infinite variety of pattern. The patterns change with time, but are not dependent on time alone. Each period, each decade, shows its unrepeatable pattern as changes come, slowly or swiftly, changes which finally replace one human appearance by another. Many small changes are no more than the expression of a passing moment, a whim, a temporary variation of decoration, slight shifts of emphasis. These changes make dress, at first glance, appear the most ephemeral, trivial and extravagant of human expressions and may obscure the importance of the major changes. Yet they catch the mood of a passing moment and can reflect a facet of their time.

Fashion in the widest sense of the word is change. Fashion in dress is the creation of one style after another as time passes and this sequence, which is a striking feature of European dress, particularly in the last five hundred years, has been the subject of much study. What has been less studied is the complexity of dress, the variations it shows from any one of these styles, which at any moment make up the whole dress of a society. The fashionable sequence and this more complex pattern, which also changes with time, have no simple relationship. There are variations according to country, or regions within a country; the natural division of sex and age; the wearer's place or function in society, through status, occupation, or way of life; the ritual occasions of life; work and leisure; and, however limited, personal choice. Even the simplest society has its patterns of dress and the more complex and changing the society the more variations of human appearance, the more complex and shifting the patterns of dress are likely to be.

Any major change affects more than fashionable dress, the dress of people who shape change and exhibit fashion. It is a major change only when it is more widely understood and accepted. Understanding and acceptance may be slow, but a readiness to accept, a response to something new, yet recognised, must be there. The last twenty years of the eighteenth century saw the shaping of a new European style. There

9

are recognisable differences between the dress of 1730 and 1770 for both men and women, but the basic style is the same. The difference between the dress of 1770 and that of 1800 is a complete difference, two distinct styles. It is often stated that this change was the result of the French Revolution: a glance at the dress of 1775 and 1795 may confirm this view. Closer examination reveals that the beginning of change, in dress as in revolution, goes back a long way. In the following chapters I hope to show something of the variety of dress worn in eighteenth-century England; the relation of clothes to the people who wore them; to what they were doing when they wore them; to opportunities for buying or otherwise acquiring them. For it was from this variety, from the gradual change in several patterns of dress coming together, that this major change emerged.

## The Evidence

Clothes surviving from the eighteenth century are a random selection which chance has preserved from the variety of clothes worn. Many of them clearly fall within the fashionable sequence. Others, though still equally clearly of eighteenth-century origin, are more difficult to place within it. Even after those mutilated at a later date are eliminated a large number remain which show only a rather basic fashion. Other garments, fewer in number, do not appear to relate to fashion at all. It is easy to dismiss both these groups—and together they form a fairly large proportion of surviving dress—simply as unfashionable. Knowledge of who wore them is generally lacking; for what occasion, where, or for how long they were worn; how they were made or acquired. But each garment has its own signs; we may not see them, we may not be able to read them correctly, but all surviving dress preserves some evidence of the total appearance of its time, of the pattern of dress of which it was part. We see the different shapings, the cut and construction which make the technical variations of form and the evolution from style to style; the variety of texture of their fabrics and the way fabric and form work together in change; the changing taste expressed in the pattern of fabrics and in the accessories and decoration of dress. What has survived is often incomplete. The accessories worn with it, originally separate—ruffles, tuckers and handkerchiefs—have been permanently separated. Trimmings, ruchings, puffs and flounces of matching material usually remain, but the added festoons of gauze and flowers and gold and silver foils, which trimmed dress in the last quarter of the century were often removed for re-use and in any case were too fragile to survive very long. The final shape of a garment depends not only on its own cut but on all its supporting garments of stays, hoop and petticoat; it is rare for these to survive with the dress with which they were worn. It depends too on the human body which wore it, for the wearer, like the clothes, was an eighteenth-century creation.

Paintings, drawings and prints give us a view of dress, reduced to two dimensions, but seen in its own time. Each artist has his own response to dress. In portraits this ranges from a careful attention to detail, so that the patterned silk of a dress or coat can be matched with surviving silks or designs, to an ignoring of detail but a confident interpretation of essential line and style, so that dress and sitter become a living image—an ideal image—of their time. Like everyone else, the artist works within the influence of his time as well as with his individual vision. Evidence of eighteenth-century dress from its portraits is confused by fashion in painting itself. From the 1730s fashionable people were often painted in a version of seventeenth-century dress, after the much-admired Vandyke. From the 1760s they submitted to the convention of being painted in a compromise between the contemporary style and the dignified ambiguity of classical draperies. Some artists imposed a dress, which though fashionable could be peculiar to the portrait and not the usual wear of the sitter: 'A note from Romney to desire me to dress myself in white Sattin before I come to him today. ... The Borrowed Gown won't satisfy him, he insists upon my having a rich white Sattin with a long train made by Tuesday and to have it left with him all summer.'[1] Lady Newdigate's sittings for this portrait continued from 1790 to 1792.

The poet, dramatist and novelist, like the artist, portray the eighteenth century in their own terms: 'Perhaps you will say I should not take my Ideas of the manners of the time from such trifling Authors, but it is more truly to be found amongst them than from any Historian.'[2] Lady Mary Wortley Montagu is commenting on contemporary novels in 1753. Dress may appear, used consciously to create character through appearance, sometimes with the edge of caricature; but often it comes effortlessly, almost unconsciously, into scene or action, a single phrase vividly evoking its physical quality or its social nuance.

Dress as it appears in letters and diaries is the real dress of men and women of known position in society, whose characters and ways of life are also revealed in these personal records. Because many people relied on letters for news of new fashions, and commissioned relatives and friends in their letters to buy garments and materials for them, exact and detailed descriptions of what was needed and what was available often appear in personal correspondence. Many of the travellers who came to England from Europe during the century kept diaries or wrote a series of letters home, describing what they saw. Their skill as observers and their range of experience is uneven and most of them did not travel far from London, but they give another view of English dress, a view which highlights its variations from other European fashion.

Journalism flourished during the century, with the essay developing as a characteristic literary form. From the years of *The Tatler* and *The Spectator* contemporary fashions were a frequent subject for comment. What was said in *The Tatler* and *The Spectator* is well known, but there were a score of periodicals of long or short life, some still remembered, some forgotten by all but specialist students of the period, which raised a constant voice on fashion and manners. Moralists of every age have never been in doubt about the relation of dress to morality or, more often, to immorality and social chaos, and much of this writing has a strong moral tone. Sometimes the morality is supporting economic pleading as writers speak for the many industries and trades which depend on dress and which could be destroyed or made prosperous by a change of fashion. Only in the last quarter of the century do journalists begin to give information of current fashion with no other intent, although comment still flows in essays in the same journals. At the same time journals produced particularly for women were fully launched as a special branch of journalism.

Apart from the large group of purely factual records, the inventories of personal possessions, the commercial transactions of buying and selling, all written evidence will be coloured by the purpose, attitudes and limits of experience of the writer. We need to know who is speaking and why, as well as what is being said. We need also to remember that what is not being said, because then taken for granted, is what we now want to know; and that we ourselves are always missing what people of the time caught and understood.

# I

# *Crown and Court*

The view that dress expressed status in society was an unchallenged commonplace of the eighteenth century. The rulers of the country and the leaders of English society were a small group of noble families, of older and newer creation, who controlled politics at home and in embassies abroad. Their power and wealth came from their large estates and the revenues from them, but they also accumulated wealth from other sources by remote control. They were an exclusive group, but from time to time their ranks opened, particularly under pressure of political expediency, to admit wealth acquired in the professions, commerce and banking, and then closed again. At the end of the century the number of peers was almost twice what it had been at the beginning.

Socially this group formed the society of the court, and the core of fashionable society. Within it the isolated majesty of the crown was emphasised in the dress of high ceremony, at coronations and royal weddings, a dress set apart by its archaic element and a display of precious metals and jewels of an assessable magnificence.

When George I came to the English throne in 1714 no queen accompanied him—divorced and disgraced, she was imprisoned in Hanover—but the two later queens who were crowned in the eighteenth century, in 1727 and 1761, and the daughters of George II at their marriages wore a form of dress already out of fashion at the time of Queen Anne's accession (Fig 1). At the Coronation of George II and Queen Caroline in 1727 all the ladies bearing the Queen's train wore stiff-bodied gowns, including the three princesses who held the tip of it: 'stiff-bodied gowns of silver tissue embroidered or quite covered with silver trimmings, with diadems upon their head, and purple mantles edged with ermine and vast long train.'[1] One of these princesses, Anne, married the Prince of Orange in 1734, again dressed in silver tissue: 'The Princess of Orange's dress was the prettiest thing that ever was seen—a corps de robe, that is in plain English, a stiff-bodied gown. The eight peers' daughters that held up her train were in the same sort of dress—all white and silver, with great quantities of jewels in their hair and long locks.' At the court which followed the day after the wedding the Prince of Orange was 'in a gold stuff embroidered with silver; it looked rich but not showy. The King was in gold stuff which made much more

1 *Augusta, Princess of Wales, 1736, wearing the stiff-bodied royal gown of ceremony.*
*Charles Philips*

2 *Mantua and petticoat, blue silk damask, embroidered in silver, showing the draping of the mantua over the hips; each embroidered motif of the petticoat is worked within a width of silk, but together form a single pattern over the joined widths. Probably a court dress of c. 1740 worn by a lady of the Morgan family.*

show, with diamond buttons to his coat. . . . The Queen's clothes were a green ground flowered with gold and several shades, but grave and handsome; her head was loaded with pearls and diamonds.'[2] In 1740 the Princess Mary married. Lady Hartford went to see a display of the bride's clothes 'all laid out in order, on two tables, which are the whole length of the poor queen's state bedchamber.' Amongst them 'the stiff-bodied gown she is to be married in, is very nearly the same as the princess royal's was.'[3]

In 1761, little more than twenty-four hours after she had landed in England from a stormy Channel crossing, Princess Charlotte dressed for her marriage to George III, 'in a Silver Tissue, stiffen-body'd Gown, embroidered and trimmed with Silver, on her head a little Cap of purple Velvet quite covered with Diamonds, a Diamond Aigrette in the form of a Crown, 3 dropt Diamond Earrings, Diamond Necklace, Diamond Sprigs of Flowers in her Sleeves and to clasp back her Robe, a diamond Stomacher, her purple Velvet Mantle was laced with Gold and lined with Ermine. It was fastened on the shoulder with long Tossels of Pearls.' The bridesmaids, peers' daughters, also wore 'stiffen-bodied gowns of white Silk, the Stays and Sleeves embroidered and their Petticoats trimmed with Silver and all adorned with a great number of Jewells.' The King also wore silver, 'stuff a new manufacture the Ground Silver flower with embossed plate and frosted silver.'[4]

The stiff-bodied gown was a boned bodice worn with a separate petticoat and train. At the time of its wearing for these ceremonial occasions the usual court wear was a mantua and petticoat. The mantua had entered fashion informally as a loose gown but had now been shaped by pleating the back and stitching the pleats to fit the upper half of the body, or rather the stays which gave it shape. The skirt fell long and full and was lifted and draped at the back, or made a train for court wear (Fig. 2).

Gold and silver in fabrics and trimming and the costly splendour of jewels marked royal dress on other formal occasions. At the Prince of Wales's birthday court in 1739 the Princess was 'In white satin, the petticoat covered with a gold trimming like embroidery, faced and robed with the same, her head and stomacher a rock of diamonds and pearls.'[5] Among the gowns of Princess Mary which Lady Hartford saw was

> 'a stuff on a gold ground, prodigiously fine, with flowers shaded up to the middle of the breadths like painting, and a kind of embossed work of blue and silver towards the edges. Mrs Purcell assured me that she bought the gold by itself, before the stuff was woven; and that there was in it no less than eighteen pounds weight. This to me sounds incredible; but she affirms it to be true.'[6]

The magnificent dress of royalty at court was, however, well matched by the dress of their noble and wealthy subjects. Lady Spencer was at court in bridal white and silver after her wedding in 1756, 'as fine as brocade and trimming could make it', but this was only a background for a magnificent display of jewels:

> 'The diamonds were worth twelve thousand pounds, her earrings, three drops, all diamonds, no paltry scrolls of silver. Her necklace most perfect brilliants, the middle stone worth a thousand pounds and set at the edge with small brilliants. . . . Her cap all brilliants (made in the fashion of a small butterfly skeleton) had a very good effect with a pompon and behind where you may suppose the bottom of the caul, a knot of diamonds, with two little puffs of diamonds where the lappets are fastened and two shaking sprigs of brilliants for her hair; six roses all brilliants for her stays.'[7]

Lady Shelburne, dressed for a royal christening of 1768 'was so illuminated with jewels and radiant with gold and silver she must have added splendour even to that magnificent assembly.'[8]

Wealth displayed was the essence of this dress, the richness of the silks, their elaborate woven patterns or intricate embroideries, fine lace and above all costly jewels. Rich embroidery all over gown and petticoat could be as costly as work in gold and silver. Mrs Montagu was having such a gown made, 'at a cheap rate', that is the embroideress was doing it at her own pace, when the Queen saw it, 'fell in love with it, gives 130 guineas for it.'[9] The magnificent embroidery of the Duchess of Queensberry's clothes in 1741 was described with admiration by Mrs Delany, herself a skilled embroideress:

> 'They were white satin embroidered, the bottom of the petticoat brown

hills covered with all sorts of weeds, and every breadth had an old stump of a tree that run up almost to the top of the petticoat broken and ragged and worked with brown chenille, round which twined nasturtians, ivy, honeysuckles, periwinkles, convolvuluses, and all sorts of twining flowers which spread and covered the petticoat, vines with the leaves variegated as you have seen them by the sun all rather smaller than nature, which made them look very light; the robings and facings were little green banks, all sorts of weeds, and the sleeves and the rest of the gown loose living branches of the same sort as those on the petticoat; many of the leaves were finished with gold and part of the stumps of the trees looked like the gilding of the sun. I never saw a piece of work so prettily fancied.'[10]

Not all birthday courts were equally brilliant. In 1737 'My daughter Verney was at Court of the birthday; there was very little finery, abondance of People in Striped Lutestring.'[11] In 1738 Mrs Delany reported that there was to be 'no finery at the Birthday, by his Majesty's desire. Princess Amelia has a stuff of 30s a yard without either gold or silver.'[12] Queen Caroline had died a year before and the court was only just out of the period of mourning. The price of the Princess's gown seems to have been well known, for Lady Hartford also wrote of it: 'I will not enter into a detail of the finery; but that you may judge of it in the general will give one instance as a specimen of the whole; and that is in the Princess Amelia who had on a yellow and silver which cost thirty shillings a yard.'[13] On the other hand, in the year following the death of the Prince of Wales, 1752, Lady Jane Coke reported that

'there was more finery at the Birthday than ever I saw; don't imagine I was at Court, but I went to Lady Betty Germain's, where great numbers came to show themselves. Lady Coventry, Lady Caroline Petersham and Mrs Watson (she was Miss Pelham) were allowed the finest; their clothes had all silver grounds and coloured flowers with silver mixed and a great quantity of jewels in their hair.'[14]

The Queen's birthday court of 1764 was one of great display: 'I never saw anything equal to the Court on Wednesday. There was hardly a gentleman or gentlewoman in London who was not expiring under a load of finery. Indeed I was one of the fools myself.'[15] Four years later it was, according to Lady Mary Coke, a poor show: 'I heard there, many people had gone to Court, on the Queen's Birthday, in Clothes they had the year before and that it was the Worst Ball that had ever been remembered.'[16]

Not every one entitled by birth or position to attend court functions was dressed with equal magnificence. Some appeared, like Mrs Delany at the Prince of Wales's birthday court in 1739, 'humbly drest in my pink damask, white and gold handkerchief, plain green ribbon, and Lady Sunderland's buckles for my stays.'[17] Jewels were often lent by relatives and friends for such occasions. Mrs Montagu at a court of 1769 said she was 'not gorgeously dressed. A corded blue tabby trimmed with

Ermine, which with fine lace and jewels, makes a respectable figure and as I had the Ermine cost me little.'[18] Lady Macartney thought in 1785 that

> 'it would be right for me to go this year, and also to have a gown rather more expensive than a plain lustring, yet I grudge any expense for my dress. I therefore determined to have some sort of trimming made at home and knowing nothing about the matter myself and my maid being as ignorant, we have together contrived an ugly thing which costs twice as much as I intended.'[19]

But with fine lace and jewels her 'ugly thing' too would have been acceptable, even if not greatly admired.

Style changed slowly in this formal dress: 'If I were to describe their clothes to you', wrote Lady Hartford about a birthday court of 1740, 'you would say you had seen them (or just such) at every birthday that you can remember.'[20] The hoop which came into wear in 1710 was accepted with the mantua of court dress and as it widened, developing its most imposing forms, oblong and fan-shaped in the 1740s and 1750s, the draped skirt of the mantua was folded back and secured as a rectangular train, with the wide petticoat now fully exposed. During the last twenty years of the century the bodice followed the changing line of fashion and its waistline rose: the hoop remained in its mid-century form but rose with the waistline, so that in 1800 it spread from just below the armpit. The hoop which disappeared from fashionable dress by the 1780s was caught and held in court wear, and there it remained, a purely court fashion until 1820 (Figs. 3, 4).

*3 Engraving from* The Lady's Magazine, *July, 1782, showing the birthday court of George III, June 1782. The hoops are still in the fashionable shape of the 1750s. For fashion plates showing court dress for 1768, 1771 see colour plate 1, and Fig. 39.*

*4 Fashion plate from* The Gallery of Fashion *by Nicholas Heideloff, 1799: court dress with the hoop still retained, making it now completely at variance with fashionable dress.*

During the first half of the century fashion was expressed in court dress mainly through change in its fabrics, the silks which spread in full display over the hoops. With new designs year by year, their patterns changed from the large, densely textured patterns of the first decades of the century to the more flowing patterns of the 1740s and 1750s, which the eighteenth-century term, 'flowered silks' describes perfectly. Gold and silver thread in these silks made them more splendid for court wear and costly to buy, but the more elaborate patterns could be costly enough without gold or silver. The gown Mrs Delany wore at court in 1729, 'the ground dark grass green, brocaded with a running pattern like lace, intermixed with festoons of flowers in faint colours,'[21] had the lace-like design fashionable in the 1720s. The silks Lady Anson looked at as she 'turned over all Carr's and Swann's shops two or three times' to find a silk for her sister-in-law for the birthday court of 1753, were of quite different character:

> 'The first is a Silk with a white Ground, a great deal of Silver, a little Gold and some fine Colors; the Silver forms diagonal Diamonds, in the midst of the Silver pattern there is a running Gold Stalk and some small and lively colored Flowers. This I would take for your Ladyship if I could venture without a farther commission to give 4£ pr yd which is the lowest price of it.'[22]

Some of these silks were made in very small quantity, so that exclusiveness was added to their value. In 1762 Lady Caroline Fox and her sister-in-law, the Duchess of Richmond, 'had much the handsomest clothes there, almost exactly alike, and the only two silks of the sort that have been made, the most beautiful shaded chenille flowers on a white satin ground without gold or silver.'[23] From the 1750s the changing character of fashionable dress, expressed in the lighter textures and patterns of its silks and a growing elaboration of accessories and trimming, was visible in court dress. Lady Anson wrote again about the gown for her sister-in-law, the Marchioness Grey:

> 'If your Ladyship would have your Sleeves with Ruffles which is the fashion, would you trim them with a Gold Blonde; a Gold Blonde round the bottom and up the Seams, Ruffles, Train, etc would not come to above 14 or 15£ and would trim a Sack after the Birthday was over, which was my project and would make it excessively pretty—But upon the modern scheme the Ruffles and Robing *must* be trimmed I think—and a stomacher and to suit (which I intended if I had taken this stuff and upon the Pettycoat too) the Ruffles may be trimmed with Silver you know.'[24]

By the 1770s the trimming could be more important and expensive than the fabric of the gown itself: 'As I always intended to have my gown highly trimmed, it would not be worth the while to bestow a high Price on a very rich Silk', Lady Polwarth, the Marchioness Grey's elder daughter, wrote to her sister:

'It must I should think be trimmed with a cheneel Blond and Flowers, chiefly blue and purple, lest it should look too yellow and staring; as to the Quantity of Trimming I can say nothing but that if it can be obtained I could wish the Mantua-maker would not make it come to much more than the Silk.'[25]

Sophie von La Roche watched her friend the Countess Reventlow dress for court in 1786:

'It was a delightful moment for me, when I offered my hand to the countess for her to step into her hoop, to which the skirt was already fixed; it was made of silver floss, with twining roses, the petals all of foil, like a rose-hedge in which a beauteous nymph, garlanded with flowers, wanted to hide, asking me to lend a hand. The sack with sleeves was of the same silver floss, trimmed with rich blonde lace, flowers and pearls. Nothing is gained by fastening up the train, for a great length is required so as to form a number of deep folds as it loops.'

She compared the hoops with those of Paris and found them just as large, but the train, which at Versailles trailed as a mark of respect, 'is here held up for the same reason.'[26]

A small cap with long lappets was the fashionable head-dress of the early years of the century. This remained as court wear, in fine lace, the lappets later pinned and looped up to the crown. A suit of lace for court wear continued to be an important and costly part of formal dress to the end of the century. When Lady Jemima Grey married Lord Ashburnham in 1723 the bill for her laces alone, omitting the materials involved in making them up into caps and ruffles, was £131. 5. 3; the 'fine loopt Brussels Sute', which cost £40 may well have been for court wear. The material for her wedding dress, a white and silver mantua and petticoat cost only a little more than this, £45.[27] Mrs Delany bought in 1743 'a very fine head, ruffles and tucker of Mrs Carter—new fashioned Brussels, it comes to near fifty pounds, is not that extravagant?'[28] Lace, like the silks, changed in pattern during the century, but these suits of lace are likely to have been worn for several years. Although lighter laces and silk gauzes were much worn in the second half of the century, lace of the finest linen thread in a suit for court wear was still the star item in any trousseau. In Miss Yorke's, in 1784, 'the Laces are beautiful especially the point suit value about 100£', and another Miss Yorke in 1790 also had 'a suit of fine point lace for Court.'[29] Feathers appeared with the lace and jewels from the 1750s and perhaps earlier, but according to Lady Louisa Stuart the Queen expressed such dislike of the towering plumes of the fashionable head-dresses of the 1770s that 'for two or three years no one ventured to wear them at Court, except some daring spirits either too supreme in fashion to respect any other kind of pre-eminence, or else connected with the Opposition and glad to set her Majesty at defiance.'[30] The Queen had practical reason for disliking the high plumes, as Fanny Burney realised: 'Charge the dear girls not to have their Feathers so long or so forward as to brush the royal cheek as they rise', she warned in 1798.[31] By this time feathers had become the orthodox head-dress. Louisa Holroyd wore two ostrich and one silver feather with silver gauze at her presentation in 1796.[32]

Men showed the same splendour at court as women. In 1700 the line of coat, waistcoat and breeches was, like that of women's dress, slim and vertical; the coat and waistcoat reached the knees, almost concealing the breeches; the vertical quality was emphasised by the wig, which rose high on the forehead and fell in long cascades of curls over the shoulders. As women's skirts spread out over the hoop, the skirts of men's coats swung out in stiffened pleats in a diagonal line from each hip: 'The Skirt of your fashionable Coats forms as large a circumference as our Petticoats; as these are set out with whalebone, so are those with Wire, to encrease and sustain the Bunch of Fold that hangs down on each side.'[33] Men and women shared the richly flowered damasks and brocades, the gold and silver and the fine embroideries. In 1722 Sarah Osborn wrote of the gentlemen at court:

> 'I believe the gentlemen will wear petticoats very soon for many of their coats were like our mantuas. Lord Essex has a silver tissue coat, and pink color lutestring waistcoat, and several had pink color and pale paduasoy coats, which looks prodigiously effeminate.'[34]

At the Prince of Wales's birthday court in 1739 Mrs Delany noticed that the gentlemen were wearing 'much finery, chiefly brown with gold or silver embroidery, rich waistcoats' and she thought the same in the following year, 'as fine as the ladies . . . my Lord Baltimore was in light brown and silver, his coat lined quite throughout with ermine.' She thought the Duke of Portland 'very fine' in 1753 in a coat of 'dark mouse-coloured velvet embroidered with silver; Jenny Glegg's work, and the finest I ever saw; the waistcoat Isabella satin, embroidered the same as the coat.'[35] There even appears to have been competition between men and women for the same material. The Countess of Hardwicke was disappointed in 1755 because 'Mr John has drest Lord Royston on the occasion in a velvet would have been agreeable to me; by which means I am at present unprovided.'[36] Velvet was much worn by men and often, at winter courts, by women. Cloth also appeared in court dress. Mrs Delany noted, with approval, in 1742, 'My Lord C. was in plain cloth; which was what it appeared to be a good warm, clean coat.'[37]

During the second half of the century the fullness of the coat skirt diminished and the pleats, no longer stiffened, moved from the side towards the back. At the same time the waistcoat shortened until by the 1780s its skirt had completely disappeared and it was cut horizontally at the waist. The high wigs lowered in the 1720s and the falling curls grew shorter; by 1750 they had shortened to the ears with a longer back section tied back. Fabric and ornament showed the same change as in women's dress. At the June drawing-room of 1778 Frederick Robinson wore a green poplin suit which had been made for him in Paris, 'verte brodée en perles, diamants et gaze' and found 'fewer cloaths handsomer or prettyer.' He reported the next year that the men were chiefly in silks with coloured borders, and particularly noted Mr Hatford in a green coat 'embroidered with real pearls and steel, very handsome and beautiful.'[38] Sir Joseph Yorke, for many years minister at the Hague, went to court in 1782, in clothes which, according to his sister-in-law, 'were the most elegant and richest embroidery I ever saw, the coat was carmelite velvet which set off his fine diamond star and order to perfection.'[39] This finery at court continued to the end of the century. Lord Sheffield's daughter saw the arrival of the Duke of Bedford at court in 1791, so grand that, 'when he arrived the Guard stood at Arms taking him for the Prince of Wales.' The dress he wore on this occasion was coat and breeches of brown striped silk shot with green, with a white waistcoat. All were embroidered in silver, blue foil and stones in wreaths of flowers for the borders and seams and the ground covered with single brilliants and silver spangles and it was estimated that it cost him £500.[40]

Until the last years of the century men's court dress was distinguished from fashionable wear only by this magnificence, although few might emulate the Duke's splendour. It followed conservatively the changing lines of coat, waistcoat and breeches, until the 1790s. Then in general wear breeches gradually lengthened down the calf to form tight-fitting pantaloons, preparing the way for the trousers, which came into fashionable wear in the first decade of the nineteenth century and made a complete change of form in men's dress. Breeches remained in court dress, and the lines of the coat and waistcoat as worn when fashion and court wear diverged, were preserved with them. Variety of fabric disappeared into plain dark silk or cloth. Embroidery, following the taste of the time became lighter, stereotyped and limited to the waistcoat. Men's court dress had become a uniform.

George III had created a uniform for the wear of the royal family and members of the royal household, the Windsor uniform, with dress and undress versions. At Chapel on the morning of the Prince of Wales's birthday in 1781 'the Gentlemen wore the undress uniform'; at the ball which followed, 'the Princes and all ... those belonging to the King's family wore the Windsor full Dress Uniform.'[41] An American loyalist saw the King on the terrace at Windsor in the same year 'drest in a blue Fly, cuffs small, open and turned up with red velvet, Cape of the same, buttons white, breeches and waistcoat white cotton, an ordinary white wig with a tail ribband, round black chip hat, smallish and of the same kind as is used in riding.' In the evening the King appeared again, this time in the 'full dressed blue uniform, Sword and Cockade, Prince of Wales the same.'[42] At the Thanksgiving Service for his recovery in 1789 the King appeared in the full-dress Windsor uniform and at the fête which was part of the celebrations the directions for dress were very precise for women as well as men.

> 'Everybody is to appear in a uniform, the men in the King's Hunt, which you have often seen, and the ladies in deep blue, trimmed with scarlet and gold the same colours. ... This dress, which by the Queen's directions is to be from Mrs Beauvais only, comes to thirty pounds.'[43]

Parson Woodforde went in a family party to see the royal family arrive at Sherborne from Weymouth to dine with Lord Digby in the same year. The royal party walked on the terrace and rode in open carriage through the park: 'The King was in his Windsor Uniform, blue coat with red Cape and Cuffs to the Sleeves, with a plain round Hat with a black Ribband round it. The Queen was in a purple Silk and white Bonnet.'[44] Samuel Curwen had seen the Queen at Windsor in the morning dressed in 'a red habit of the same colour and primings as the King's, having a fashionable bonnet with a bright feather therein.'[45] This, for her, was occasional wear only, and the women's dress version created by Mrs Beauvais for the 1789 celebrations seems to have gained no permanent place.

The presence of royalty increased the formality of dress. When Mary Hamilton was first introduced into the Queen's household in 1777 she was told: 'As you come to the Queen's House by her Majesty's order, you will of course be as much dressed as you would be for a large Assembly.'[46] The personal inclination of the royal family tended, however, to limit the occasions of ceremonial wear. The undress Windsor uniform was a simple dress and in 1769 the Queen was wearing nightgown and apron for undress wear: 'Ly Charlotte told me that the Queen wears an english Night Gown and a white apron, and had ordered her to do the same: 'tis a dress his Majesty likes: formerly Nobody could appear before the Royal Family with a white apron.'[47] When the German scholar, Lichtenberg, was given an audience in 1775 he contrasted 'the evening before last . . . the Queen being covered with jewels and the King, majestic beyond description, in an embroidered costume with his order over the coat; this morning after nine o'clock I again had to wait on the Queen, who was in a cap and black easy gown, quite en famille.'[48] In contrast to the command to Mary Hamilton in 1777, when Maria, Countess of Ilchester was made an extra Lady of the Bedchamber in 1804, the Queen told her: 'You may dress in a muslin gown with a hat on, and shall be presented to the King after dinner.'[49]

The royal family had one far-reaching and recurrent effect on dress, in the mourning ordered when its members died. There were two types of mourning for which orders were issued. Court mourning was observed for distant connections and other sovereigns; for this the period of mourning was short, the mourning slight and a matter for the court and court occasions only. Public mourning ordered for the monarch and members of the royal family was a very different matter. The orders for this were actually 'to all persons'; it was observed particularly by those within the orbit of the court when appearing there or in the presence of the royal family; but it was also observed much more generally.

Mourning was deepest and most widespread at the death of the monarch, which came three times in the eighteenth century. Full mourning was worn for three months, and was usually, for women, black bombazine, plain muslin or long lawn linen, crape hoods, shamoy shoes and gloves and crape fans, and for undress dark Norwich crape;★ for men, black cloth without buttons on sleeves and pockets, plain muslin or lawn cravats and weepers, shamoy shoes and gloves, crape hatbands and black swords and buckles, and for undress, dark grey frocks. Second mourning followed, also lasting for three months. The bombazine might then be replaced by black silk and black gloves with white; undress was grey or white silk; men's linen could be fringed or plain. Even for the death of a monarch it was only at court that the strictest mourning was observed throughout the whole period. In 1727, after the death of George I, Mrs Delany wrote: 'Undrest people wear all sorts of second mourning, unless they go to court when they must wear black silk or velvet.'[50] When Queen Caroline died in 1737 the King ordered public mourning 'as for a wife', that is six months' deep mourning and six months' second mourning and 'all the world cry out upon the hardship of it with respect to trade and private families.'[51] The mourning for Frederick, Prince of Wales, in 1751, was shorter, a six-month mourning. Mrs Delany bought a dark grey Irish poplin sack for this as she already had an unwatered tabby nightgown and two black and white washing gowns: 'I shall make shift with them till the second mourning— it is only for three months.'[52] She was apparently not wearing the bombazine of deep mourning which would have been needed had she been more closely involved at court.

The 1750s brought several deaths in the royal family. For the King's sister, the Queen of Denmark, mourning was almost as universal and as deep as for the Prince of Wales and Lady Jane Coke was surprised to find that her friends in Derbyshire were not mourning too, 'as I thought Derby too genteel to be out of the fashion.'[53] When the King's daughter, Princess Caroline, died in 1758 he was very strict about this mourning. Talbot Williamson, who was gentleman usher to her sister, Princess Amelia, wrote to his brother: 'Everybody that thinks themselves anybody wear deep mourning and at court all belonging to it chamois shoes. The King even took notice of the ladies having put flounces on their bombazine and they were stripped off.'[54] In 1760 the King himself died and once again mourning was deep and widespread.

Purple was the mourning colour worn by royalty only. George II was seen in purple with crape knots on his sleeves when his father died in 1727, and George III appeared in purple coat and silver waistcoat, in

★This was a worsted stuff, not the crimped fabric of the nineteenth century

mourning for his sister, Princess Louisa in 1768. The Queen on this occasion had given her ladies the order to appear either in black or in white and silver in full dress but not in white.[55] The King wore a white and silver waistcoat at a birthday court in 1774 as he 'had not pulled off his mourning for his brother of France, though he followed the modern fashion of his subjects in wearing a white and silver waistcoat with it.'[56]

In the country mourning was generally more relaxed. When the Queen of Denmark died in 1775 the Marchioness Grey wrote to her daughter in Bedfordshire:

> 'I heartily condole with you on the Death of the Queen of Denmark—or at least on the Orders for General Mourning which I thought you would have been Exempted from in the Country. Whether you are Genteel enough in Bedfordshire to comply with these Orders and reckon yourselves amongst the *All Persons* addressed to, I don't know, but if you are, I can only say for your comfort that any old Black Silk or plain Linnen will do for the occasion by the Exemptions Visible on *Ourselves* (here at Home) and many Others.'

Mourning came to England not only with deaths in the English royal family but when members of the Queen's family of Mecklenburg, a tiny duchy smaller than Wales, died. In 1778 Frederick Robinson lamented that because the court was in mourning for the Queen's aunt he would have no opportunity of wearing his green poplin again, that green poplin which had recently been 'much admired'. The death of Prince Charles of Mecklenburg in 1782 caused anxiety to Mary Yorke, wife of the bishop of Ely. The effect of the mourning orders tended to diminish with distance from St James's and according to place and occasion, how 'genteel' place and persons were. She wrote to her sister-in-law, the Marchioness Grey for advice:

> 'Desire you will be so kind as to direct me (and my Neighbours who refer themselves to me) how we are to act with respect to this long Court mourning? I should suppose at Ely it would scarcely be necessary to put it on but as I am so soon to appear at Cambridge at a Publick Meeting I am more uncertain.'

The death of Prince George of Mecklenburg three years later drew from Lady Grantham the remark: 'There is no end of deep mourning for the poor Queen's relations', though she hoped that being in the country, 'we shall escape the blackest part.'[57]

# II

# *People of Fashion*

The court circle, with its houses and regular seasons in London, its attendance at court, its wealth and power, was at the centre of fashionable society. But fashionable clothes were available to all who had the money and opportunity to acquire them and who led the life to display them. The wealthier gentry followed the same pattern of life, with houses in London, rented for the season, or with regular visits to relatives for the entertainments and pleasures of the capital. There was also a London-based group of those whose achievements opened society to them. The theatre, art and literature linked people outside it in social status with those with like interests within it.

The nobility held their own courts, full-dress receptions as splendid as those of the court. At 'her Grace of Bedford's drawing room' in 1760, Mrs Delany waited 'with many fine ladies in *beaten silver* and glittering with jewels, till half an hour after three.' In this exclusive group there were 'very fine ladies' who were leaders of fashion, who in their gatherings displayed new styles with a greater freedom than was possible at court. There were also those who, like Mrs Delany, kept only 'a decent compliance with the fashion, which is less affected than any remarkable negligence of it.'[1] Lord Chesterfield's attitude was much the same, set out in a letter to his son in 1748; 'A man of sense . . . dresses as well, and in the same manner as the people of sense and fashion of the place where he is. If he dresses better, as he thinks, that is more than they, he is a fop; if he dresses worse, he is unpardonably negligent. ... Dress yourself fine where others are fine, and plain where others are plain.'[2] In Richardson's novel, *The History of Sir Charles Grandison,* Sir Charles almost echoes Lord Chesterfield:

'In my own dress I am generally a conformist to the fashion. Singularity is usually the indication of something wrong in judgment. I rather, perhaps, dress too shewy, though a young man, for one who builds nothing on outward appearance. But my father loved to be dressed. In matters which regard not morals, I choose to appear to his friends and tenants, as not doing discredit to his magnificent spirit.'[3]

By the 1760s and 1770s it was not only members of the nobility who were acknowledged as leaders of fashion. Mrs Abington, the actress, was closely observed: 'The style of her clothes and headdress is always in the most exquisite taste, as I have been assured by ladies, whose opinion I advance both to complement and accredit my own; thus she seldom appears on the stage when the mode in genteel society does not follow her.'[4]

## Full Dress

In women's dress the sack-back gown was replacing the mantua at full-dress balls and assemblies during the 1730s. Like the mantua the sack had begun as a loose, informal robe; unlike the mantua it kept its flowing back, held in place by pleating at the shoulders, but it developed a bodice-front shaped to the figure. Until the 1770s this was open over a stomacher; then the fronts met with a centre fastening. A version with a closed skirt disappeared during the 1750s and the sack, open down the centre front, was worn with a matching petticoat: 'Everybody wears flounced sleeves and all the sacks are made open.'[5] (Figs 5, 6). Until the 1770s, when it began to disappear, the sack was worn on a wide range of occasions. For balls it was made more formal by the loose back being lengthened into a train, and by its fabric and trimming, the 'dressed' or 'full-trimmed' sack, whose fabric and ornament was similar to the court gown. Lady Anson planned to take off the trimming from a court gown in 1753, 'to trim a sack after the Birthday was over.' In 1776 Lady Polwarth ordered twenty yards of silk for a 'highly trimmed' gown for court, 'for it will make a good Sack by and by.'[6] Full-trimmed and trained the sack was a formal dress, but it appeared almost everywhere in its plainer versions. Lady Jane Coke wrote from London in 1751: 'You ask me whether sacks are generally worn; I am so partial to 'em that I

5   *The Andrews Family, 1749. Joseph Andrews (1691–1753) of Shaw, Berkshire, Paymaster to the Forces, is plainly dressed in brown, probably velvet, with a silk waistcoat, in contrast to his elder son (b. 1727) in grey laced with silver and a waistcoat of silver brocaded in red and green. The difference of generation also appears in the wigs. The sack worn by Mrs Andrews over an oblong hoop, meeting at the front and with wing cuffs to the sleeves shows a fashionable form of the 1740s. The other gown with ruched trimmings down the front opening and falling cuffs looks forward to the 1750s. James Wills*

6 *Susannah Beckford, 1756. Her blue and silver gown is open both in bodice and skirt, with a wide matching stomacher and a matching petticoat, and is worn with only a small hoop. The treble ruffles, handkerchief and ruff, a fashion of the 1750s, are a suit of blonde and blue silk lace. These and the serpentine ruchings with trimmed edges, soften the lines of the dress in the decorative phase of the eighteenth-century style. Sir Joshua Reynolds*

have nothing else—a sack and apron, with a very small hoop, when I am undressed, and the whole ones when I am to be set out.'[7]

The hoop, its size and shape, varied with the formality or informality of dress as well as changing in shape with time. It was at its widest in the 1740s and 1750s, oblong or fan-shaped, but the large forms were limited to full-dress wear. When Mrs Boscawen came from the country to London in 1747, she wrote: 'I have been here 6 days, but have never yet parted with my short hoop—that is, I have neither seen or been seen.'[8] They were, even then, not universally worn for formal occasions. At Chipping Norton in 1754, 'at the two last Balls all the Ladies danced without Hoops', and when Lady Pomfret appeared without a hoop twice at Oxford, 'Mrs Jones took occasion to commend her chiefly for throwing off the Tyranny of French Fashions and respiring the Grecian Dress ... well, but behold on the third day Lady Pomfret appeared in a Hoop.'[9] In Bath in 1761 it was still the rule that 'The Ladies who intend to dance a minuet wear large hooped dresses, but others do not.'[10] The size of the hoop, apart from the court hoop, diminished from the 1760s, but it did not go completely out of wear until the 1780s. The

27

7 *Lady Sefton, 1769. Her gown and petticoat of light silk, worn without a hoop, or with a very small one, shows the less formal wear of a fashionable woman. The looping up of the skirt of the gown is the beginning of the polonaise style of the 1770s, and the hair, dressed high, the beginning of its elaborate hairdressing.*
Thomas Gainsborough

Queen at an evening concert in 1784 wore a sack with a hoop, 'much smaller than the Court hoop and those of the Princesses only of a size to lift the dress from clinging.'[11]

As the hoop grew smaller the character of dress changed. In the more informal gown, with fitted back, the fullness of the skirt moved towards the back, and the line of dress was broken and softened by the skirt being lifted up in loose puffs of material, making a new style called a polonaise (Fig. 7). This was worn at balls, instead of the sack, from the 1770s; 'if they should remonstrate at Edinburgh at being not enough dressed, tell them there is nothing but Polonaises worn here at Balls and even at Assemblies.'[12]

In the 1780s the new lines were shaping themselves under a camouflage of trimming and the fabrics of dress changing (Fig. 8). Gowns were now often of plain satins covered with festoons and flounces of gauze, flowers and gold and silver foil. At court, in 1781, 'Lady Salisbury's was White with the Petticoat trimmed entirely over with Festoons and of Gauze lined with Yellow Silk which being further decorated with Fringes and Tassles of Gold gave the whole a rich appearance. Miss North, Miss Lucy Pelham, Miss Cowper and several others were entirely in White like Brides.' White was becoming more and more evident; in 1788, 'the Dresses were showy in point of trimming in Gold, Silver or Foil, most of them White Petticoats with Gowns of some other colour.' By 1790 muslin was the fashionable fabric: 'Tell the Ladies Miss Y's Cloaths are chiefly muslins—a gold one India, rich; a very fine worked one sprigged and trimmed with bath lace to be married in.'[13] A dress gown worn by Betsy Sheridan in 1785 shows the transition between the old and the new, 'a robe à la Turque—violet colour—the petticoat and vest white—Tiffany guaze [*sic*] and pale yellow ribbons—with that a sash and buckle under the robe.'[14] The gown has become of less importance; the white petticoat and vest with the waist marked with a sash, now partially revealed beneath it, will soon emerge as the new form. A wide sash had appeared on the still rigid bodices of the early 1780s, helping to raise the line at the waist. As it rose the stiff shaping of the bodice at last relaxed. Skirts for a time remained full over accustomed petticoats and small bustles, although in more flowing lines from light muslins or silks. Then in the last decade of the century, over a single petticoat, light as the dress, the new form, new in line, texture and colour, a major change in dress, was fully revealed.

Men wore a suit of coat, waistcoat and breeches, all three garments matching in material and ornament; or two of them, coat and waistcoat, or coat and breeches, with a contrasting third. A contrasting waistcoat often appeared in court and dress wear and was likely to be the most richly patterned and ornamented garment of the three. In the first half of the century the fabrics used were the same as those of women's dress, gold and silver brocades for the grander occasions, damasks and corded and flowered silks for dress wear. Velvet, plain or figured in cut and

uncut patterns, with or without embroidery, is more often found in men's suits than in women's gowns (Fig. 11). Cloth also appeared in men's dress wear, trimmed with gold or silver and worn with a rich waistcoat. A bridegroom in 1769 wore a light cloth with a silver tissue waistcoat. [15] The gold or silver was often concentrated as a border, or around the buttons and buttonholes. In the second half of the century the silks grew lighter in pattern, with small units of design scattered over the surface and embroidery was lighter both in all-over work and in borders (Fig. 9). Embroidered suits often had coat and breeches in coloured silk and a waistcoat of white or cream repeating the embroidery of the coat but in contrasting colours. Lord Stormont's wedding coat in 1776 was brown cloth lined with straw colour and embroidered with foils, the waistcoat straw colour embroidered with gold and foils. [16]

The wig had been an important part of a man's appearance since the middle of the previous century; it remained so throughout the century, with change only in the final years. It was a sensitive point of fashion, but wigs also had a difference according to occasion. The full-dress wig of the beginning of the century was a particularly costly item of dress, with its mass of curls, rising high on the forehead each side of a centre parting and falling over and well below the shoulders. Lord Bristol usually paid £20 for the 'long perruques' he wore between 1701 and 1715 and he bought one every two or three years. During this time he also bought a 'campaign perruque' and a 'tying perruque', both cheaper at £12 18s

*8 Queen Charlotte, 1789. The painting of her gown of silvery blue, trimmed with fringe, shows a quality of lightness and delicacy, still within the main eighteenth-century form but helping to re-shape it.*
*Sir Thomas Lawrence*
(Reproduced by courtesy of The Trustees, The National Gallery, London)

*9 Waistcoat for dress wear, white satin, embroidered in coloured silks, brilliants and spangles, 1770–80.*

and £10. In the 1720s and 1730s he had bob wigs at £3 3s and tie wigs at £7 7s and his last long periwig in 1728 was only £10 as the long periwig or full-bottom wig had then lost both height and length.[17] The campaign wig was shorter, with the curls knotted at the back and over each shoulder, and was an undress or travelling wig. The bob, the plainest of all and always an undress wig, stopped short of the shoulders and was curled up all round. The tie wig had the curls drawn back and tied in a single tail with a bow of ribbon, the tail sometimes being enclosed in a bag. There were several variants of all these wigs (Fig. 10). From the 1740s all wigs grew smaller and smoother, and the tie wig became the main wig of dress wear, with side curls above the ears. The treatment of the hair over the forehead—the toupee—varied, low and smooth in the 1750s, rising in the 1760s and 1770s and broadening in the 1780s, so showing in slighter degree the same movement as the hairdressing of women. Although there was a fashion for wearing the natural hair in the 1760s, the wig remained an essential part of dress until the 1790s, when fashionable young men began to appear with their own hair cropped short, the first entry of the new style. The tie wig still remained in full-dress wear. Full-dress wigs were always powdered and powder was general in the dressing of wigs. Gay's poem, *Trivia* mentioned the powdered full-bottom wig of the early years of the century as one of the hazards of London streets:

> *You sometimes meet a Fop of nicest Tread*
> *Whose mantling Peruke veils his empty Head .   .   .*
> *Him, like the Miller, pass with Caution by,*
> *Lest from his Shoulders Clouds of powder fly.*

10  *A Group of Vertuosi, 1735. At the centre of this group is the fashionable and wealthy Sir Matthew Robinson, father of Mrs Montagu, in a suit of greyish-gold, laced with silver. On the far right William Kent has gold-laced buttonholes to a brown coat and John Wootton, a gold binding to his waistcoat. All the others, artists, painters, engravers are more plainly dressed in browns and greys. Rysbrack has the functional plain slit cuff to his coat, a detail of a working coat. The artist has painted himself in the background even more informally dressed, without a wig, in a blue cap. The wigs all show variants of the campaign wig or a shortening long wig. Some of the group still wear the scarf-like cravat; others the newer form, a pleated band round the neck, buckled at the back.*
*Gawen Hamilton*

The hat was always worn or carried, indoors as well as out. Sir Charles Grandison, before dancing with Harriet Byron in a minuet, 'reached his hat, and took me out.'[18]

By the middle of the century the coat was losing its stiffness, and the pleats of its skirts, now unpadded, were set further back (Fig. 11). The fronts were cut back in the 1770s and then curved away still further towards the back so that by the 1790s all that remained of the coat skirt was a narrow tail. The waistcoat, which started the century almost as long as the coat, also lost its skirt gradually until by the 1780s it ended in a horizontal line just above the hips and continued to shorten to the end of the century. Within this main change of line there were changing details, the size and shaping of cuffs, the placing and treatment of pockets. By the 1770s a small standing collar had appeared on the plain round neck of both coat and waistcoat and this grew higher. The sleeved waistcoats which were sometimes worn, the upper sleeves plain like the back or made in one material throughout to appear without a coat, did not survive in fashionable wear beyond the first half of the century.

Breeches, almost invisible at the beginning of the century, were gradually revealed by the shortening of the waistcoat and the backward movement of the coat and were cut high to meet the rising line of the waistcoat. With this emergence of the breeches from obscurity a flap or fall-front was added to cover the vertical front fastening, sometimes made as a narrow central section, sometimes extending from seam to seam over the whole of the front.

An elegant leg in a white silk stocking was an important part of fashionable appearance; after the 1770s the breeches, closely moulding the leg above the knee, extended this display. Fine buckles which fastened the straps of the shoe over the tongue gave the final touch of costly elegance to the leg. In 1749 Lord Chesterfield sent his son a pair of diamond shoe-buckles. During the 1770s and 1780s buckles became larger before disappearing in the 1790s. Parson Woodforde in 1784 noted the shoe-buckles of his host: 'Mr Micklethwaite had in his shoes a Pair of Silver Buckles which cost between 7 and 8 Pounds.'[20]

The change in full dress in the second half of the century was not only a change in line, fabric and ornament. Growing informality lessened the number of occasions for wearing it. Frederick Robinson, longing to wear the handsome suit he had bought in Paris, found in June 1778 that 'At this time of year in England a dress coat is wanted for nothing but court, nor do I foresee the occasion I can ever have for putting on my green poplin again.' The weather had been too cold earlier in the year and now he was frustrated by court mourning. So in the following year he had to put on 'my old finery, viz my poplin embroidered with blue and silver; I have added a little cape to the coat', that is a standing collar. Because it was too cold for spring velvets when he arrived in 1778 he ordered a vicuna cloth suit with a plain gold lace, 'with black silk breeches very fashionable' and also a *marron* frock with a gold binding

11 *Francis Beckford, 1756, in a plain dress suit of matching coat, waistcoat and breeches in blue velvet with lace ruffles matching the lace of the shirt. Fashionable wigs are now smooth over the forehead, with curls or wings at the sides, sometimes now set high to show the ears. The tied-back hair in a bag, the sword and cocked hat under the arm complete the full dress.*
*Sir Joshua Reynolds*

for Ranelagh. The next year he went to the Opera in a vicuna frock, white waistcoat and black satin breeches; 'there is rather an affectation of negligence and men go to the opera in plain frocks and white waistcoats.'[21]

These white waistcoats had formerly been a seasonal change, a sign of summer in undress wear. The black breeches had become increasingly fashionable worn with a coloured cloth coat and waistcoat, or a silk waistcoat, plain or embroidered. Coat, waistcoat and breeches need not be a suit at all, but the black and white which was in the nineteenth century to become the established uniform of dress wear was already a strong element there from the 1770s.

The frock in the first half of the century was a coat for easier informal wear, distinguished by its turn-down collar and unstiffened pleats. It was usually of plain cloth; if there was trimming it was limited to a binding of gold or silver lace. When Mrs Boscawen saw Admiral Byng in 1748 in 'an undressed frock very richly embroidered with silver, which in my eyes is a strange dress' she thought it odd enough to mention in a letter to her husband.[22] It was worn for formal morning visits. Peregrine Pickle in Smollett's novel dressed himself for such an occasion in a 'genteel grey frock trimmed with silver binding.'[23]

In 1761 Lord Huntingdon presented himself, in a frock, at a ball at Norfolk House pretending he had just come from the country. The frock was not yet quite acceptable at a ball of this standing, but it might have been excused for this reason. Unfortunately Lord Huntingdon had been at court, full-dressed, that morning. [24] This plainer version was gradually becoming more and more accepted where previously a dress coat would have been worn, and taking the place of the more decorative coat for all but the formal court occasions.

## The Influence of France

Fashionable people in England looked to France as the source of new fashions, but not all French fashions established themselves in English dress. French dress had at one extreme a stiffness and formal elegance — the stiff-bodied gown which was by the early eighteenth century worn only by royalty on its ceremonial occasions remained the regulation court dress in France until the Revolution — and at the other a loose, *negligé* quality generally rejected in England. The Earl Orrery, a young man of eighteen, visiting Paris in 1722, was impressed by this difference: 'The French ladies most of them for what I can perceive may be very beautiful but they dress themselves in a new face every day. ... Their shapes also may possibly be fine but of this no certainty for they wear Sacs or Robes de Chambres that will hide the roundest Shoulders.' [25]

Fashion dolls came regularly across the Channel to bring the latest French fashions to England. They came as a normal trade device to the milliners or were brought or sent by individuals. *The Spectator* in 1712 wrote:

> 'Before our Correspondence with France was unhappily interrupted by the War, the Ladies had all their Fashions from thence; which the Milleners took care to furnish them with by means of a Jointed Baby that came regularly over, once a Month, habited after the eminent Toasts in Paris. ... Last Sunday I heard a Lady in the next Pew to me, whisper another that at the Seven Stars in King Street, Covent Garden, there was a Mademoiselle compleatly dressed just come from Paris.'[26]

Lady Lansdowne sent one from Paris in 1727 to Mrs Howard, bedchamber woman to the Queen, to show the Queen and 'when she has done with it to let Mrs Tempest have it. She was dressed by the person that dresses all the princesses here.'[27] Mrs Tempest was a fashionable milliner. In 1748 Lady Anson was sent a dress made in France which had been fitted on a lady judged to be near her size, a 'very fine

Green and White and Gold Sack, very finely adorned with a most elegant French trimming, with Tippet, Stomacher, Sleeve Knot, Ruffles, etc, etc, all properly suited to it.' She regretted that 'the Poupée which is coming over dressed exactly like Madame de Pompadour did not arrive time enough for me to be able to adjust my coiffure quite in the Taste it ought to have been in, which indeed was the only thing defective in my appearance.' Eventually the doll arrived:

> 'She has three compleat Dresses, one the habit de Sage-Femme, which is de Grande Ceremonie; a Robe (or Sack) pour les Spectacles, les Promenades, etc, etc, and one Robe de negligé for her morning wear; with all sorts of Coiffures, Agréments suited to them all, and written explanations and directions to every part of her Attire.'[28]

Englishmen also brought back from Paris, or ordered through friends there, suits for dress wear. Frederick Robinson, travelling back to England from Spain by way of Paris in 1778, had a spring suit made there. The tailor, le Duc, had the previous year sent patterns of silk to Lord Grantham in Spain, a light brown striped and corded silk, the colour described as 'cheveux de la Reine' and 'absolument nouvelle' which was for Lord Grantham, a similar silk 'cerise' with black dots between the striping for his brother, Frederick; it was suggested that the waistcoats of both should be of white satin ground with embroideries.[29]

The ordinary Englishman recognised French clothes when he saw them in the street. In 1726 de Saussure wrote home: 'When people see a well-dressed person in the streets, especially if he is wearing a braided coat, a plume in his hat, or his hair tied in a bow, he will without a doubt be called "French dog" twenty times.'[30] An Englishman wearing French clothes might get the same treatment. A young Englishman dressed in 'a little green frock he had bought from Paris' was taken for a Frenchman and abused and those who had insulted him thought no better of him when they discovered he was an Englishman wearing a French coat.[31] When de la Rochefoucauld first appeared in the streets of Bury St Edmunds in 1784 he was met with cries of 'Frenchies, Frenchies'.[32]

The French Ambassadress was carefully observed for new fashions. Lady Jane Coke reported from the birthday court of 1749: 'The French Ambassadress and the Duchess of Bedford were the two finest women; the first is the pattern for dress .   . her hair is curled in small ringlets round her face, pinned up behind a cap not near so big as your hand and nothing round her neck.' The next year she wrote again: 'As for fashions, according to the English custom we follow the French Ambassadress'; and in 1751: 'The short caps you mention are only worn by young people who curl their hair after the French Ambassadress's fashion.' In 1754 she found the fashions 'too various to describe. One thing is new, which is, there is not such a thing as a decent old woman left, everybody curls their hair, shews their neck and wears pink, but

12 *Lady Hertford (1726–82), 1765. At the time this portrait was painted Lady Hertford was living in Paris where her husband was British Ambassador Extraordinary. She is therefore 'dressed French' and shows the French style of hairdressing, adopted also by some Englishwomen, a richly brocaded gown and petticoat over a full-dress hoop and a full display of jewels. Alexander Roslin*

your humble servant. People who have covered their heads for forty years now leave off their caps and think it becomes them, in short try to out-do our patterns the French in every ridiculous vanity.'[33] (Fig. 12).

   The hair lowered after 1710 from the high dressing of curls above the forehead in front of the cap with its standing frill, to a plainer dressing, drawn back from the face into a bun high at the back or with ringlets falling on the neck. Although it was curled and powdered for court wear, the plainer styles were general: 'few women curl or powder their hair and they seldom wear ribbons, feathers or flowers, but little headdresses, of cambric or of magnificent lace on their pretty, well-kept hair.'[34] Lady Mary Wortley Montagu in Paris in 1718 had no liking for the style she saw there:

'Their Hair cut short and curled round their faces, loaded with powder that makes it look like white wool, and then on their cheeks to their chins, unmercifully laid on, a shineing red japan that glisters in a most flameing manner that they seem to have no resemblance to human faces, and I am apt to believe took the first hint of their dress from a fair sheep new raddled.'[35]

During the 1760s the hairdressing rose higher over pads and rolls, and in the 1770s all the extravagance of ephemeral fashion concentrated on it. Much time was spent in the hands of the hairdressers. Marie Antoinette, now Queen of France, was regarded as the source of the most elaborate fancies: 'These fashions are newly come from France where it is said the Queen invents them for the King's amusement. ... Mrs Beauvais says she is now able to set fashion and oblige others to follow it, whereas before she was obliged to be tied up to Etiquette.'[36]

Lady Hartford, writing to her friend, Lady Pomfret in 1741, discussed the effect of French fashion on the dress of fashionable young ladies in England:

'This on the whole is neither quite French nor quite English; their hair being cut and curled after the mode of the former, and their bodies dressed in the way of the latter, though with French hoops. Few unmarried women appear abroad in robes or sacques; and as few married ones would be thought genteel in anything else.'[37]

Madame du Bocage, who visited England in 1750, admired the informal dress of English women but thought they made 'a less brilliant appearance in the evening at their assemblies, and in the morning at court, when dressed according to the French fashion.' Her general comment on Englishwomen was: 'The women use no paint and are always laced.'[38] The wearing of rouge on one side of the Channel and not the other struck visitors in both directions, but after the middle of the century rouge appeared more in England, though it was still a matter for comment, especially if generously applied. The wearing of a gown closely fitted in the bodice, 'always laced', that is, wearing stays with the bodice shaped over them, was a constantly noted characteristic.

French skill in the arts of dress, the inventiveness and expert handling of all ornament and accessories, the ability to shape the whole appearance into a minor work of art, was fully recognised, but there were not many Englishwomen who consistently 'dressed French'. The difference was less a matter of style than of degree of dress. When the Marchioness Grey in 1785 met the lady her brother-in-law, ambassador to the Hague, had just married, she wrote a revealing description of her dress:

'The lady is extremely well-dressed, her hair well-curled (like any of yours for the fullest Dress). ... She wears only Dressed Sacques with a larger Hoop than we do now (That on Saturday was a Striped Lustring, full-trimmed with Crape and Blond, Blond Ruffles, Tippet etc) and not adopting the white apron will look at all parts of the Day more dressed than we are now used to. She said she was always used to that Dress (the Robe) and asked if she must now wear the Night gown and straight bodied Dresses, to which I assured her she might do whatever she liked best. She understood they were much worn at Paris she said and our Fashions much adopted as here, and that her Daughter had brought back from Paris where she had been last Winter nothing but tight Buttoned gowns.'[39]

## Masquerade

One of the most fashionable entertainments of the century was the masquerade, a gathering where people escaped from the limitations of formal dress into a variety of dresses of fantasy, and dressed 'in what they have a mind to be.'[40] They wore either fancy dress or enveloped themselves uniformly in concealing dominos. Two kinds of dominos were distinguished by Lady Mary Coke in 1768, quoting Mrs Spilsbury: 'there was but two kinds of Dominos and that the french one was certainly what you meant and is wore with a hoop.' The Venetian one was 'really exactly a Parson's gown.'[41] Whichever dress was chosen, masks were worn and an unmasking moment part of the entertainment. Masquerades were held throughout Western Europe. When Lady Polwarth was in Nice in 1778 she wrote of a masquerade there, 'not very unlike a shabby masquerade in England', and after describing some of the dresses, adds, 'but this sounds so like a paragraph in some English paper that you think perhaps I am copying one.' She also noted that 'All agree that this is very different from the common style of carnival Masquerades in Italy at Venice and Florence particularly where Dominos are the only disguises.'[42]

The year 1768, when the King of Denmark paid a visit to England, was a year for masquerades of the grandest kind. The Duke and Duchess of Northumberland gave one at Sion House, which according to Mrs Delany 'beat all others', the Duke and Duchess of Portland gave one at Welbeck and in return the King of Denmark gave one at the Haymarket. The next year the Duke of Bolton gave a magnificent one, at which the Duchess appeared first in a man's domino and then unveiled to show herself as 'the most brilliant Sultana that ever was seen, covered with pearls and diamonds.' Lady Waldegrave appeared as a Sultana too, in the same dress she had worn at the King of Denmark's masquerade the year before.[43] Women sometimes disguised themselves as men with the help of dominos. Judith Milbanke and her sister appeared in 1778 'in Men's Dominos our Hair immensely well dressed, smart Bags, Fierce Hats and Feathers, etc and we made two smart Beaux, but I think "I wore my Rapier with the better grace and proved the prettiest Fellow of the two".'[44] The possibilities of disguise at the masquerades, attractive to some, made others view them doubtfully as, with good reason, Harriet Byron did, in Richardson's *The History of Sir Charles Grandison*. The demand for masquerade dress was great enough for shops to be set up for the making and hiring of masquerade habits and dominos. One of these was Jackson's Habit-Warehouse in Covent Garden.[45] The mass production of stock masquerade garments was exploited, dramatically, in Mrs Cowley's play *The Belle's Stratagem*.

There were many variants of the masquerade. In 1774 Lord Stanley gave a *Fête Champêtre* at the Oaks, near Epsom, appearing himself as Rubens. Another variant was a *Fiera Maschata*. For one of these, in 1775, the Marchioness Grey, suggesting that her daughters should go as Country Girls come to see the fair, thought 'common nightgowns of silk (plain) or linen is alone wanting, gauze handkerchiefs and apron, round-eared caps (or no caps) and chip hats with ribbons; a plain toupee for the hair without curls or powder; so that not even the attendance of a Hair-dresser is wanting.' Masquerades were also part of the life of family parties in country ·houses. Lady Heathcote arrived at her husband's home in 1755 to find a *bal masqué* imminent, and another arranged for the following week, for which she made herself a 'peasant's dress of pink and white.' Much care was given to dresses for the grander masquerades. For the Danish King's masquerade, Agneta Yorke had 'a fine nabob's dress cut to pieces to make the vest I wore.' Someone else at this masquerade was also in 'a sort of Persian dress' which had been made from 'the King of Misore's dress which he gave General Lawrence.'[46] Betsy Sheridan went to a masquerade in 1789 as one of a group, transformed in almost exact detail into gipsies, in brown stuff jackets and blue stuff petticoats, straw hats tied under the chin; but their red cloaks were silk 'in imitation of the red cloaks worn by these Ladies', which would have been wool.[47]

Masquerade dress had its own fashions. Horace Walpole wrote to Horace Mann about a masquerade given by the Duke of Norfolk in 1742: 'There were quantities of pretty Vandykes and all kinds of old pictures walked out of their frames.' He himself went as Aurengzebe.[48] At a subscription masquerade at the Haymarket in 1749, the Marchioness Grey

> 'pretended to nothing more I assure you than a tolerably handsome pretty Habit. . . . It was what we call Spanish and composed of a Pink Sattin Curtained Petticoat trimmed a Black Sattin Waistcoat trimmed also with silver with close sleeves slashed with Pink and a small Hat and Feather. . . . Lady Mary Capell was *Volage* and quitted her first husband Rubens to be Queen to Charles the first but she was paid for her Inconstancy by not looking near so well as in her first state. She was the fine Vandyke with her Hair hanging about her Ears but somehow or other it did not suit her.'[49]

Harriet Byron dressed reluctantly as an Arcadian princess, disliking the gaudiness of her dress: 'It falls not with any of my notions of the pastoral dress of Arcadia—I am not to have a hoop— they wore not hoops in Arcadia.'[50]

Some of the fancies of the masquerade were drawn into the main stream of women's dress. The Marchioness Grey wrote of the 'most irresistable Fashion lately sprung upon us—the true Vandyke Hankerchief' in 1752, and Lady Jane Coke also reported it amongst the fashions of that year: 'New fashions I am bad at remembering. However, one is so remarkable it is not easily forgot, which is a variety of Vandyke handkerchiefs; they are not worn in full dress.'[51] Masquerade caps and hats reappeared as fashionable head-dresses and

hats in the 1770s and 1780s. In 1775 one cap 'at its first appearance raised an outcry and looked more like a masquerade Bergers Hat than anything else.' At a wedding of 1784 the hat worn by the bride was described by one guest as a 'white Spanish hat' and by another as an 'Air Balloon Hat of Feathers, or rather a Rubins of white Satin', the current fashion of 'everything Balloon' after the flights of 1783-4 merging with the inspiration of the hats painted by Rubens.

It was not only the details of dress which reflected the fancies of the masquerade; the whole style of dress of the late 1770s seemed to Frederick Robinson, on his return to England, theatrical: 'There is at present much more expence and taste in the trimmings of the Ladys Gowns than in the stuffs; they are full and in almost a theatrical style, but I think very handsome.' And after a year in England he still thought the dresses 'beyond measure capricious, a few years ago they would have been thought fantastick for a Masquerade.'⁵²

The pastoral dress of Arcadia, nymphs, shepherds and shepherdesses; images of the past from Vandyke and Rubens; Gothic abbesses and pilgrims; the exotic east, Persian princesses: these were the recurrent themes of masquerade dress. Its fashions were also the fashions of portraiture (Fig. 13). Fashionable women appeared as shepherdesses, in a

*13 Sir William Young (1725–88) and family, 1765–7. Sir William's family had settled in the West Indies and he was Lieutenant Governor of St Dominica and Tobago. The family were friends of Garrick and took part in theatrical productions of their own. All appear here in varying degrees of 'Vandyke' dress, except the eldest daughter whose wrapping gown seems classically inspired and the youngest in her normal dress. The hairdressing is within the fashion of the 1760s, although Sir William seems to have added a few flowing cavalier locks to his wig.*
J. Zoffany

simple gown and straw hat, with a crook and perhaps an attendant lamb. Both men and women were painted à la Vandyke from the 1730s to the 1780s, wearing a masquerade dress copied from a Vandyke or Rubens portrait, a dress copied direct from one of their portraits, or in eighteenth-century dress with a few seventeenth-century details added. Sitters who were from the beginning antique could never look merely out-of-date. Even the unsophisticated wife and daughters of the *Vicar of Wakefield* are made to have ambitions of being portrayed in this way. Mrs Primrose 'desired to be represented as Venus ... Olivia would be drawn as an Amazon, sitting on a bank of flowers, dressed in a green joseph, richly laced in gold and a whip in her hand. Sophia was to be a shepherdess.'[53]

In the 1750s a new phase of interest in Greek art strengthened the strong classical background of English culture, and from the 1760s fashionable women saw themselves re-created on canvas in the flowing lines of classical draperies, in portraits by Sir Joshua Reynolds and others—draperies which linked them more closely with classical sculpture than with the earlier visions of Arcadia. The escape to Arcadia, that indefinite golden past, the interest in the historic past, the lure of distant places and people expressed in the dresses of the masquerade, reflected an underlying romantic mood. The lines of dress had already softened in the 1750s and they continued to grow more flowing and lighter in texture. The artists' image merged with the evolving style and helped to guide it towards a classical form, but its creating spirit was romantic.

## Fashion at Home

The looser version of the sack, falling wide and free from the shoulders, as worn in France, is rare in England. For practical reasons this kind of garment, with its almost untouched widths of fabric, is less likely to survive, but it is also rare in English portraits. What does appear is a loose gown, overlapping and fastening on one side or secured round the waist with a girdle. Even in the most domestic surroundings the Englishwoman modified the loose form in this way; 'What gives a Lady a more easie Air than the Wrapping Gown in the Morning at the Tea Table?'[54] The sack was adopted, not in its original loose form but in its more formal version, with the bodice-fronts cut and shaped to the figure. It was then worn informally as well as formally for the whole period 1740-80 and for a wide range of occasions. Lady Polwarth, planning visits following her wedding, saw it as an all-purpose gown: 'I think I must have 3 Sacks, a plain one I intended to go to Mrs Yorke's in and then wear every day, another for company and a third for Assemblies.' She chose the new silks with flowered stripes for the last two.[55] Mrs Delany had a sack in green and white linen which she seems to have worn when painting as 'it hangs in the painting room.'[56] Lady

14 *Yellow silk gown of informal wear, showing the bodice-back which links it in construcion to both mantua and sack. The central section is pleated, the pleats stitched down to the fitted lining and shaped to taper to the waist and then fall free into the skirt. The sleeves which have a weight at the elbow to keep them in place would probably have a shaped cuff fitting over them, either of matching silk or of ruched and frilled muslin. The joins in the silk suggest re-making from an earlier gown, probably a sack; they would be concealed by the handkerchief, 1770–80.*

Jane Coke was so partial to this form that she wore nothing else.

The other type of gown which has survived in large numbers from the same period, in a wide range of silks, linen and cotton, is one which is linked with the fitted mantua, also a development from an earlier loose gown, by the characteristic shaping of the back, with the central section of the bodice pleated and sewn down, following the shape of the stays and extending without a waist seam into the skirt; another version of this, developing later, has a complete division at the waist, with the skirt pleated on to the bodice all round (Fig. 14). This is the nightgown, the English nightgown, known to the French as *robe à l'anglaise*. It was an informal gown, particularly English in character and very generally worn. The name is confusing. Early in the century it may have meant a loose gown. Lady Mary Wortley Montagu's request to her sister in Paris to send her a ready-made nightgown in 1722 suggests that fit was not important. She had written a few years before, in a poem satirizing fashionable life:

15  *Quilted cream silk waistcoat with concealed lacing at the front; probably worn in place of stays under a loose wrapping gown or for warmth, as an additional undergarment.*

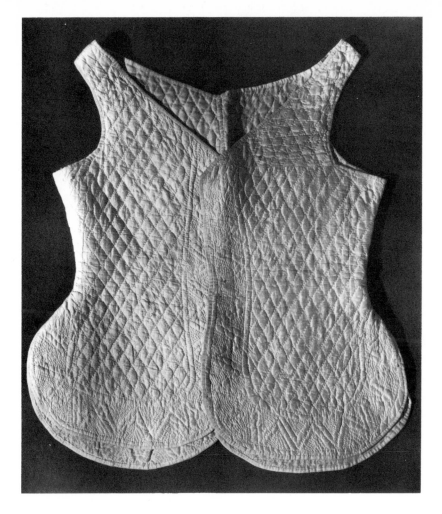

*I drank bohea in Celia's dressing-room:*
*Warm from her bed, to me alone within*
*Her night-gown fastened with a single pin;*
*Her night-clothes tumbled with resistless grace,*
*And her bright hair played careless round her face;*
*Reaching the kettle made her gown unpin,*
*She wore no waistcoat, and her shift was thin.*[57]

The waistcoat mentioned here was probably silk or linen lightly quilted and embroidered. Many of these survive, although literary and graphic references to them are few (Fig. 15). By the 1740s the word nightgown has a more general meaning. When Mrs Delany said she would, as her sister advised, bring with her on a visit 'nothing but nightgowns', the loose garment of the poem would hardly meet all her needs.[58] Nightgowns were listed amongst the wedding clothes of Princess Mary in 1740: 'There are four nightgowns (three trimmed) and one blue tabby embroidered with silver; four sacks or robes, all trimmed ... four more fine gowns besides',[59] and of Miss Poyntz in 1756, who had four negligées, four nightgowns, four mantuas and petticoats.[60] As it is unlikely that a trousseau of this date would be without sacks, and nightgowns are listed, the term negligée seems more likely to refer to a sack than to be an alternative name for a nightgown. Although night-gowns of royal and noble wearers could still be rich garments, they are generally the less costly gowns. Mrs Delany, preparing to visit Ireland in 1731, bought a gown and petticoat of flowered satin with trimmings which cost £16 and pink damask for a nightgown at 7s a yard, which would work out at about half the price of the satin gown.[61]

The nightgown is often mentioned alone, not as a gown and petticoat. Originally it probably did not reveal the petticoat; and although satisfying the English preference for a fitting gown, was informal in that it completely covered all that was worn, or not worn, beneath. This could be achieved by the skirt meeting at centre front, or by a closed front in which the front section was open at the top of the side seams and fastened like an apron round the waist beneath the back of the gown. The open bodice-front was closed by lacing over a handkerchief. Both these forms survive. Later the front opening widened to reveal the petticoat. Although matching petticoats are found with gowns of this form, many of those which survive alone were probably worn with a contrasting petticoat. What was at first an invisible upper petticoat, quilted for warmth, and also used instead of a hoop—'There is not one of us but has reduced our outward Petticoat to its ancient Sizable Circumference, tho' indeed we retain still a Quilted one underneath, which makes us not altogether unconformable to the Fashion'[62]— became visible and was then quilted for ornament. The wearing of a gown with a contrasting quilted petticoat is seen in many informal portraits, and is characteristic of informal English dress (Fig. 16).

The practical character of the nightgown was emphasised by its being worn without hoops or with very small ones, and with an apron. Lady Hartford said in 1740 that she did not feel at home in her own house without an apron, 'nor can endure a hoop that would overturn all the chairs and stools in my closet.'[63] In 1754 Lady Jane Coke, reporting the popularity of hoops, still made an exception for morning dress. Much later, in 1780, the Marchioness Grey wrote to her daughter from Richmond: 'Dress is not required, no Company of any sort will be there, we having no Relations in Town and we Part immediately. Any common Nightgown there is sufficient.'[64] It was often worn at weddings because these were regarded as private domestic occasions. Horace Walpole's niece, Lady Waldegrave, was married in a white silver nightgown and a hat in 1759.[65]

The apron, in spite of Beau Nash's famous attack on the Duchess of Queensberry's apron at a Bath Assembly, had established itself in all but full dress. It had a complete range of fashionable wear from the 'working

16 Le Lecteur or The Judicious
Lover, 1743–5. This is fashionable
dress of the 1740s with a fairly large
hoop, but otherwise in its plain form
for informal, indoor wear. The green
gown is open over a pink quilted
petticoat and worn with a white
apron, plain ruffles and a small
round cap trimmed with pink ribbon.
The quality of the dress, with the
stiffly shaped bodice above the
billowing shape of the hoop when
the wearer was seated, has been
caught in this scene, painted by a
French artist.
H. F. Gravelot

apron', which Lady Mary Coke, an enthusiastic gardener, hardly had
time to throw off, when the Princess Amelia unexpectedly called [66], to
the dress aprons of silk with rich embroidery in coloured silks and silver
thread and foil or finely embroidered and lace-trimmed muslin, which
survive in large numbers (Fig. 17). In 1785 Judith Milbanke ordered a
suit, apron, ruffles and handkerchief, 'to wear for dining visits and
undress balls.'[67]

In the 1770s once again a looser form from undress made its way into
morning dress. It surprised Judith Milbanke in 1779: 'a sort of Loose
Robe tyed carelessly round her Waist with a Blue Persian Sash.'[68] This
was the chemise gown with unshaped bodice, open down the front,
meeting at the centre and held in place by a sash and with gatherings at
the waist (Figs 18, 19). By 1784 it was worn for dining visits: 'The
Thompsons dined here. ... She looks very well and very smart in a
Chemise de la Reine.'[69] The French name came from its wear by Marie

44

Antoinette. The nightgown, with its back shaping, its bodice-front now closed and the skirt closing again with the apron front which had been worn earlier in the century, continued to be worn during the 1780s, in chintz, cotton or light silk, often with a broad sash like the chemise gowns. As the two forms appeared side by side in formal dress, the chemise gown brought the final change to the nightgown and to the whole of late eighteenth-century dress, by its loosening of the bodice.

Men also relaxed, privately and at their ease in a nightgown. This term, like the same word in women's dress, is ambiguous, and later the word morning gown was used. The nightgown was a long garment, full-length or at least covering the knees, and always much easier in cut than any coat. It survives in several forms, the basic straight-cut form, shared with the women's mantua, of widths of material passing over the shoulders from back to front without shoulder seams, sleeves in one with the gown, or set in with or without added shaping. The more fitted forms differ from coat or frock in having simple side vents without pleats or a back vent with or without an inverted pleat. The loose form was often worn wrapped over and secured with a sash, like the women's wrapping gowns. The more fitted form sometimes has a wrap-over front with ties for each side, to wrap right over left or left over right. It is sometimes found with attached waistcoat fronts, sometimes with a matching waistcoat (Fig. 20). The gowns are of silk, damask or brocaded, or plain, of printed cotton or woollen damask. Lord Bristol bought six between 1720 and 1739. When he notes the material, it is damask; all were blue or red except the last one which was 'dark-

17 *A dress apron, 1725–50, cream silk embroidered in coloured silks, mainly in shades of purple and green, and silver thread.*

18 *A chemise gown of figured muslin, edged with a narrow cotton fringe, drawn up across the bodice by three cotton cords which tie at the centre front to close the opening. The sleeves of plain muslin have slots for drawing up with ribbons, as shown. Ribbons, sash and handkerchief although of the same date as the gown, 1780–90, are not those originally worn with it. Frilled muslin scarves which cross over the front of the bodice and tie at the back may still be called handkerchiefs.*

19 Sir Robert and Lady Buxton and
their daughter Anne, in informal
indoor dress of the 1780s. Lady
Buxton's gown is similar to that of
fig. 18 with the large muslin
handkerchief puffed over the ribbon
drawing the bodice fronts together;
and she is wearing mittens. Before
her on the table is her embroidery
frame. The girl's dress shows the
freedom which came to children's
dress in the second half of the
century. Women's dress has already
taken the sash from it and will take
over the whole style by the end of the
century.
J. H. Mortimer

coloured' damask, the only one for which a separate price is entered, £4 18s.[70] Nightgowns were sometimes quilted for warmth. The term Indian nightgowns, which often occurs, may refer to their fabric, silk or cotton, or to their loose, kimono-like form. The term banyan, which is also used for them, is another link with the East Indies. The loose forms seem to have been worn for most of the century; most of the fitted ones which survive have a standing collar, of varying height, which, related to the formal coat, would place them in the second half of the century. But if they were inspired by an eastern original, or took from the loose robe the rectangular section added for fit to the neck at the back, the standing collar could have come to the formal coat from this source.

The nightgown was a garment of slippered and wigless ease. When Jonathan Swift had 'a cruel cold' in 1710 he 'staid within all this day in my nightgown.' He makes a distinction between this gown, which he puts on when he gets up in the morning, and a 'bed nightgown' made for him, which was probably what he actually wore in bed.[71] Dr Morris was ill in May 1726, 'through walking in the Garden above an hour (4 a.m.) with only my Bed Night Gound on.'[72] John Byng, however, in 1789 seems to use the term bedgown for nightgown: 'At last home I come, so happy, clap on my bedgown, my slippers, take off my garters, ease my neckcloth.'[73] Men received visitors in their nightgowns as a sign of intimacy and informality. They were sometimes, in certain places, seen out-of-doors. In 1711, Steele, writing of coffee houses, referred to those who 'come in their Nightgowns to Saunter away their time.' When the wig was taken off, a cap, often called a nightcap, was put on.

46

This was sometimes of similar material to the gown and sometimes of silk or linen, finely embroidered, especially those of the early part of the century. Nightcaps actually worn in bed were usually plain and of wool, cotton or linen, although they might be quilted for warmth.

In the winter months the large, elegant rooms of eighteenth-century houses could be chilly. For women wadded gowns were a great comfort. Lady Holland wrote in January 1763: 'At present I live in a wadded gown, which is so warm and light how I shall leave it off I don't know.'[74] In December 1740 Mrs Delany wrote to her sister: 'I hope you are as wise as I am and sit with hood and cloak on by the fireside.'[75] Examples of quilted and hooded short gowns which were probably worn in this way, survive (Fig. 21).

Men wore under-waistcoats of flannel for warmth; 'the stern answer of a greatcoat or a flannel waistcoat and take care of yourself', Mrs Boscawen wrote to her husband the Admiral in October 1754.[76] Lord Chesterfield wrote gratefully to Dr Chevenix in 1764: 'I have the warmest sense of your kindness in providing my old and chilled carcase with such a quantity of flannel. I have cut my waistcoats according to my cloth, and they come half way down my thigh.'[77]

Muffs carried out-of-doors by men were regarded as the mark of a

*21  A satin hooded jacket, cut as a loose sack, with pleats falling over the shoulders in front as well as at the back, quilted and trimmed with ruffles edged with silk fringe. The long sleeves fitting from the elbow make a style which can also be seen in the small fashion plate of colour plate 1 on a jacket called The Brunswick. There it is clearly an outdoor garment, but this example was probably one of the cloaks and hoods worn for warmth indoors, 1750–75.*

*20  Lord Burlington in a scarlet nightgown of the more fitted form, and matching nightcap, with turn-up brim and loose crown, 1717–20. The wearing of a nightgown in this portrait gives emphasis to Lord Burlington as an architect, rather than a peer, for it is particularly artists, men of letters, musicians and scholars who are painted in this dress. For an example of a nightgown of the looser form, see fig. 47.*
*J. Richardson*

fop, but they were used indoors for comfort: 'I wish you would buy me a muff; it must be grave and warm, for as I and my brother pass many evenings alone I grow cold by my fireside with reading.' Horace Walpole bought George Montagu his muff, 'a decent smallish muff that you may put in your pocket and it costs but fourteen shillings.'[78]

## Fashion Out-of-Doors

Out-of-doors for morning walks in St James's Park and for informal visits, the morning dress of indoors, nightgown or sack, and white apron again appeared, with the addition of a hat. In 1727 de Saussure had noticed the hats, 'small hats of straw that are vastly becoming. Ladies even of the highest rank are thus attired when they go walking or make a simple visit.'[79] At the beginning of the century a hood was fashionable wear and, over a full-dress head-dress, remained in use, but from the 1720s a hat was being worn with morning dress. It was this dress which Madame du Bocage admired in 1750, 'with the white apron and the pretty straw hat.' The gowns were short, that is they cleared the ground, and she adopted the style herself for her later travels, 'the short English dress which I wear in my journey.'[80] Grosley also noticed the ladies walking in St James's Park in the morning, 'in a short gown, a long white apron and a hat.'[81] (Fig. 22). When Lady Mary Coke was surprised that Lady Grosvenor went to Lady Harrington's 'straight from

22  *The women in this sketch show two versions of 1750s' dress, the plain, out-of-door style with hat and apron, which may be either fashionable undress or the dress of a woman of lesser rank, and the full-trimmed fashionable style.*
*P. Sandby*

walking in the Park in a hat, nightgown and white apron, yet she did not seem ashamed of her dress', it was surprise that she should attend a social gathering in that dress, not that she was wearing it to walk in the Park, for which it was normal; it would also have been acceptable for an informal call. With this dress only small hoops, or no hoops at all, were worn. Lady Mary, always particular about wearing the hoop in formal dress, never, if she could help it, wore one for walking. Visiting Princess Amelia at Gunnersbury, 'I had put on a Hoop to be very respectful, which I was sorry for, as we walked all round the grounds in the rain which being dressed was not agreeable.'[82]

The hat, which had come into fashionable dress from being worn out-of-doors in the country, was a plain hat, often of straw, with a flat crown and fairly wide brim. In town these hats became more elegant, covered with silk and trimmed. Worn first for walking in the park, they then became indispensable for the English woman out-of-doors. The undress character of the hats was modified and they became 'dressed' according to occasion. They appeared at Vauxhall and Ranelagh, where in the 1760s fashionable women wore 'their favourite undress'. Grosley wrote this in 1765, but his translator of 1772 added a note that 'when our author was in England the undress of Ranelagh corresponded with that of Vauxhall, but the ladies now rather make a distinction and generally appear dressed at Ranelagh.'[83] When Lady Polwarth was in Nice in 1778 she was astonished that 'the better sort of people' walked out 'full-dressed without any kind of shelter', although the country women wore large cane hats. She kept to her English habit: 'For my part I boldly wear an English hat and bonnet.'[84] By the 1780s hats were worn for all but full dress. Dress hats perched on top of the high hairdressing of the 1770s, tilting over the forehead; wide ballooning hats spread above the wider hairdressing of the 1780s and were impressively trimmed. The undress hats, though following fashionable change, kept the plain character of their origin and were of 'straw, chip, Cellbridge or cane of the dimensions pretty nearly of your round tea-table, two rows of narrow ribbon or one of broad, round the crown and three or four yards pinned loosely at the back. I have got a Cellbridge for the honour of Ireland.'[85] (Fig. 23).

When Grosley saw the ladies walking in St James's Park, he thought; 'The country life led by these ladies during a great part of the year and the freedom which accompanies that way of life make them continue an agreeable negligence in dress which never gives disgust.'[86] In their country dress they walked in the London parklands. Duties at court, attendance at the House of Lords or House of Commons and the pleasures and resources of a capital city brought families to their London houses, but it was the great country houses, many of them built, altered or enlarged during the century which were their chief homes. Time and money were devoted to them; parks, often landscaping village or hamlet out of existence, spread round them; a family's wealth and

23 *St. James's Park, with Buckingham House in the background, 1790, a place of fashionable parade. The women show different stages of the rising waistline and loss of fullness in the skirt and most of them wear a high-crowned style of hat fashionable in the late 1780s and early 1790s, although one or two of the wide-brimmed, full-crowned hats of the mid-1780s still appear. A woman in a habit shows a plain version of the high-crowned hat, very similar to that worn by most men, although amongst them a few cocked hats can still be seen.*
F. Dayes

24–25 *The Gardens at Hartwell House, Buckinghamshire, 1738, with the family or a group of visitors in riding-dress and members of the household; maid-servants in plain dress, one with hat and pinned-back gown; men-servants without wigs, the gardeners wearing jackets and wide-brimmed hats, uncocked.*
B. Nebot

position was displayed there (Figs. 24, 25). Some of the fine, fashionable ladies preferred life in London, but many joyfully returned to the country for the summer months. And when they were in London, they usually had a nearby retreat in London's countryside, a villa on the Thames. After an autumn of 'fine walking weather', Lady Hartford left her country house reluctantly in 1740: 'We go to London for the winter tomorrow. This gives me no joy on my own account. . . . I find our lawns (though at present covered with snow) a more agreeable prospect than dirty streets, and our sheep-bells more musical than the clamour of hawkers.'[87] Lady Hartford's writing often reflects a literary approach to the country, and echo of the classic pastoral, but there is no reason to doubt her enjoyment of it; even less to doubt the pleasure of Mary Yorke, who thought 'the pleasures of the country are certainly beyond any other amusement in my esteem.' Her sister-in-law, Lady Grey, wrote of her in 1773 that she was 'really happy I believe in being at *Liberty* this year to enjoy it, and scrambling over Hedge and Ditch, anywhere, having run wild she says all over the Fields in the first two days she was there, endulged herself in the supreme Felicity of getting over half the Stiles in the Parish and to all points of View.'[88] Mrs Montagu, fresh from a visit to Paris, in 1776, wrote:

'From a gay Parisian Dame . . . I am at once metamorphosed into a plain Country Farmeress. . . . A French Lady told me she thought the english women not so happy as the french; I smiled and said I was not sure of that. She gave it as one reason that they were obliged to spend part of the year in the Country. I combated her opinion, but found it impossible to make her comprehend the pleasure of a morning or evening walk, the delight of animating industry or relieving the little wants of a district.'

In another letter written at the same time she repeated this view: 'The

change we make in our amusements and mode of life by spending the summer in the country is I think much in our favour.'[89]

Riding was a country pleasure which had long made its mark on women's dress. The satire of *The Spectator* was directed against it several times between 1711 and 1714. John Gay in *The Guardian* wrote in 1713:

'There is another kind of Occasional Dress in Use among the Ladies, I mean the Riding Habit, which some have not injudiciously stiled the Hermophroditical, by Reason of its Masculine and Feminine Composition; but I shall rather chuse to call it the Pindaric; as its first Institution was at a New-market Horse Race, and as it is a mixture of the Sublimity of the Epic with the easie Softness of the Ode.'[90]

Neither style nor complaints were new. Pepys had disapproved of the riding habit nearly sixty years before:

'I find the Ladies of Honour dressed in their riding garb, with coats and doublets with deep skirts, just for all the world like mine, and buttoned their doublets up the breast, with perriwigs and hats; so that only for a long petticoat dragging under their men's coats, nobody could take them for women in any part whatever—which was an odd sight, and a sight did not please me.'[91]

Von Uffenbach, who was in England in 1710, went to Epsom and saw there 'vast crowds on horseback, both men and females; many of the latter wore men's clothes and feathered hats, which is quite usual in England.'[92] (Fig. 26).

The riding habit was a petticoat, jacket and waistcoat, or waistcoat fronts attached to the jacket, which followed the lines of men's coats until the 1780s, except that it had a waist seam. It was worn with a cocked hat or jockey cap. In the first half of the century it was usually made of camlet, a closely woven worsted sometimes mixed with silk, rather harsh to the touch; later the usual cloth was broadcloth. Habits were sometimes laced with silver, or had collar, cuffs and waistcoat of a contrasting colour: 'I sent to desire Knox to make you a stone colour riding-habit lined with green and a green waistcoat, as it is quite the fashion now to have them lined with different colours', Lady Stormont wrote to her sister in 1776.[93] Materials of lighter weight, like nankeen, were sometimes used for summer wear. A number of riding jackets, but few complete habits, survive (Fig. 27).

The habit was not only a riding dress, but soon became a dress for travelling. Lady Mary Montagu wrote from Adrianople in 1717: 'I was in my travelling habit, which is a riding dress.'[94] This caused amazement at Adrianople, but was strange to European eyes as well. When the Duchess of Queensberry was in Europe in 1734, she must have worn a habit, for her brother wrote that 'She has been called *sir* upon the road above twenty times.'[95] From Macon in 1777, Lady Polwarth wrote: 'I think our stay produced nothing else remarkable except the admiration of the maid at Mrs Barker's riding habit which she put on for the sake of

warmth. The girl calls it being *habillé en homme* and told her she was *joli comme un coeur* in it and deserved to be made love to.'[96]

Lady Polwarth herself does not seem to have travelled in a habit. A year before her mother had sent her a new dress for her travels:

'I liked the form (by name half Polonaise) which I think smarter and more convenient than a Nightgown; and it goes to see places or with the addition of a Hat and Cap that suits it even makes Visits on the Road or in a morning with great Success. I had some notion that after so many weeks trapising at Tunbridge another morning apparel could never be useless.'

The name half-polonaise suggests that this was the fitted jacket, cut without seam at the waist, its fronts below the waist curving to the back, rather than a version of the polonaise with looped-up skirt. A fitted short gown or jacket would be convenient for travelling, but less masculine than the habit. Lady Polwarth thought it 'much fitter for the road and much smarter than any other of my gowns' and wore it at church at Tunbridge 'with much approbation'. But if she did wear this dress on her journey through France, it did not do very well: 'The gown Mrs Watson made up for me was only fit for a bonfire on my arrival . . . but . . . an old nightgown and old everyday sack, which came packed in the

*26 The Countess of Mar and Kellie, 1715, in a pink riding habit laced with silver. Her flowing hair or wig, cravat, coat and waistcoat and the cocked hat beneath her arm are all in the style of men's dress. Sir Godfrey Kneller*

*27 Riding jacket, brown camlet, lined with brown linen and twilled silk, believed to have been worn by Susannah Watts (d. 1809) at the age of sixteen in 1735.*

53

trunk, were not hurt by the carriage and serve very well for common use.'[97]

Riding dress was accepted not only for travelling but to some extent as an alternative morning dress (Fig. 28). Mrs Delany's younger sister, having travelled to London in 1737, was taken straight into the company 'just as I was in my riding dress and cap.' While she was in London she acquired a new habit, 'which I shall long to wear but I think I must keep it for some extraordinary occasion it being too great a beauty for vulgar rides or visits.'[98] In 1783 Mary Hamilton one day entered in her diary that on getting up she had her hair dressed for the day, though she put on as usual a riding habit for the morning. There was some indecision about actually riding, but she noted changing back into the habit from a riding skirt; which makes a distinction between the habit worn as a morning dress and the skirt actually worn for riding. In the following year she got up before six one morning to enjoy the 'freshness of the morning air and the beauty of the Thames', but could not go into the garden as the maid 'had taken my Habit out of my room to get it brushed.'[99]

Throughout the century, until the 1780s, the main outer garment was a cloak, full-length, short or three-quarters length, with or without hood, and with variations in shaping and name. As the skirts of the gowns lost their fullness a fitted over-garment became possible. A form

*28  Lady and Gentleman in a Phaeton, 1787. The wearing of a large, full-trimmed hat with a habit, often appears in the 1780s, even with a habit as plain as this one (see also colour plate 2). The man is dressed as for riding in a brown riding frock, buff breeches and riding boots.*
*G. Stubbs*
(Reproduced by courtesy of The Trustees, The National Gallery, London)

29 *Lord Irwin, 1700, in a shooting coat. Apart from the pockets being unusually low this coat differs from a dress coat in its cloth, its looseness of cut and the small round cuffs. The belt added to it is part of his sporting equipment. The wig is the undress campaign wig of the time, and the cravat worn in this way was also a fashion of the early years of the century. The breeches brought down and tied over the knees is the working countryman's style; fashionably at this time stockings came up over the breeches, fastened by garters and turned down over them.*
L. Knyff

of riding greatcoat, buttoned down the front, or open in the skirt to reveal a little of the petticoat, with lapels, a deep or multiple collar, with a large white handkerchief at the neck, was worn as an overcoat, in place of the habit for travelling or morning dress.

Life in the country had an even stronger influence on men's dress. The dress they wore for riding and shooting had a cloth coat of easy fit, shaped for use and plain, though still influenced by the changing lines of dress (Fig. 29). These plainer versions were modified for town wear early in the century. De Saussure, writing home in 1726 said:

'Englishmen are usually very plainly dressed, they scarcely ever wear gold on their clothes; they wear little coats called "frocks", without facings and without pleats, with a short cape above. Almost all wear small round wigs, plain hats and carry canes in their hands but no swords. Their cloth and linen are of the best and finest. You will see rich merchants and gentlemen thus dressed and sometimes even noblemen of high rank, especially in the morning, walking through the filthy and muddy streets. ... Peers and other persons of rank are richly dressed when they go to Court especially on gala days.'

Not all 'noblemen of high rank' approved of this habit. De Saussure later tells a story of the Duke of Bolton 'simply dressed in a plain frock, a small round wig and carrying a stick in his hand' being pushed by the Duke of Somerset's footman, and getting no sympathy from the Duke who 'could not understand how a person of his rank could walk alone through the streets dressed after the manner of a common gentleman, that if anything unpleasant occurred he had only himself to blame and that under the circumstances no one was obliged to recognize him.'[100] Others like Lord Orrery ('I who can so suddenly quit my frock and bob-wig to put on a tye and laced coat') kept their expression of rank for full dress.[101]

As the dress coat began to lose its stiffness in the middle of the century and the frock became accepted for all wear but full dress, the two became more alike. The frock was still marked by its turn-down collar and its plainness, but as it became part of dress wear it developed as a more fitting garment. From the late 1770s it had lapels, 'a lapelled frock, sometimes spotted, with buttons of Mother-of-pearl, short white quilted waistcoats, leather breeches and boots and everybody rides about town.'[102] The plainness was relieved during the 1770s and 1780s by highly decorative buttons, often very large, 'The custom of wearing rich buttons prevails more than ever within these few years; so that a simple frock often costs more than a laced one.'[103] With the lapelled frock, double-breasted frocks also began to appear and became general in the last years of the century.

The leather breeches and boots worn with the frock were the result of the habit noted by Frederick Robinson: 'everybody rides about town.' Travelling from the country into town and riding in town brought a fresh wave of influence from the dress of the country, the dress of riding. Kalm noticed in 1748 that unless a man was sitting on a horse he was rarely seen in boots: 'If anyone in any case walked in the town with boots, he always had a riding whip in his hand as a sign that he had ridden in. If he did not do this he was looked on as a foreigner.'[104] The American loyalist, Samuel Curwen, saw Lord Shelburne walking in London in 1783, 'his dress a brown frock, in boots and a whip in his hand.'[105] C.P. Moritz, the year before, noticed that members of the House of Commons came to the House 'in their great coats, and with boots and spurs.'[106]

Samuel Curwen was surprised to see that Lord Effingham, taking his seat in the House of Lords, 'had the appearance both in his person and dress of a Common Country Farmer, a great coat with brass buttons, frock fashion, his hair short, strait, and to appearance uncombed, his face rough, vulgar and brown, as also his hands. In short he had the look of a labouring farmer or grazier.'[107] The House of Lords was socially a homogeneous body, the peers of England gathered together for the purpose of taking part in the government of the country, but a member could appear in the dress of a farmer. The Duke of Norfolk at Deepdene made the same impression on Betsy Sheridan in 1788: 'The Duke in appearance gives one the idea of a good honest Gentleman Farmer dressed in a plain grey frock.'[108] Many of the great landowners were also great farmers, and on occasion displayed themselves as such. Wraxall recalled in his Memoirs the change of appearance in the House of Lords

with a change of ministry in 1782, when Lord North and his colleagues, now dispersed amongst the Opposition benches, were difficult to recognise, 'wrapped in great coats or habited in frocks and boots' while their successors 'having thrown off their blue and buff uniforms, now ornamented with the appendages of full dress, or returning from court decorated with swords, lace and hair powder, excited still more astonishment.' Ministers wore full dress and the interest was the greater because the blue and buff uniforms of the opposition which they had to throw off had been worn to show sympathy with the Americans in the War of Independence. Wraxall wrote of one of the foremost of them, Charles James Fox: 'At five and twenty I have seen him apparelled *en petit maître* with a hat and feather even in the House of Commons; but in 1781 he constantly, or at least usually, wore in that assembly a blue frock coat and a buff waistcoat, neither of which seemed in general new and sometimes threadbare.'[109] (Fig. 30).

In the middle years of the century, fashionable young men were making their revolt against established dress. To Lord Chesterfield this was an affectation which implied

*30 The House of Commons, with William Pitt announcing the declaration of war with France in 1793. This painting shows the variety of dress and hairdressing worn by members. Fox is sitting on the front bench on the right, wearing a large round hat, with Sheridan on his left.*
*K. A. Hickel*

'a flaw in the understanding. Most of our young fellows here, display some character or other by their dress; some affect the tremendous, and wear a great and fiercely-cocked hat, an enormous sword, a short waistcoat, and a black cravat. ... Others go in brown frocks, leather breeches, great oaken cudgels in their hands, their hats uncocked, and their hair unpowdered; and imitate grooms, stage-coachmen and country bumkins so well in their outsides, that I do not make the least doubt of their resembling them equally in their insides.'[110]

The horse has had a very strong influence on English dress. Macky in his *Journey Through England* wrote of Newmarket: 'All Mankind are here upon an equal Level, from the Duke to Country Peasant! Nobody wear Swords, but without distinction are cloathed suitable to the Humour and Design of the Place for Horse Sports.'[111] Such equality should not be taken as absolute, but the sport and the place together dominated dress, and were a stronger element than social distinction. In Francis Coventry's novel, *Pompey the Little* (1752), Mr Chace is a character whom Lord Chesterfield would have recognised:

> 'Usually called Jack Chace among his intimates, possessed an estate of fifteen hundred pounds a year; which was just sufficient to furnish him with a variety of riding-frocks, jockey-boots, Khevenhullar hats, and coach whips. His great ambition was to be deemed a jemmy fellow, for which purpose he appeared always in the morning in a Newmarket frock, decorated with a great number of green, red or blue capes; he wore a short bob wig, neat buckskin breeches, white silk stockings, and carried a cane switch in his hand.'

Riding and shooting frocks were often shorter than the normal form, and were sometimes double-breasted. Waistcoats too were shorter, some without skirts, with the horizontal 'square-cut' at the waist before this appeared in other dress. These and the riding coats had the name 'Newmarket'. The form of hat worn for most of the century was the cocked hat, that is a hat with the brim turned up in three sections against the crown. There was variety in the size of brim; the angle of wearing, the pinching of the cock; the binding of the edge and the wearing of cockade, button or jewel. The hats were made of beaver or felt or were silk-covered. By the 1780s there was an alternative form, the brim cocked twice only front and back. The round hat, with uncocked brim, a fashionable affectation of common dress in the middle of the century, appeared as a riding hat in the 1770s, and gradually replaced the cocked hat in both forms. By the end of the century this had passed out of wear except in full dress, where, cocked back and front, and made with a collapsible crown, the hat was carried flat under the arm, not worn.

The military, sporting and country life images were met by the opposing image of the Macaronis during the 1760s and 1770s. A few of their fashionable extravagances, like the large buttons and shoe-buckles, passed into general wear in the 1770s and 1780s, but their underlying tendency, a move towards more fastidious and precise dress merged with the main movement, balancing the sporting and country element which gave it direction. The dress worn for sporting activities was worn for much of the day in the country. The young Frenchman, François de la Rochefoucauld, who stayed in Suffolk in 1784, described this life and noted the difference in the approach to day and evening dress:

> 'The commonest breakfast hour is 9 o'clock and by that time the ladies are fully dressed with their hair properly done for the day.... At 10 o'clock or 10.30 each member of the party goes off on his own pursuit—hunting, fishing, or walking. So the day passes till 4 o'clock precisely when you must present yourself in the drawing room with a great deal more ceremony than we are accustomed to in France ... in the morning they come down in riding boots and a shabby coat.... But in the evening unless you have just arrived, you must be well-washed and well-groomed.'[112]

While in the country formal dress was kept within this limit, in town the dress of the country was continually gaining ground, not only by appearing on all but the most formal occasions as an acceptable type of dress, but as a source of change. When Samuel Curwen saw the royal family on the terrace at Windsor in 1781, he thought the Prince of Wales 'affects much the Jemmy dress and air. Age will doubtless soften down the juvenile taste and affectation.'[113] (Fig. 31). The dress of the mature Prince of Wales at the end of the century was a softened down Jemmy dress, its final refinement expressed, but not created by Beau Brummell.

*31  The Prince of Wales, c. 1786, wearing a riding frock with breeches extended into pantaloons, meeting short boots; the loose bush wig is a style of the 1780s and the high-crowned hat, now general for riding, will soon become general wear.*
*G. Stubbs*
(Reproduced by Gracious Permission of Her Majesty The Queen)

## Mourning

Fashionable dress, which was often darkened by periods of court mourning, was also affected by family mourning. This varied in intensity and duration according to the degree of relationship; it also changed in detail during the century. For all except the shortest mourning the period was divided, half deep and half second mourning, with the second period sometimes divided again to make a more relaxed final quarter before dress in full colours and trimmings was once more worn. Short mourning for distant relations was comparable with second mourning and was expressed rather by lack of colour than by wearing black. In 1722 a slight mourning gave Mrs Delany the excuse to buy a new gown, 'my mourning, though a slight one, was a good pretence for me to have a white lutestring.' In 1753 she told her sister to wear 'a week's mourning (grey or white) for Lord Gower' and in the next year they had a fortnight's mourning in grey or white.[114] In 1789 Betsy Sheridan asked her sister in Dublin to get her two poplin gowns and petticoats: 'The colour I wish is a kind of silver-grey which may be worn in slight mourning, but is also to be worn out of mourning.'[115]

Mourning for people of fashion was not a simple expression of private grief and loss. Like other dress it was subject to the occasion of wearing and it had its own full dress and undress, its public and private wear. When Lady Tufton's daughter died in 1710, she and her surviving daughters went to church 'in long scarfs and allamode hoods over their faces not a bit to be seen of them, soe they sat all churchtime.'[116] In 1747, Mrs Delany in mourning for her sister's brother-in-law wore black bombazine in a manteau and petticoat for full dress; but 'at home a dark grey poplin, and abroad, undrest, a dark grey unwatered tabby.' After three months the bombazine was replaced by black silk. When their father died at the end of 1723, she wrote to her sister in the following March: 'You should if you keep strictly to the rules of mourning, wear your shammy gloves two months longer, but in the country, if it is more convenient to you, you may wear black silk.' The wearing of black chamois leather gloves was a sign of the deepest mourning, dullness of surface being an essential quality; glazed black gloves or silk ones followed and then white. But the minutiae of mourning were generally relaxed in country wear. In the following year Mrs Delany replied to an enquiry from Mrs Carter:

'I think her right in buying a white satin to top her black, for the reasons she gives me; but that she can only wear as a nightgown, and if she was in town she should wear only mourning when she is dressed, but in the country that will not be minded, white gloves, coloured fan and coloured shoes and edgings if she pleases, and black or white short apron and girdle, which she likes best.'[117]

In 1779 the Marchioness Grey instructed her daughter Lady Polwarth about the family mourning when the death of one relative came within the mourning period for another:

'But I have now a longer Mourning to announce to you ... the death of old Mrs Cocks. ... This is an Aunt's Mourning and the same sort exactly as we now wear only longer, and this week we shall reckon into part of the other. ... A Black Nightgown I will get for you and desire Mrs Watson will make it with all Speed, but nothing can carry it to you before Tuesday next. The Sack trimmed with Lace is not I believe improper and I have not untrimmed mine. As to Linnen—worked or plain Muslin—Gauzes plain or striped, Fringed or Edged—made up plain or trimmed with Gauze or Ribbon or Tiffany or anything may all be worn. *As to Time* we shall not I suppose hold out Six Weeks, but putting the two together make out a Month in all, perhaps three weeks, black buckles, ribbons and one week coloured ribbon. But you may really do as you please and wear it or not. For Caps too I would add that all Dressed Caps now and undressed being composed of Gauze a bit of Black and White Ribbon makes them all fit and worked round Ruffles and Aprons are very fit.'

In a year's time Lady Polwarth was herself a widow, after only eight years of marriage and the Marchioness wrote sadly, but practically to her younger daughter:

'Send to Mrs Watson and speak to her to get a proper Dress for your Sister. It is I know Silk and not stuff but of a particular kind, a thick Rusty not Shining Black and known I believe as Alas! the *Widows* kind of Silk. The Form too which used to be more different from other Persons may now I believe be what is more commonly worn, a close-bodied Nightgown and Pettycoat but without any Trimmings and the sort of half-close Sleeves with Cuffs (worn this winter) but not to the wrist that allow of little Ruffles would I should think be a proper sort. It is not necessary to be higher in the neck or button as a Jesuit but she might (for Dispatch) get and send with it a Black Crape Handkerchief and a Black Silk Short Apron, trimmed plain with Crape.'

Of all mourning a widow's was the deepest and of longest duration, but difference from normal dress has lessened and silk is worn for deep mourning, instead of the earlier and regulation bombazine or crape of court mourning (Fig.32).

There was a nice balance of convention when private mourning coincided with a court appearance. In 1780 Lady Grantham was busy choosing her gown and trimmings for her presentation at court after her marriage, when the death of a relative of her husband raised the question whether she should attend or not. In the end it was decided that she should go: 'Lord Grantham thinks it would be proper to go to Court on Thursday in mourning ... and to defer the presentation is very inconvenient to me in particular as it delays my returning visits.' She thought she had better go in a black gown and petticoat and had 'bespoke a suit of gauze linnen, for Lace, I imagine is improper at first', but 'I went at last in White—Gold with Black ornaments and Black

32 Mrs Salusbury (1707–73), mother of Mrs Thrale, c. 1766. Her husband had died in 1762 but she still wears a frilled cap, pleated ruff and black veil of widow's mourning. It was this dress which the Marchioness Grey must have had in mind when she wrote in 1780 that a widow's dress was then less different from that of other people than it had been formerly.
J. Zoffany

Ribbon in the Cap; having determined it was better not to go the first time entirely in Black.'[118]

For men mourning was simpler: black suits for deep mourning and grey for second mourning, with the details of weepers, the linen bands worn on the cuffs, hat bands, black buckles and swords, as the special signs of mourning. With these details another dark material seems to have been acceptable as well as grey. When Admiral Boscawen's sister died, his wife prepared his mourning:

> 'I have this day made you (alas) 3 pairs of cuffs. I have likewise examined your wardrobe and found you have a coat for deep mourning but no frock, so I've sent for Regnier and as I could not venture to fancy grey, I ordered the same superfine blue you used to have with black buttons and black cape and it will be ready tomorrow. This I thought necessary as you would not like to go abroad in colours and you won't be able to stay at home.'[119]

The deep mourning coat was there for full dress, but the frock was needed for undress wear. In 1771 Lady Grey's father, Lord Breadalbane, wrote to her from Edinburgh when his son and her step-brother died, asking what the present regulations were about mourning:

> 'I am so out of the world that I don't know the regulations about

mourning, which have gone through several alterations. Here they wear weepers for Uncles and Nephews (which I think they don't in England) and even for cousins, and their mournings are very long, but as I think all ceremonial fashions should be regulated by those of the Court, I wish you would let me know how long I should wear weepers if I were in London, and how long black wax is used. I think weepers are worn half the *whole* mourning, black swords and Buckles without weepers during half the *remainder* and slight mourning of the last quarter of the time, but I don't know how long the whole amounts to.'[120]

Children joined in this family mourning. When Mrs Delany's great-niece was about to pay her a long visit she wrote in November 1780: 'You may send up GMA's coloured coat as should you be willing to leave her behind till June, her mourning will be out at the end of the 3 qrs of the year mourning. Perhaps rules are altered but I speak of ancient days.' The child's grandfather had died in August so, according to 'ancient days', she would have been in mourning till the following April. She was at this time nine years old.[121] Charlotte Jerningham, at a convent in Paris for her education, was in 1785 wearing mourning for her grandmother: 'If you do not like to wear your Black Linnen at present, keep it for second Mourning or at Christmas. You shall have a Black silk, and it will be better to wear that only on Sundays, and the Linnen every day.'[122]

Servants too, in and out of livery, were put into mourning. In 1712 Lady Strafford wrote: 'My brother Arundell has got the small pox ... which makes me defer making up my men's surtout coats till I see whether he lives or dyes; for, for a brother's mourning all people put there [*sic*] servants in gray.'[123] Servants were not usually put in mourning for public mourning, although George II had ordered it for Queen Caroline. The Marchioness Grey wrote to her daughter on this point: 'As to Mourning, your Livery Servants you know only wear your *own* Mourning and when that ends they of Course go out of it into the Coloured Livery. It has been customary in Deep Mourning for the nearest Relations to put the Upper Servants (men and women) into it and then they wear it the whole time and in the different changes of it, as their Masters do.'[124]

# III

# *The Gentry*

## The Country

Although not all of the gentry were country-dwellers, most were country-based. The wealthier members followed the nobility in regular seasons in London. From the point of view of fashion this divided the country gentry into those who had regular contacts with fashionable society and those who would not have regarded themselves as people of fashion, but kept what Mrs Delany called 'a decent compliance with it.' The great houses and estates of the nobility, a dominating presence in the countryside, were the social centres of a local group of smaller landowners, gentry and clergy. In turn these gentry, some of whom had steadily held the same manorial estate for centuries, and others who had recently established themselves, were leaders of their smaller local society and through their contact with people of fashion set the local standards. For many of the smaller gentry, particularly in the first half of the century much of their knowledge of fashion was gained indirectly, through contacts with noble or more fashionable neighbours and through correspondence with relatives and friends more conveniently placed for discovering the news of fashion.

An essay in *The Spectator* of 1711 gives the impression that the time-lag of fashion increased with the distance from London. An imagined lady of a justice of the peace near Salisbury was said to be 'at least ten years behindhand in her Dress but at the same time as fine as Hands could make her. She was flounced and furbelowed from Head to Foot, every ribbon was wrinkled and every part of her Garments in Curl. ... The greatest Beau at our next Country Sessions was dressed in a most monstrous Flaxen Periwig that was made in King William's Reign.'[1] The plays of the time constantly make comedy of country fashion. In Steele's *The Tender Husband* (1705), Sir Harry Gubbins dresses his son Humphrey 'in the very Suit I had at my own Wedding' and Humphrey is mocked by the fashionable London lady: 'Mr Gubbins I am extreamly pleased with your suit 'tis Antique and originally from France. ... 'Twould make a very pretty Dance Suit in a Mask.' Such garments of festive wear, or more than usual cost, were preserved for other special occasions, so that it was the grand clothes which were the unfashionable ones.

Yet even early in the century distant country gentry bought such clothes in London. Nicholas Blundell of Crosby, Lancashire, bought there as part of his marriage expenses in 1703 'a Campaign Perry-Wigg' for £10. This was only a little less than Lord Bristol paid for a similar wig. Nicholas Blundell's wedding clothes were of blue cloth with silver thread for the button holes and silver buttons. The cloth at 18s a yard cost £4. 12. 3; the silver thread for the buttonholes was £2. 12. 6. and the buttons £1. 6. 3. In the following year his wife had a calico mantua and petticoat from London, costing £3. They again bought clothes in London in 1706, 1709 and 1710 and 1717, when they also bought outfits for their two daughters, Mally, thirteen and Fanny, eleven, who were about to set off for a convent school in Bruges. Six years later the girls returned with material for gowns bought in Paris and more bought in London. From Paris there was damask, lemon-coloured for Mally, red for Fanny, enough for a gown and petticoat at 8s 4d a yard. There were nightgowns and petticoats, probably one each, at a cost of £8. 14. 7., with materials and making up, half the price of the damask; the material for a single mantua and petticoat at £1. 6. 4. and materials for altering and enlarging others. Quilted petticoats cost £3. 19. 2. There were a pair of stays each, riding habits with hoop petticoats and 'Linnen for riding in', other hoop petticoats and 'Barmoodas' hats. There were silk aprons, black silk hoods, gloves, stockings, shoes and clogs, buckles, girdles and fans, diamond and gold earrings. A large item was holland for shifts and aprons, cambric for 'Carchaffs' which cost £14. 18s., and cambric muslin and holland for heads, ruffles, aprons and handkerchiefs, £8. 19s. The largest and most costly item was Flanders lace for heads and ruffs at £42. 15s. far more costly than the damask for gowns and petticoats which came to £18. 15s.[2] Amongst the country gentry as well as within the court circle fine lace was the important item of full dress.

Squire Sullen in Farquhar's play, *The Beaux Stratagem* and Squire Western in Fielding's *Tom Jones* are only two of a long line of country squires in fiction and drama in the first half of the century with no interests beyond their own property, country sports and drinking, playing cards and smoking. The Rev. William Cole of Bletchley in 1766 wrote of one of these young men, one of the smaller gentry, son of a fellow clergyman, whose wife had brought to the marriage the property on which they lived. She, however, unlike Mrs Sullen, enjoyed the same way of life as her husband, 'the most sensible match that was ever made in point of Tempers, they equally living on horseback, in the Fields, by the sides of Rivers, or anywhere but in the house, which is at Mursley, where her Father established them in a Farm.'[3] Most of the country gentry enjoyed some of the country sports, but many had wider interests and a greater concern with the practical business of local society, looking after their own estates and taking an active part in local affairs (Figs. 33, 34).

One of these was Henry Purefoy of Shalstone, Buckinghamshire, who had succeeded his father in 1704 when he was a boy of seven. The

33 *Thomas Cook of Thoresby, aged*
*85, 1725. The coat appears to fasten*
*not centrally, but right over left and*
*the large hat to be erratically cocked;*
*the stockings are pulled up over the*
*breeches.*
*Peter Tillemans*

34 *A scene from Isaac Bickerstaffe's*
*opera,* Love in a Village, *first*
*performed in 1762, showing Justice*
*Woodcock, a pompous country*
*squire, Hawthorn his easy-going,*
*sporting neighbour and Hodge his*
*servant. The different styles of dress*
*of Woodcock and Hawthorn, one in*
*a laced suit, the other in frock and*
*riding boots, reflect their two ways of*
*life.*
*Mezzotint by J. Finlayson, 1768,*
*after J. Zoffany*

Purefoys owned the manor and had lived there since the fifteenth century. Henry's mother, Elizabeth, was daughter of 'a citizen of London' but was also of 'an antient family' in Hertfordshire. Henry Purefoy, having read law at Oxford, settled down to look after his estate. He took a careful interest in the parish, often acting on behalf of his poorer neighbours against any encroachment of their rights, 'for I think it a pity the Poor should be deprived of their Right only because they are poor.' He was not a great sportsman although he rode, coursed and did a little hunting. He bought books on many subjects and was a regular subscriber to *The Gentleman's Magazine*. He was not active in public affairs outside the county, but was sheriff of Buckinghamshire in 1748-9. He and his mother travelled locally, mainly in summer, but visits to London and Bath were rare and much of their knowledge of what was fashionable—and they considered this when they bought their clothes—they had by proxy.

They bought clothes, or material for them, locally, in Brackley or Buckingham and at the little more distant Bicester or Chipping Norton. They also bought a good deal from London through tradesmen or connections who acted as agents. In 1736 Henry wrote to Mr Boyce, Surrey Street, Strand, asking for patterns of superfine cloth and for news of the current fashion for suits, 'whether they button their Cloaths with silver or Gold buttons or continue to wear laced waistcoats of silk or cloath and whether dressed or undressed coats.' (Figs 35, 36). He wanted his breeches made with no flap to the codpiece—this was still a fairly new device in the 1730s. The colour of the cloth coat and breeches is not revealed, but the waistcoat was of green, unwatered tabby, had sleeves, was trimmed with silver buttons and silver lace about the same breadth as he had in gold for a waistcoat the year before, 'a showy lace of the common price by the ounce'. When the clothes arrived he found the coat sleeves longer than his last year's coat and wanted to know 'if they wear their coat sleeves longer than they did last year'. In 1745 he had a suit from a Chipping Norton tailor and pointed out that his breeches had been made with holes for strings at the back waist, instead of straps; he always used a buckle. In 1746 he had red cloth breeches and a waistcoat from the same tailor and in 1747 ordered 'cinnamon colour or very light colour' coat and breeches only as 'I have so many waistcoats by me.' He does not mention material, but probably these, like most of his coats and breeches, were cloth, worn with either cloth or silk waistcoats. He was always particular about the gold or silver lace trimming and that the buttons should be fashionable. In 1744 he ordered from George Vaughan, laceman in the Strand, '5 yards of silver Lace to bind a waistcoat as good and fashionable as any is worn; and also two dozen and four silver twist buttons for the waistcoat.' Two months later his mother wrote for '2 dozen and an half of silvered coat buttons with catgutt stalks to them and 20 silvered breast buttons with catt gutt stalks, also the newest fashion.'

35 Portrait of a gentleman of the
1740s wearing cloth coat and breeches
with a contrasting waistcoat, laced
with silver.
J. Highmore

He wore nightgowns or morning gowns. Mrs Purefoy, again writing
on his behalf, asked Mr Robotham, their chief agent in London—whose
wife had been a maid in the Purefoy household—to enquire 'what sort of
sashes the Gentlemen tie their fine nightgowns about with.' In 1744 she
ordered green alapeen 'to line my son's nightgown' and in 1749 he wrote
to Anthony Baxter of Covent Garden for 'nine yards of flowered cotton
with a brown ground and coloured flowers yard wide ... it is for my
own morning gown so that if half of it be of one sort and half of another
it will do but both of them must have brown Grounds.' His nightcaps
were of 'fine thick plain white Dimmothy or I think it is called
Vomilion, it has a little nap on it on one side.' He wrote again for
'vermilion or Dimmothy' for night caps, in 1744.

His wigs were made by a barber and wigmaker at Buckingham. In
1747 he found that 'The new Periwigg you made mee has some Hair on
top of the Crown that don't curl and when I put on my Hat or the wind
blows it stares and rises all up. I have minded other folks' periwigs and I
think it should have another row of Curls higher towards the Crown.' In
1753 he ordered a dark brown one 'instead of a Grizzel one' at fifteen

36 *Waistcoat of green watered silk
trimmed with silver lace, 1760–70.*

shillings. He used a good deal of powder; '6 pounds of grounds to
powder Periwigs' are recorded in 1736, 1737 and 1740. He was
particular that his beaver hats were beaver: 'the last you sent they tell me
was not all Beaver.' In 1737 Mrs Purefoy asked Mr Robotham to check
the fashion in men's hats: 'The Brim is but 4 inches wide. The
Gentlemen here wear 'em with larger Brim but I desire you will enquire
whether that is the fashionable size or No.'

He wore half-jack boots, with spur leathers and a pair of strong spurs
in 1736 and liked the boot soles thick for riding. In January 1735 he
found 'every place now so deep in dirt where one walks that my
Galloshes are of no service to me' and the Buckingham shoemaker was
asked to call so that he could have something else made from them. He
got spatterdashes or leggings from another shoemaker, in Brackley.
Inside his boots he wore white thread over-stockings.

In 1735 Mrs Purefoy, then sixty-three years old, was interested in
'workt chintz for a gown and petticoat.' Her son wrote to Anthony
Baxter: 'They are generally worked in very fine Change stitch and in all
colours as chintzes are printed, let us know of it, or if not enough for a

gown and petticoat enough for a wrapper.' She sent a blue damask gown to London for cleaning or dyeing in 1746 'any colour it will take best' and at the same time enquired about new materials: 'They say Sattins are much worn, I desire to know if they be; if they are pray send me patterns of a beautiful green Sattin and some patterns of a fine pretty deep-blue Lutestring.' In 1753, now eighty years old, she was still interested in new materials and asked for 'a fine Cotton for a gown with a Cinnamon or yellowish ground Flowered very handsomely with shades of Colours and enough for another gown of fashionable cotton with white Ground flowered with coloures of a crown a yard.'

She bought hoop petticoats from Long's warehouse in 1738, 'for one who is not half an Ell [22½ in] in the waist' and in 1741 'a good whalebone hoop Petticoat of the newest fashion. It must be 3 yards and a quarter round the bottom and it must draw in a Top for a waist half a yard and a nail round [20½ in] and the length upon the hip to the bottom a yard and half a quarter.' A quilted petticoat had to be returned in 1739 because it was too heavy to wear; in 1742 she was wearing underpetticoats of 'tufted Dimmothy' beneath her hoop.

She wore wrapping gowns of printed cotton. Anthony Baxter was asked to send in 1739 'fine thick printed cotton enough to make two wrappers for my mother, they must be of different handsome patterns' and in 1746 'chintz with a brown ground or anything that is very fine that imitates it . . . it is for a wrapper for my mother.' In 1738 she ordered enough white satin to make the satin she had bought for a wrapper, price eight shillings a yard, into a gown and petticoat. At this time she was in mourning, both for a nephew and for Queen Caroline.

For dress wear she ordered in 1736 'a long Alamode Hood with a very good black lace round it (as wide as anybody wears) to wear when I am dressed or a Manteel hood if they be most worn.' Another hood, 'a short flourished hood', cost half-a-guinea in 1744. More expensive was the 'Genteel fashionable Capuchin of about three pounds price and an Handsome Ermine Tippett' in 1746. She was interested in the 'new french gold and Silver Hatts', sold at the White Bear in Fleet Street, 'some say here they be made of leather', in 1740, but ordered a little later 'a fine fashionable Leghorn hat for myself. They wear them here small crowns and narrow Brimms.' She also bought a straw hat from Dunstable for 3s 6d, which was most likely of local making.

Both mother and son were anxious to know the changes in dress worn in London when they bought new items, but they also took careful note of what was being worn in Buckinghamshire and modified their requests accordingly. Mrs Purefoy refers to her dresses simply as gown, gown and petticoat or wrapper. The wrappers of 'fine thick cotton' were probably her morning wear as a housewife, for she was active in the management of house and dairy and her letters reveal her as a competent woman of business.[4]

Clarissa Harlowe, in Richardson's novel, *Clarissa* (1747-8), is a young

country gentlewoman in this tradition. It is one of her virtues that she was skilled 'in all the parts of dairy management' and 'whether full-dressed or in the housewife's more humble garb, equally elegant and lovely.' She is also shown as a leader of fashion in her neighbourhood: 'The neighbouring ladies used to say that they need not fetch fashions from London; since whatever Miss Clarissa Harlowe wore was the best fashion.' (Fig. 37). Richardson uses clothes to convey the attitudes and pressures of her family when they are trying to force her into marriage against her will. Patterns of rich silks are sent for, for wedding clothes, 'the newest as well as the richest we could procure answerable to our station in the world', expressing in this way their complete satisfaction with a marriage which they saw only in material terms. At the same time they try to overwhelm the reluctant Clarissa with material generosity, while completely disregarding her own feelings: 'Your father intends you six suits (three of them dressed suits) at his expense. You have an entire new suit; and one besides, which I think you never wore but twice. As the new suit is rich, if you choose to make that one of the six your father will present you with a hundred guineas in lieu.' That implies that her dressed wedding suits would cost each about a hundred pounds, which brings them into the range of dress worn by the nobility.

*37 Robert Lovelace abducting Clarissa. Her dress was described by Lovelace: 'her morning gown was a pale primrose-coloured paduasoy; the cuffs and robings curiously embroidered by the fingers of the ever-charming Arachne, in a running pattern of violets and leaves; the light in the flowers silver, gold in the leaves ... her coat white satin quilted.' The artist followed the text except for the petticoat which is here embroidered to match the gown. She is shown without hat or hood because 'she seems to have intended to show me that she was determined not to stand to her appointment' of leaving her home with him.*
*F. Hayman*

71

38 *Gown of printed linen, white with lilac stripes, sprigs in red, yellow and brown; the type of gown which could have been the morning wear of the daughter of 'a plain country squire' and later pass, like Nancy Woodforde's, to be the best dress of a maid, 1775–90.*

39 *Page from Barbara Johnson's album, 1771, showing purple and white linen which she bought for a gown at Northampton.*

The prospective, but thwarted bridegroom appeared 'as fine as a lord, with a charming white peruke, fine laced shirt and ruffles, coat trimmed with silver, and a waistcoat standing on end with lace.' In the early days of her captivity by Lovelace, Clarissa wears 'a brown lustring nightgown, fresh and looking like new, as everything else she wears does, whether new or not, from an elegance natural to her. A beaver hat, a black ribbon about her neck and blue knots on her breast. A quilted petticoat of carnation-coloured satin.' A plain silk gown over a contrasting quilted petticoat, the undress of the country gentlewoman, eighteenth-century dress in its basic, simple form, is the dress which Clarissa later gives to the maid of the house for 'Sunday wear'. As her trials and persecutions increase she wears, continually, a white nightgown, 'white flowing robes (for she had not a hoop)', and all the emotive overtones of white come into play, as her dress is from time to time described.[5]

Dresses of printed linen or cotton were general morning wear in the households of country gentry (Figs 38, 39). In *The School for Scandal* (1777) Sir Peter Teazle reminds his wife, now a fashionable lady in London, of her dress before he married her: 'You were then in somewhat humbler style—the daughter of a plain country squire. Recollect Lady Teazle, when I first saw you sitting at your tambour, in a pretty figured linen gown with a bunch of keys at your side.' Goldsmith's comedy *She Stoops to Conquer* is based on the possibility of mistaking the house of a country squire for an inn and his daughter for a maid when she appears in her morning dress. The mistress of the house kept certain tasks to herself and her morning dress was to this extent a working dress. Fanny Burney tells the story of friends expecting a visit from French emigrés in the district, caught in their linen morning gowns: 'Miss Kitty was in *dishbill* and Mrs Hamilton finishing washing up her China from Breakfast. A Maid who was out on the Pump first saw the arrival ran in to give Miss Kitty time to escape for she was in her round dress, nightcap and without her roll and curls. However he followed too quick and Mrs Hamilton was seen in her linen gown and mob, though she had put on a silk one in expectation for every noon these four or five days past.'[6]

The Williamsons acquired the manor of Husborne Crawley in Bedfordshire early in the century. Talbot Williamson, who inherited in 1737, was gentleman usher to Princess Amelia and lived in London. His younger brother Edmond, rector of the neighbouring parish of Millbrook, looked after the estate. Their sister Christian—Tidy to her brothers—was married to a naval officer, Jonathan Russel, but they also lived in London. In 1760, Edmond, a widower of forty-seven with an eight-year-old daughter, married Mary Tipping, the nineteen-year-old daughter of another Bedfordshire rector. Tidy, Talbot and his wife were asked to buy wedding clothes in London, and Tidy wrote for practical details: 'How many yards of $\frac{1}{2}$ Ell she takes for a Negligée and petticoat

A Gentleman and Lady in the
Undress of the Year 1771.

a Garnet Damask Gown
eleven shillings a yard.
eleven yards.

January 1771.

a black Italian Lutestring
Negligee. eighteen yards.
three qrs. wide. seven shillings
a yard:

Northampton May 1771

Mourning for my
Uncle Johnson

a purple and white copper-plate
linnen Gown. seven yards
3. 2 a yard.

Northampton May 1771

A Gentleman and Lady in the
Court Dress of the Year 1771.

and also the bigness of her arm for the Ruffles as 'tis worth while to have them made up in London and no great expence, indeed if her Cloaths could by sending an old Nightgown that fitted her to be sure it would have been better but that must be as they think proper.' Talbot reported the results of their shopping:

> 'We have been all three this morning to buy a silk and have bought a very pretty one, white damasked with shades of white in pattern and a few coloured flowers interspersed. Silks are dear and negligées are a prodigal fashion—20 yards at 13s.... Your sisters wish the gown was to be made up in London, but as that cannot be we suppose, still they hope the cap and ruffles may be, preferring *à la mode de Londres* to Bedford.'

Mary Tipping and her mother did not think a gown made in London could be made to fit, but she sent her arm size for the ruffles and these and the cap were made up, of blonde lace, in London.

Mrs Purefoy had written only of gowns and petticoats and of wrappers. The next generation of country gentry took up both the fashionable term negligée and the 'prodigal fashion' of it. In 1764 Mary Williamson had a new sack, this time made in London, and again her sister-in-law was involved, sending careful details of it with sketches for approval (Fig. 40). In 1769 Mrs Russel wrote again about the trimming

*40  Letter from Christian Russel to Edmond Williamson describing the trimming of a new sack for Edmond's wife, Mary, 1764.*

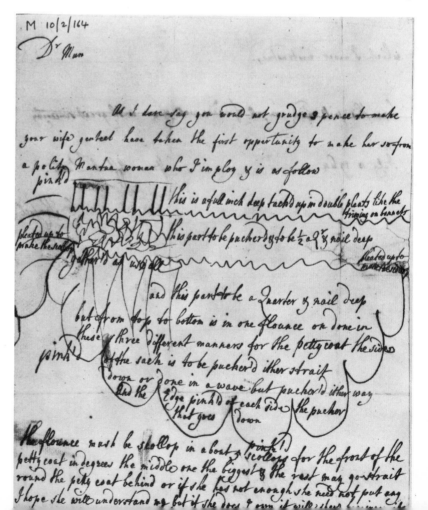

of a gown: 'It must be Shaneel of what colour you please or mixed with two colours.' This was 3d or 4d a yard and she would need a dozen and a half yards; 'I have $2\frac{1}{2}$ for my Nightgown, but that is trimming down to the bottom which takes up to the 2nd Dozen.' Mrs Williamson's gowns seem to have been sacks, although it may have been only these dress gowns that needed help from London. In 1771 Mrs Russel wrote again: 'Your sack is trimmed and paid for and looks very smart. Miss Hyde thinks a Blond Lace Stomacher will look the best as your Sack is trimmed with Lace.' In an undated letter she asks how Lady Ossory liked Mrs Williamson's new sack. More practical clothing came from London to Millbrook in 1761, a winter petticoat and cardinal, 'the prunella is esteemed very strong wear and warm, price 13s unmade up, which will be better done to fit at home; the cardinal 14s. You will not find that like the scarlet men wear; such a one would be 25s; but this is common woman's wear and wove 8 qrs wide.' In gratitude for her help with the wedding shopping Edmond offered Tidy a habit which had probably been made for his first wife. She thought she would have small use for it as she rode little and generally went in the post chaise, so she declined it, adding: 'Now I don't see why it might not do at home, as I think it was never worn, and might save the expense of one, but you know best.'

Letters between brothers and sister have few references to Edmond's clothes, but Talbot sent him in 1762 five and a half yards of thick cloth for 'a good double-breasted surtout coat with a cape, unless you are for bestowing a piece of black velvet or black Manchester velvet (which is cotton and of which I have 2 pair of breeches that look and wear very well).'[7]

John Salusbury was a contemporary of Edmond Williamson and lived about ten miles away, at Leighton Buzzard. A diary of three years of his life, 1757-9, survives. He seems to have had no profession or occupation, but drew rents from a little property, acted as justice of the peace, turnpike trustee, officer in the militia and trustee of a Leighton Buzzard charity. He belonged to a local society, a group of men who each in turn was responsible for an evening meeting of entertainment at one of the local inns, and he often walked or rode to visit friends in the district. He went regularly to church, not always his own, and often to Aspley Guise, near Husborne Crawley and Millbrook, but there is no reference to the Williamsons in his diary and none in their correspondence to him although they had common acquaintances. He was a bachelor with one maidservant and a boy and help in the garden and orchard which supplied him with fruit and vegetables. He did a little shooting and fishing, saw visiting players perform *Oroonoko*, *The Recruiting Officer* and *Richard III* at Leighton in the summer of 1759 and played a great deal at cards.

Throughout the three years he made half-yearly payments of 5s for having his hair powdered regularly. In May 1759 he bought a new-cut wig for a guinea which he noted as part of his expenses as a militia officer.

The clothes he acquired during these three years were of cloth, fustian or leather. In 1758 he bought buckskin breeches, a pair of cloth breeches, 'to my best coat', a fustian coat and waistcoat costing £3.16s and another coat and waistcoat. In 1759 he bought another pair of leather breeches. He paid a bill for mourning for Princess Caroline in 1758 and put on mourning again for the Princess of Orange the next year. He bought two pairs of shoes in 1757 for 11s and another two pairs and a pair of boots costing £1.12s in all in 1758. In August 1757 he went to the Assembly held at the time of the Bedford Races when the ball was opened by Lord Russell and Lady Caroline Russell. The younger people danced: Mr Salusbury played whist.[8]

There had been races at Bedford since 1730 and the evening assemblies held with them were major social events in the county, assemblies attended by local gentry and some of the nobility. In 1778 Fanny Cater, seventeen years old, was looking forward to one of these balls. She and her twin sister Sophia had been working themselves gowns to wear and they were concerned about their shoes. Mrs Cater wrote to her friend Mrs Williamson, now a widow, living with Mrs Russel in London to ask her to let Wilmer, the shoemaker, know 'that Fanny will have them not so round at the top of the toe as the last, nor the Roses so deep Coloured—also that they are to dance in so begs he will be careful that they will keep up well behind.' Fanny wrote to ask if Batson, a hairdresser, could be persuaded to come down and stay at Kempston to dress her and her sister's hair and perhaps that of some friends: 'I hope we shall be able to get several heads for him to dress besides ourselves as we shall be sorry for it not to answer for him.' She also wanted to know 'what they now wear on their Heads and likewise on their necks.'[9]

There were regular subscription balls at many towns, with the attendance at them carefully controlled. Printed copies of the rules of the Derby Assemblies show that these balls were for the gentry only. By the end of the century there were less exclusive balls, like those at Bury St Edmunds, where to French eyes, in 1784, 'The ladies are always dressed for the occasion yet with simplicity. . . . The men's dress is very simple, black breeches and silk stockings such is the correct dress for occasions like these. The well-dressed men wear a new coat every time, but a plain coat of cloth with nothing sumptuous about it'. Public balls were also held every fortnight in the Assembly Room at Colchester.[10]

There were some sporting young men who carried their informality a little too far. Jane Austen wrote to her sister about a ball in 1796, wondering 'How many of the Gentlemen, Musicians and Waiters he will have persuaded to come in their shooting jackets.' A year later, working on the first draft of *Northanger Abbey,* she created John Thorpe, 'who seemed fearful of being thought too handsome unless he wore the dress of a groom.'[11]

Barbara Johnson (1738-1825), daughter of a vicar of Olney, Buckinghamshire, compiled an album of samples of material from her dresses, sometimes noting full details of the lengths of material used, its width and price. Small fashion plates from the pocket books of the year appear amongst the samples. Diaries, letters and accounts give the types and quantity of dress, the names of fabrics and the cost of clothes, but this album, now in the Victoria and Albert Museum, is a kaleidoscope of change in texture, colour and pattern during one woman's lifetime.[12]

From 1751, when she was thirteen years old, until 1756, she records a suit in yellow tabby and a short sack and petticoat, both in 1752; in 1753 a blue camlet riding habit. During these years she also had several mourning garments, a gown of black stuff for the Prince of Wales in 1751 and a long sack of grey poplin for second mourning, showing that even a girl of thirteen or fourteen wore public mourning for a member of the royal family. She had another long sack in grey figured stuff, which was second mourning for her grandmother in 1753, when the black gown of 1751 was perhaps still available for first mourning. Her father, who left the Olney living in 1753, died in 1756, and she then had a black-stuff short sack, a grey-stuff negligée and white lustring nightgown, the last two second mourning. The rest of her clothes are listed as negligées, nightgowns, sacks and short sacks and petticoats. The negligée of 1755 was of flowered silk; the nightgowns of blue watered tabby, 1753 and brown tabby, 1755; the sack of 1752 of Irish stuff, the two short sacks, 1754, of red and white linen (Fig. 41).

In the next ten years between the age of eighteen and twenty-eight she had two more riding dresses, brown fustian, 1757, and pompadour broadcloth, 1760, this one a present from her brother. She had a nightgown and petticoat of green damask, and a negligée and puckered petticoat of white satin, 1762. There were two nightgowns, brown figured lustring, 1758 and a green and white stuff, 1763; six negligées, two of them mourning dress for her mother, 1759, bombazine and dark grey poplin; others in striped buff taffety, 1758, blue and white spotted lustring, 1761—this for her brother's birthday—pink and white striped lustring, 1765 and garnet-coloured paduasoy, 1761-2. There were besides ten gowns, dark grey tabby, another mourning dress for her mother, 1759, a 'massareen' blue lutestring, 1766, purple and white cotton, 1762, purple and white linen, 1763, yellow and white striped linen, 1766, blue and white copper plate linen, 1764, India dimity, 1765, flowered lawn, 1764, and two of scarlet stuff, December 1759 and Christmas, 1764 (Fig. 42). The term negligée appears first in 1755 and after 1756 she no longer uses the term sack. After 1777 she drops both negligée and nightgown and uses only the general term gown until 'round gown' appears in 1798; she gives a name to one gown, a Stormont gown and petticoat, mourning for an aunt in 1789. The only other named style is a Manchester Brunswick in 1772, a blue and white check cotton, twelve yards of three-quarter-yard wide material. A Brunswick is illustrated in the small fashion plate under the year 1768. There are gaps in the records between 1772 and 1776 and between 1781

41  *Page from Barbara Johnson's album, 1752–6  showing flowered silks of 1755 and the grey stuffs and white lutestring worn for second mourning, 1753 and 1756. The small heads have been added from later fashion plates.*

42  *Page from Barbara Johnson's album, 1764–6, showing other examples of flowered and striped linens and Indian dimity.*

and 1789 and from this time the entries are more sparse. Between 1792 and 1800 there was a gown and petticoat, brown and white cotton, 1794; gowns of Irish stuff, 1792, clouded French satin, 1795, a Manchester gown 1794, blue Canterbury muslin, 1795, six calico gowns, a round gown in 1798, a gingham round gown, and black taffety— mourning for her brother Robert—in 1799.

Her most expensive dress was the negligée of garnet paduasoy which took twenty-two yards of silk at 10s and was trimmed with fringe. A figured ducape negligée of 1767 cost £6. 6. 6. and its trimming £2. 4s (colour plate 1). This she noted was for Stamford Races, that is for the evening assembly at the time of the race meeting. After her father's death she seems to have lived in Lincolnshire, perhaps with a brother. Her yellow and white linen gown of 1766 cost £1. 4s, which was about the same price as the calico gowns of the 1790s; her satin gown of 1795 cost £3. 10s.

Nancy Woodforde came to live with her uncle, James Woodforde, in the parsonage of Weston Longeville in Norfolk in 1770 when she was a young woman of twenty-two. She remained with him until his death in 1803 and seems sometimes to have found her life in this country parish rather dull. There were visits to the houses of neighbouring clergy and local gentry and their return visits to the parsonage; regular visits to Norwich for shopping, the rector's church business and occasionally for a theatre or concert. Every three or four years she and her uncle went on a long summer visit, June to October, to see their relations in Somerset, breaking the journeys by spending a few days in London and sometimes in Bath. In intervening years some of their Somerset relations came to Norfolk. Life would have been much less pleasant without the friendship of Mrs Custance, the wife of the squire of Weston, whose grandfather had acquired the property in 1726. John Custance held a minor court appointment as a gentleman of the Privy Chamber. The rector greatly admired 'my Squire' and his wife, 'the best lady I ever knew', and there was constant contact between hall and parsonage. Nancy and Mrs Custance and visitors to hall and parsonage exchanged news of fashions. From time to time Mrs Custance made Nancy presents of fashionable items, 'a fine India fan, another for common use but all the Fashion at London' in 1781, a full-dressed cap in 1782, a Camperdown Bonnet in 1798. Nancy did not, however, have to rely on Mrs Custance for London fashions. Her brother sent her a balloon hat from London in 1784. Her own visits with her uncle gave her a London milliner and it was she who sometimes first wore a new style in Weston. In June 1802 she was able to show Mrs Custance 'a new Bonnet (by name Pick-Nick) which she had sent her from London by Miss Rider. . . . Mrs Custance said it was very handsome and had seen nothing like it at Norwich as yet, tho' only at Norwich last week to see the new Fashions.'

In 1779 Mr Woodforde saw Mrs Townshend, wife of the member of Parliament for Yarmouth, fashionably dressed 'in a scarlet riding dress, her head dressed very high and no cap at all on.' In 1781 Mrs Custance, who often walked to the parsonage for a morning visit came on foot in a riding habit. Soon afterwards Mr Woodforde bought Nancy a habit, of pompadour broadcloth, a guinea a yard, with a white dimity waistcoat, both lapelled, habit shirt of long lawn, habit gloves and a riding hat with a feather. She wore it for the first time when she went out with the Custances in their coach. A week or two later she set off with her uncle for the Somerset visit, probably travelling in her new habit. She had another habit made in 1793 which cost £7. 4s and there was also a new black beaver hat with purple cockade and band. She does not seem to have done much riding, but drove about the neighbourhood in what her uncle called 'her little cart'.

In 1782 Nancy was given by her uncle an 'old brown silk gown, very good nevertheless, and was my late Aunt Parr's.' Aunt Parr had died in 1771. Nancy had the gown re-made by Miss Bell, mantua-maker of Norwich. In 1790 her uncle gave her another of Aunt Parr's gowns, a green silk damask, a fabric by then completely out of fashion. This time Nancy re-made it herself. She had six yards of pink silk lutestring at 5s 9d a yard for a petticoat in 1783 and in the following year there was a bill of £6. 1s for silk for a gown. Otherwise her gowns were mainly of cotton, chintz or muslin. There was a new cotton gown, trimmed with green ribbon in 1780 and five and a half yards of Chintz in 1781. In 1782, a present from her uncle, she had 'a very pretty new-fashioned calico', which cost £1. 4. 3. Eight yards of blue muslin came from London in 1791 and when it was made up and trimmed with steel buttons 'Mrs Custance liked it extremely well.' In the same year she bought a chintz gown for £2. 10s. She wore the blue muslin with a straw-coloured and purple bonnet to meet the fashionable Mrs Townshend at Weston Hall in 1792:

> 'Mrs T ... in a worked Muslin Jacket a dark Green Sash and a Hat trimmed with dark Green Ribbon in two Cockades before. The Miss Townshend were also in Jackets and hats trimmed in the same manner with two sorts of ribbon, Straw colour and Brown. Mrs Custance in a worked Muslin Gown and petticoat, Broad coloured Sash and a Hat trimmed with a Handkerchief.'

Mr Woodforde bought her muslin in Bath in 1793 and she bought, or received as a present from her uncle, cotton or muslin in 1794, 1795 and 1798. In 1802 she had a new gown of blue and white muslin from Miss Ryder in London. She had an allowance of £10 a year from her uncle for clothes and pocket money, but he was also generous with gifts of clothes.

Mrs Custance seemed to feel the fashionable change to scanty muslin gowns, for on a cool day in July 1802 she arrived at the parsonage in 'a fur tippet, a bosom friend and a Muff and a Winter Cloke'. In November 1800 she and her eldest daughter arrived wearing 'brown silk Pellices, alias Great Coats.'

The living at Weston was a good one, about £300 a year, and James Woodforde also had some income from property in Somerset. There was land to farm at Weston which was managed by 'my farming man, Ben Leggatt', the most highly paid of all the parsonage household at £10 a year.

As a young man at Oxford in the late 1750s James Woodforde had a superfine blue suit of cloth, very good cloth, which cost £4. 10s and a chocolate suit, 'bad', which cost £3. After his arrival at Weston he gave few details about his suits. He had coat, waistcoat and breeches in 1781. This may have been the 'good black striped coat and waistcoat' which, with a pair of velveret breeches and powdered wig, he gave to his parish clerk in 1790. In 1788 he bought five yards of black velveret for two pairs of breeches and in 1790 bespoke a new coat and waistcoat and bought another five yards of velveret. In 1793 he had coat, waistcoat and breeches of black cloth; in 1795 a grey coat of Bath coating; and in 1800 another coat 'black cloth not superfine, but what is called second-cloth' at 7s a yard, and another pair of black velveret breeches.

When he dined with the Bishop, or with the Custances when the Bishop was also a guest, he wore gown and cassock. Visiting the Bishop in Norwich on church business in 1783 he put on his best suit and waistcoat and 'walked down in my boots.' There is no reference to any of his suits being of silk and he was in 1787 very critical of the dress of a neighbouring clergyman who was in 'a very frenchyfied Dress, black silk Coat, Waistcoat and Breeches with a Chappeau de brache under his left Arm.' After the early suits at Oxford, black and grey are the only colours actually mentioned for his coats and breeches; the breeches were often of the hard-wearing cotton velvet, 'velveret', which Talbot Williamson had recommended to his brother in 1762. He wore black silk stockings which were expensive, at 12s and 14s 6d a pair, or the less expensive silk and cotton mixture at 8s 6d.

He enjoyed the outdoor activities of fishing and coursing with his neighbours and worked in his garden. He had a 'fishing frock' made in 1781 and while he was in Somerset in 1793 a pair of shoes 'for fishing flannel lined' which he thought exorbitant at 9s. In the same year he had a coat and waistcoat made at Castle Cary: from the entry in the diary one or both of these may have been of fustian, though it is not quite clear. He bought special stockings to wear when coursing, '2pr. of coursing stockings made of wool from the sheeps back without ever being dressed at all, and knit.' His stockings show great variety, silk ones for dress wear, coarse ribbed stockings, fine black and white, small ribbs, woven, ash-coloured Welch stockings, white worsted boot stockings and also 'brown thread stockings to wear under boots' bought at Castle Cary. For the gout which afflicted him in the 1790s he had coarse white lambswool stockings, knitted, and also white worsted gauze ones which he wore as bedsocks on his gouty foot.

Boots, shoes and hats are recorded without detail, except a pair of 'wooden slippers' in 1792 for 1s. In 1774 he bought a wig, 'a more fashionable one than my old ones are, a one curled wigg, with two curls of the sides' and in 1794 a 'two-curled bob' for £1. 5s at Norwich and another from London in 1795. Hair powder had carried a tax since 1786, but in 1795 there was an additional personal tax of a guinea per head which he paid in 1796.

Informally, at home, he wore a lined cotton morning gown, the earlier nightgown, and more than once records being caught 'on the hop being in my garden dressed in my cotton morning gown and old wigg and hat.' He must have worn his morning gown a good deal, for he regularly bought cotton for one, six yards before 1788, then seven yards every year until 1800, except 1793, once or twice a year, with calico to line them. He usually bought purple and white cotton, but there was a

*43 Mrs Ashton (1710–78) widow of a Liverpool merchant who died in 1759. This portrait, probably painted about ten years later, shows her in matching gown and petticoat of black silk, with white muslin and black ribbons, but unlike Mrs Salusbury (fig. 32) her dress is otherwise in fashion.*
*J. Wright of Derby*

black ground in 1781, black, purple and green in 1794 and, in 1796 'a bright striped cotton for a morning gown of a kind of plad colour.' The price of the cotton ranged between 1s 10d and 2s 6d a yard. In 1790 when he was fifty he began to have a flannel lining round the arms and shoulders and in September 1797 put on a flannel underwaistcoat 'for the first time during my life.'

He had a brown worsted cap for travelling. There were nightcaps in the list of clothes of his Oxford days, but later he seems to have preferred night handkerchiefs of long lawn; four yards of it made five of them. Linen and cambric were bought for shirts and muslin for shirt frills and cravats which were generally made at home.

In the inventory of goods prepared after his death, his wearing apparel with money in his purse was valued at £120.[13]

Public mourning was carefully observed at this level of society. De Saussure noted how general mourning was in London when George I died: 'Everyone is in deep mourning . . . the nobles, gentlemen, officers, merchants and citizens are in mourning. So are the women. One would think everyone was mourning a father or mother. A well-dressed man wearing a sword could not venture to go into any public place dressed in colours; he would be insulted.'[14] Even small gentry in a country market town, like John Salusbury of Leighton Buzzard, put on mourning dress for Princess Caroline in 1758 and the Princess of Orange in 1759. When Queen Caroline died in November 1737 Mrs Purefoy wrote to Mr Robotham: 'Pray let me know what sort of mourning will be proper for my son who will have but one suit for the whole six months and wear it every day, and pray send him some patterns of Cloath.' The following June she asked about second mourning, 'whether they wear coat, waistcoat and Breeches all alike or wear black waistcoat and breeches', probably with a grey coat. Public and private mourning were at this time coinciding for the Purefoys: 'my nephew Leonard Porter is dead so we mourn somewhat longer on that account.' When the Prince of Wales died in 1751 Henry Purefoy had to order a suit of second mourning for his attendance at the Assize to sit on the Grand Jury.[15]

Talbot Williamson, a member of Princess Amelia's household, was well placed to send directions to Bedfordshire when George II died in 1760. He wrote on 30 October that his wife had bought twenty-eight yards of crape,

> 'for it is equally worn with bombazine and by people of the best fashion. . . . You desire 3 yards of gauze. It is not the thing. Muslin is the wear and that is 10s a yard. . . . Note as the mourning is meant to be as deep as possible, women's hats are plain, black silk with crape round the crown with a bow knot; and their silk cloaks of the genteelest kind should be garnished at the bottom with ditto (hatband) crape, not with ribbon.'

Tidy, who was in Cornwall, had sent for 'her mourning ding-dong' which would take a week to reach her. This family carefully observed

public mourning. When Tidy wrote to Mrs Williamson about some mourning in 1765, probably for Talbot Williamson who died that year, she added, 'how soon Prince Fred may follow is uncertain.' In 1771 she warned again: 'Take care of all your mourning for they talk much of the Princess of Wales being in great danger and it is to be a deep mourning.'

Mrs Russel's letter when Mrs Williamson was in mourning for her mother in 1770 reveals the meticulous attention paid to the details of

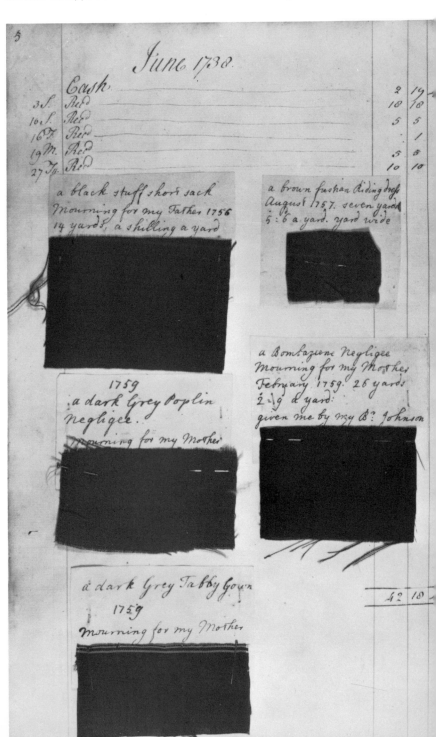

*44 Page from Barbara Johnson's album, 1756–9 with different types of material used in mourning dress and also the fustian for a riding habit.*

mourning accessories in family mourning (Figs 43, 44):

'Imprimis, when you are full drest you see it is with the black and white ribbon with which you may ware all white stomacher and sleeve knots or all black, or when you please to lower your high dress by wearing the undress cap then by all means wear the Grey Ribbon with the Cap. 2ndly the black ribbon with a bow is for your neck when full drest, the other bow I send for any other Cap you may chance to make up as I suppose you have stomacher of black to your Sack, but if not and you dont want it for a Cap you may wear it occasionally for your stomacher. 3rdly you need not wear black Earrings nor glazed gloves without you have a mind to save white ones or wear a white gown. 4thly as to your bonnet I think you might well take off the love [ribbon] and so wear it plain with a black ribbon round the crown and as to your cloak you know you dont sett it so that it is an indifferent matter at present but if you should want it by and by as a cloak you must have an Edging but that will do sometime hence but as you say you have silk by you, you may make it up and turn it with the same but really I think it most a pity to cut it as you may want it by and by to alter your Sack. 5thly the Grey Gloves and 6 pr of white ones are with Mrs Hervy bespoke the Mitts and 3 prs of Gloves are just as you and she can agree but the Mitts are 10d as well as the 3 pr. of Gloves.'

Mrs Williamson was, in her turn, in 1778 asked by her friend Mrs Cater to get her

'a suit of linning to wear with a Nightgown. It is for a 4th Cousin, so desire you will send what upon enquiry is thought most proper and genteel whether musling or Gause . . . I must have a $\frac{1}{2}$ dressed Cap to wear with my new Nightgown, a long apron, Handkerchief and Round Ruffles and a large Cap to ware everyday. . . . I shall likewise want a neat black bonnet for this melancholy occasion, and I suppose for the first mourning, a black paper Fan will be right. . . . If Wilmer can send me a pair of black calamanco shoes . . . they may come down with the other things.'

This was not just formal observance for a fourth cousin for Mrs Cater had been very fond of her 'cousin Grant'.[16]

James Woodforde gave his niece five guineas to buy mourning when her sister died in 1788, and he bought black buckles for himself. When they both dined at Weston Hall a few days later, Nancy went 'in full mourning, black silk gown and coat, and I was also in mourning.' The following year Nancy's father died. She then had twenty yards of bombazine for a gown with long sleeves and a petticoat, and nine yards of wildebore, which was perhaps the material used to make the 'black stuff German great coat for her to wear in common.' This was probably a long-sleeved gown like a coat, fastening down the front, so that the petticoat was not visible, which would have been a current style. James Woodforde had a black coat and waistcoat. After his own death in 1803, Nancy's mourning dress from Miss Ryder in London was a black silk sarsnet costing £5. 6s.[17]

## The City

When Jane Austen introduces Mr Weston into *Emma* (1816) she writes that he was 'born of a respectable family which for the last two or three generations had been rising into gentility and prosperity.' He had received a good education and a small independence, had turned to trade and through his brothers' well-established connections gained an opening in a concern which brought him 'just employment enough' and after some years a modest fortune also and the leisure to enjoy the pleasure of society in Highbury. Country gentlemen and merchant merge in Mr Weston, as they did in so many men of the time, blurring the distinction between town and country and between gentry and merchant (Fig. 45).

The merchants of foreign trade and banking were the first rank of the trading hierarchy; already at the beginning of the century some of them were more wealthy than many noble families (Fig. 46). Their heiresses

*45  Benjamin Bond-Hopkins (1747–94), of a family of London merchants. He bought Pains Hill, Surrey and built a house there, 1790, at about the time this portrait was painted. Here he appears as the country gentleman, in brown frock, white waistcoat, buff breeches, riding-boots and high-crowned, broad-brimmed hat.*
*F. Wheatley*

46  *Andrew Drummond
(1688–1769), 1766, founder of
Drummond's Bank, who bought an
estate at Stanmore, Middlesex in
1729. He wears pale grey coat and
waistcoat with black breeches, with
the type of wig, known as the
physical wig, much worn by
professional men, particularly
doctors, in the second half of the
century. He is wearing an old-
fashioned tied cravat and it was not
usual in fashionable dress to wear
garters as shown here. He has a
snuff-box and the handkerchief used
with snuff-taking in his left hand.
J. Zoffany*

married into the nobility and noble daughters married men whose estates had been bought from fortunes made in trade. Sons of gentry had been apprenticed to trade from the seventeenth century and many had returned again to country estates. Between the fashionable district of St James's in the west and commercial London to the east of Covent Garden was legal London, the centre of a profession which also often led its members from one social group to another. Sons of traders became lawyers and academics; and the hierarchy of the professions also had a range which made links at every level with gentry and nobility.

Dudley Ryder was son of a linen draper in Cheapside and the family lived at Hackney. His elder brother was also a draper and an uncle was in the same trade at Nuneaton. He had an excellent education at Edinburgh University and at Leyden and was called to the bar in 1719. When he was a student at the Middle Temple in 1715 he had a suit of cloth at 18s a yard, spent £5 on a wig and bought a sword of silver gilt which cost £3. 4s without the blade. This gave him great pleasure: 'I cannot but observe how much I am myself touched with external show; having a new sword on I could not help looking at it several times with a peculiar kind of pleasure.'[18] The sword was at this time the mark of a gentleman, so that there was more than the elegance of the sword which pleased Dudley Ryder in his new possession. Lord Chesterfield directed his wit against this idea and its consequence: 'A gentleman is every man, who with a tolerable suit of clothes, a sword by his side, and a watch and a snuff box in his pockets, asserts himself to be a gentleman, swears with energy he will be treated as such and that he will cut the throat of any man who presumes to say the contrary.'[19] Dudley Ryder's new ambitions conflicted with what his father, the draper, thought was suitable dress for a tradesman's son. When he went to his father's shop to get a nightgown, he looked at silks, which displeased his father, who 'would have me have a calimanco.' In the following year his father 'was unwilling I should have cloth' for a suit of clothes 'so I chose a stuff.' His maternal grandmother was also offended at his dress: 'looks with a great deal of indignation that the son of a tradesman should go as fine as her husband the counsellor.' By dressing in his best clothes and laced ruffles he was able to get 'through the bar' at a court at St James's, on two occasions in 1715 and 1716.[20] He had a successful career in the law and politics, which might have mollified his grandmother. He was knighted in 1740, made a privy councillor and died in 1756 just as he was about to be raised to the peerage.

The status of the city of London and its wealth meant that its dignitaries were present, by command, at court functions. 'I curled, powdered, dressed and went to Mrs Montagu at one; from thence to Court; where we were touzed and hunched about to make room for citizens in their fur gowns.'[21] The aldermen appeared in their civic robes, but their wives had the freedom and means to rival all comers in the richness of their garments. De Saussure recorded a story which was probably London gossip of 1727. A merchant had offered a rich gold-brocaded silk to the Princess of Wales, who had not bought it because it was too brilliant and costly. The wife of a city alderman, a wealthy brewer, hearing of it, bought the silk and wore it at the next drawing-room she attended. De Saussure added, 'no Frenchwoman would have dared to pay court in such a fashion.'[22] Mrs Delany, describing the dresses at a court in 1741, included that of Lady Godschall, 'a suit of clothes that were designed for her in case she had been Lady Mayoress, white satin, embroidered with gold and browns, very fine.'[23]

City society had its own full-dress occasions with a richness of fabric and jewels which brought the dress close to the conservative dress of court occasions. Catherine Hutton described a City Assembly of 1783:

'The men were chiefly in dress coats with their hair in bags; those who were not wore cloth coats trimmed with narrow gold lace, white waistcoats of silver tissue, or ornamented with gilt spangles, and their hair in a short thick queue with curls flying out each side of the head. Many of the elderly ladies were almost covered with diamonds ... the subscribers are all the first people in the city.'

She wrote again of the Assembly of 1796: 'The men were all, with the exception of one individual, dressed in silk, lace or embroidery. The women had fine shapes, large hoops and danced gracefully.' The hoop was preserved here as well as at court, although now well out of fashion, and so were the sword and lace ruffles of men's dress. The City Assemblies were for the 'first people' in the city, for this society too had its hierarchy. Miss Hutton also went in 1783 to the London Assembly, held at the London Tavern, in 'the finest room my eyes ever beheld.' This was a less exclusive gathering; 'the requisites for appearing are a dressed coat or a laced frock. After all it is much less Genteel than the City Assembly.' Nevertheless her partner, who was in mourning, wore a black sword and carried a *chapeau bras*. Because he was in mourning laced frill and ruffles were replaced by broad-hemmed muslin.[24]

When Defoe wrote of the increasing prosperity of the English tradesman in the 1720s he had in mind not only these 'first people', the merchants of foreign trade and the bankers, but 'all sorts of warehouse keepers, shopkeepers, whether wholesale dealers or retailers of goods.' He wrote not only of London tradesmen:

'An ordinary tradesman now, not in the city only but in the country, shall spend more money by the year, than a gentleman of four or five hundred a year can do, and shall increase and lay up every year too ... and as for the lower gentry, from a hundred pounds a year to three hundred or thereabouts, though they are often as proud and high in their appearance as the other; as to them, I say, a shoemaker in London shall keep a better house, spend more money, clothe his family better, and yet grown rich too ... an estate's a pond, but trade's a spring.'

This increased prosperity brought a visible change, a change in dress:

47 *Maurice Greene (1696–1755), professor of music at Cambridge, and John Hoadly (1711–55), clergyman, poet and dramatist, 1747. The clergyman wears a deep blue suit, with an unusual deeply slit cuff with four buttons. His cocked hat lies on the stool. The musician wears a nightgown of red damask in the loose, straight-cut form, with a nightcap with full, tasselled crown and turn-back brim.*
*F. Hayman*

'The shopkeepers wear different garbs from what they were wont to do, are decked with long wigs and swords, and all the frugal badges of their trade are quite disdained and thrown aside.'[25]

The plays of the early eighteenth century make their comedy as much from encounters between fashionable London and commercial London, the 'city knights', as from encounters between fashionable affectation and rustic naivety. In one of Burnaby's comedies, *The Modish Husband* (1702)—Burnaby's father was a successful brewer, and Burnaby, like Dudley Ryder, had a university education in preparation for a career in law—a fashionable character says, 'my shoulders are so sore that I shall be under necessity of wearing my Perriwig like a Citizen all before for one week.' The fashionable wig and the citizen wig were of the same style but each wore them in his own way. In Garrick and Colman's *The Clandestine Marriage* (1766) the wig is still an immediate social sign. The wealthy mercer wears 'a smug wig round his broad face, as close as a new-cut yew hedge, and his shoes so black that they shine again.' The status of a particular trade advanced with the fashionable need of it, 'an Haughty Thriving Covent-Garden Mercer, Silk or Laceman, Your Lordship gives your most Humble Service to him.'[26] The smug wig and shining shoes appear again in the 1770s in Colman's *The Spleen or Islington Spa* (1776). Doyley, whose name emphasises his trade, is teased by a friend: 'Do you fancy that your old St Clement's foppery of a clean shirt, shining shoes, smug wig and neatly brushed coat, worn

90

threadbare, without a spot, will have sufficient charms for her?' Defoe, disapproving of the more expensive dressing of tradesmen, referred especially to 'fine wigs, fine hollands shirts of six and seven shilling an ell, and perhaps laced also, all lately brought down to the level of the apron and become the common wear of tradesmen.'[27]

Professional men wore distinctive garments for their formal duties, but their professions were revealed in their everyday dress also. The full-bottomed wig was still worn until the middle of the century by lawyers, clergymen and physicians; with other wigs it then became embedded in judicial uniform until the present day. In Henry Fielding's farce *The Mock Doctor* (1732) the character of the title says: 'If I must go with you I must have a physician's habit; for a physician can no more prescribe without a full wig, than without a fee.' A young physician in *Pompey the Little* (1752) equipped himself with 'a gilt-headed cane, a black suit of cloathes, a wise mysterious face, a full-bottomed flowing peruke and all the other externals of his profession.'[28] After the middle of the century the full-bottomed wig gradually disappeared from everyday wear by members of the learned professions, but the habit of wearing black and dark clothes continued (Fig. 47 and colour plate 2). Clergymen generally wore black or grey. When Mrs Russel was buying worsted for her brother Edmond Williamson in 1760 she sent a hank 'which is called the parson's grey.'[29]

Merchants tended to link themselves with this professional group in

*48 Edward Wakefield, London merchant, and his wife Priscilla, philanthropist and writer of children's books, with her sister Elizabeth Bell, afterwards Mrs Gurney and mother of Elizabeth Fry; showing fashion of the mid-1770s as worn in a Quaker family. H. Walton*

their dress. The connection of trade and nonconformity may also have strengthened the tendency to plain and sober clothing. Nonconformists were still banned from many offices and excluded from the universities. Many who might otherwise have entered the professions turned to trade (Fig. 48). The Quakers in particular were active in developing trade and industries which did not run counter to their beliefs and many of them achieved great worldly success. They had always discouraged luxury and extravagance, and were marked by the plainness of their dress, but 'Quakers' clothes though of the simplest and plainest cut are of excellent quality, their hats, clothes and linen are of the finest and so are the silken tissues the women wear.'[30] The Quakers' reputation for success in business, as well as for honesty and fair-dealing made this outward appearance, with its inconspicuous but telling statement of fine cloth, fine linen and silk stockings, inspire confidence and no doubt encouraged its wear as a business uniform. The emphasis on clean linen, well-brushed cloth coat and shining shoes became the 'foppery' of the lesser tradesmen, the essence of dress for all young men who wished to make their way in the world. When Roderick Random, in Smollett's novel of that name, came to London to seek his fortune, he had with him one suit of clothes, but 'half a dozen of ruffled shirts and as many plain.' At the end of the century Archenholz wrote: 'The English in general, even those of the middling classes wear very excellent linen and change it daily. The fineness of the shirt and stockings, a good hat and the best shoes distinguish a man in opulent circumstances.'[31] Moritz, before he left London to explore the English countryside, wrote of the dress he had noted there: 'The most usual dress is, in summer, a short white waistcoat, black breeches, white silk stockings, and a frock, generally of a very dark blue cloth, which looks like black; and the English seem, in general, to prefer dark colours. If you wish to be full drest you wear black.'[32] What is often regarded as a nineteenth-century, or post-revolutionary change in men's dress, was firmly rooted by the early 1780s.

When Arthur Young, on one of his agricultural journeys, called on John Howard at Cardington, Bedfordshire, he was surprised to see the way he was dressed:

> 'We found him in a parlour ... dressed as for an evening in London—a powdered bag wig, white silk stockings, thin shoes and every other circumstance of his habilments excluding the possibility of a country walk. ... I asked Mr Whitbread if Mr Howard was usually thus dressed. ... He had never seen him otherwise he said.'[33]

John Howard had not yet taken up his great work of prison reform. The son of a London upholsterer, his father's trade had left him with sufficient means to settle on this small property he had inherited, but he had little interest in the usual outdoor activities of country life; his interest in agriculture, which was the reason for Young's visit, was

49  Sir Joshua Reynolds, artist, Sir William Chambers, architect, and Joseph Wilton, sculptor, 1782. Reynolds has scarlet coat and waistcoat, fur-lined; Chambers a plain coat but with the large decorative buttons of the 1780s and the fabric of his waistcoat is silk woven with foil, much used in ornament and trimming in the 1780s. J. F. Rigaud

50  William Cowper (1731–1800), 1792, poet, wearing a double-breasted, horizontally cut waistcoat fastening to the neck with a standing collar, and a lapelled frock; the wig with pointed toupee and single curls is in a style worn since the 1760s. L. F. Abbott

51  Thomas Hearne (1744–1817), 1800, draughtsman, wearing a double-breasted waistcoat, horizontally cut, and lapelled frock; the tie wig is in its freer style of the end of the century. His low-heeled shoes fasten with ties; these have been replacing buckles during the 1780s and 1790s. H. Edridge

scientific rather than practical. John Howard was a citizen living in the country, not the citizen become country gentleman, and he had not altered his dress to conform to country appearance (Figs 49, 50, 51).

London citizens shared the amenities and entertainments of the pleasure gardens of Ranelagh and Vauxhall with people of fashion. In 1765 Grosley thought that 'their favourite undress' worn by fashionable women at Ranelagh 'brings them near a level with citizens' wives' and, 'the uniformity of appearance gives that air of freedom and ease to the whole assembly which is the constant concomitant of equality.'[34] (Figs 52, 53). Although Ranelagh later became more fashionable and visitors dressed for the entertainments there, while Vauxhall remained informal, it still did not become exclusive. Moritz went in 1782 and found 'those of the lower class who go there, always dress themselves in their best; and thus endeavour to copy the great. Here I saw no one who had not silk stockings on.' His landlady, a tailor's widow, went once a year.[35]

F.A.Wendeborn, who wrote on England after spending more than twenty years in London as minister of a German congregation, remarked on 'the splendid manner in which many of the shopkeepers live, and the short time in which some of them acquire fortunes', and he also referred to the increasing quantity of clothing which people were acquiring:

'In former time, people of some consequence and fortune, thought themselves to appear very decently, if they had every year a new suit of cloaths, but at the present three and more are annually required by a man in a middling station of life who wishes to make what is called a decent appearance. Besides the fashions alter in these days so much that a man can hardly wear a coat two months, before it is out of fashion.'[36]

52  *Bagnigge Wells on a Sunday Evening, 1779. Bagnigge Wells, Finsbury. Unlike Ranelagh and Vauxhall this was one of the pleasure gardens frequented mainly by middle and lower classes and had acquired a reputation as the haunt of prostitutes and city fops.*
*J. Sanders*

Samuel Curwen, a merchant of Salem, a loyalist during the American War of Independence, spent most of the last quarter of the century in England and kept journals of his first stay, between 1775 and 1784. He made entries about his clothes and on two occasions compiled an inventory of them. He must have brought a good deal of clothing with him, so some of his wardrobe may show American detail rather than English; but his journal reveals that he was in the habit of selling clothes he did not need and in the first inventory, which was not made until 1780, five years after his arrival, only a few items are annotated 'brought from home'. As soon as he arrived he got his spectacles mended, gave a sempstress directions about some new shirts and bespoke 'a new surtout'. Early in the next year he bespoke a new suit of dark slate-coloured cloth. He had got rid of this and 'purged my trunks of useless lumber' by the time he made his 1780 inventory. He then listed one suit in brown superfine cloth; a drab cloth coat and breeches, with an extra pair of breeches. He had four other pairs of black breeches, silk, silk satin, worsted florant and double stuff. There were two striped silk waistcoats, black and green and red and green, a brown silk velvet which was perhaps worn with the brown suit as an alternative, and two of white cotton. He had two overcoats, the surtout of 1775, dark brown and a drab one 'brought from home'. This list shows how widespread the habit of wearing black breeches was, and the fashion for wearing different combinations of coat, waistcoat and breeches. He had two flannel underwaistcoats faced with silk. There was also a pair of white baize sleeves, which could be tied on to the waistcoat for extra warmth. He had four pairs of linen drawers, three pairs of leather drawers and one pair of flannel. His twenty-three 'fine irish linen shirts' and nine 'cotton

*53 Mayday in the streets, showing children celebrating, imitating the festival of milkmaids and chimney-sweeps (see fig. 74) to the annoyance of passers by. The women wear short-skirted walking gowns, now with long sleeves, of the early 1780s' style and small, comparatively plain versions of fashionable hats of 1780–3 over fashionable hairdressing. The man has a double-breasted frock, with tabs which fasten well over the shoulders, the style of a shooting frock, with a round hat with curved brim.*
*E. F. Burney*

and linen winter ditto', twenty stocks and thirteen cravats in cambric muslin once again confirm the importance of fine linen, constantly changed, in merchant wear. He had a number of stockings, in great variety, in all thirty-nine pairs: in silk, white, mottled, black and blue striped, speckled blue, purple and white speckled, dark mottled and black; in silk and worsted, brown and black and white; in thread, white; and in thread and cotton, white. He had understockings in worsted and thread, coarse and fine. There were four wigs, handkerchiefs, nightcaps, cuffs and sleeves, gloves, one pair of boots and seven pairs of shoes. In the second list, 1782 there was only one coat, 'light yellow coat on my back'. The black silk waistcoat and breeches and the four pairs of black breeches, two silk, two worsted, remain, the worsted now called 'florinet' and 'Denmark satin' [double stuff]. A pair of black fine-knitted silk breeches had been added. One of the striped waistcoats, which cost 'more than 2 guineas' had been stolen, but the green and red one remained and there were new waistcoats, dove and gold striped silk, yellow, black-spotted silk, green, black-spotted Manchester silk and another black silk. No white cotton ones were in this list, but later in the year he referred to a Marseilles quilted one in white cotton. He also had a black shagreen one lengthened and bought a 'black moleskin or long piled velvet as 'tis so called.' Eight of his shirts had been stolen and there was now only one flannel underwaistcoat and no baize sleeves. Other linen shows a natural wastage. New leather gloves appear and '1 pair of Shoes and Cloggs' amongst the shoes. He had acquired a 'Freemason's Apron'. He notes in the journal from time to time his seasonal habits of dress; in June 1779, the putting-off of his underwaistcoat, and in January 1783 the putting-on of his winter shirts, that is changing from linen to cotton; in April 1782 he noted 'for the first time these many months without a greatcoat', and again in April, 1783, 'Walkt for the first time these 6 months without great coat.'[37]

In cities and towns, away from London, the dress worn was fashionable in the sense that it was within the main stream of fashion (Fig. 54). In some towns there was a tendency to exaggerate new styles, as Sylas Neville noticed in the theatre at Plymouth in 1768: 'The ladies wear their hats almost perpendicular, but in many country towns they add to the absurdity of the London modes.'[38] Mrs Montagu, who, like Dr Johnson, liked no city but London, wrote from Bath: 'Bath reports like Bath headdresses (tho' in the mode of the times) are a little exaggerated.'[39] Some towns and cities were notably fashionable: Salisbury, Exeter, Norwich, Nottingham, York and Chester were centres of local society; people seen in the streets and goods seen in the shops reflected this and influenced local dress, for many of the local nobility and gentry maintained social links in their county towns. In Salisbury in 1786 Mr Woodforde found 'all the ladies highly dressed.'[40] Agneta Yorke wrote about an Assize Ball at Exeter in 1789: 'I never saw more beautiful women assembled; and all magnificently dressed and

*Page from Barbara Johnson's album, 1767-8, showing fringed trimmings and the amounts needed, 54 yards for a sack for the Races, 18 yards for a nightgown. It was trimming of this kind which Mrs Russel discussed with her sister-in-law in 1769, saying she had 30 yards for a nightgown. (Victoria and Albert Museum, Crown Copyright)*

*The Sharp Family's musical party on the Thames, 1779-81, showing the variety of dress worn on the same occasion within one family. William Sharp, standing, was surgeon to George III and wears the Windsor uniform; on the right in black is John Sharp, Archdeacon of Northumberland, wearing a wig like that of Andrew Drummond (fig. 46). There are two riding habits, one pale blue with white waistcoat, worn by William Sharp's wife, the other by Judith Sharp, fawn with matching waistcoat; both wear full-trimmed hats with these habits. A quilted petticoat is still being worn by Mrs James Sharp.*
*J. Zoffany (Reproduced by permission of The Executors of Miss Olive Lloyd-Baker)*

with much more care and propriety than in London I can assure you.'[41] Early in the century Macky thought that ladies at the York assemblies were as well dressed as at a drawing-room at St James's. When he was at Chester, Coronation day fell on an assembly day, 'and although that is as Tory a City as any in England, I counted Fifty Ladies as finely dressed as at an Opera in the Haymarket.'[42] Mrs Montagu wrote critically about tradesmen's daughters at a ball at the Mansion House in Newbury:

'Should you have expected to find the vanities of Versailles in a shop at Newbury ... I believe there was as much folly in the World in the last century as now, but then the follies fitted those who wore them. ... Vanity has overruled and established an uniform for all ranks ages and characters, and with distinctions of dress, many moral and civil distinctions are lost. The Newbury misses caps and garments have led me into reflections too serious for a letter.'[43]

The new towns of industry made a different impression. Catherine

*54  Mr and Mrs Atherton. William Atherton (c. 1704–47) was Mayor of Preston, Lancashire in 1732 and 1738. He wears a plain dress, brown coat and waistcoat, lightened by a plain white silk waistcoat. Mrs Atherton's dress of white satin over a blue quilted petticoat, with the stiff, cone-shape of the stays beneath the bodice, also makes this portrait a clear statement of the plainer version of dress worn about 1740.*
*A. Devis*

Hutton, who lived there, wrote that Birmingham was 'celebrated neither for fashion nor taste. We are showy enough, but nothing more.' She noted the difference between dress in Birmingham and in Nottingham, a centre of county society before industry came to it:

> 'At Birmingham one may walk till one is weary and not see a Christian above the quality of a journeyman draper or a mantua-maker; but here it is the fashion to walk, and the first people of the town make a practice of it. The women are, many of them, extremely elegant; I think but few of them handsome; but there is an air in their dress and their manner that is seldom seen at Birmingham.'[44]

Samuel Curwen wrote of Manchester in 1777: 'The dress of the people here savours not much of the London mode.' In 1780 he was in Liverpool where 'we scarce saw a well-dressed person, not half-a-dozen gentlemen', and where he thought 'Few of the shops have the appearance to be seen in all other great Towns, dress and looks more like the inhabitants of Wapping, Shadwell and Rotherhithe than in the neibourhood of Exchange or London anywhere above the Tower.'[45] His division of London brings the west end and city together, moving the division of appearance further east. It is unlikely that fashionable dress was not worn by wealthy merchants and their families in Liverpool, but neither Liverpool nor Manchester were social centres and fashionable dress was not dominant.

Catherine Hutton was the daughter of William Hutton, who had settled in Birmingham a few years before she was born in 1756. He had worked as a child in the silk mills at Derby and had then been apprenticed to his uncle at Nottingham, to the stocking frame. He set out in 1741 to make his way in the world and by 1750 had settled in Birmingham as a bookbinder. When the Prince of Wales died in 1751 he bought a suit of mourning and 'my new clothes introduced me to some new acquaintances', for he had not bought new clothes for some time, 'my best coat had now been my best coat five years.' Public mourning had a certain levelling tendency amongst all the differing social groups who wore it, as William Hutton found. He opened a circulating library and in 1756 started a paper warehouse. A successful man of business, he was able before the end of the century to fulfil his ambition and own land: 'from infancy land was my favourite object.'[46] The family then had a town house in Birmingham and a country estate in Herefordshire. They were Unitarians and suffered in the sectarian riots of 1791 when their house was attacked. Catherine travelled about England and Wales with parents and friends and visited London where she often bought clothes. When she travelled with her father she rode pillion behind a servant, otherwise by coach or chaise. Before she went to Derbyshire with her mother in 1781 her father made her a present of a habit in scarlet broadcloth. She wrote to a friend in London for a plain black hat to go with it, adding that 'one might suppose that one plain hat would be very like another; yet there is a style, a manner in a London hat which our untutored hats in the country cannot equal.' Two years later she had another habit, this time in dark blue with a buff velvet collar, small gilt buttons, white waistcoat with gilt spangles, ruffles and frills of Mechlin lace and a black hat with feather, gold lace and fringe: 'I believe I never looked so well in my life.'[47]

## Spas and Watering Places

Those who travelled on the Continent often visited Spa, a place which gave its name to all towns which, possessing springs of curative waters, became health resorts. The search for health was joined by the search for relaxation and pleasure, and in England spas had developed into fashionable resorts by the end of the seventeenth century. They flourished throughout the eighteenth century until they were rivalled by watering places on the coast, for the new medical fashion of sea-bathing.

The spas were places of fashion, but they were also places where fashion relaxed. At Spa itself the gathering of visitors from all over Europe made the ballroom, as Mrs Greville wrote to Lady Sarah Lennox in 1764, 'absolutely a Mascarade: some with large hats which Lady Mary Coke has taught them to turn up behind telling them 'tis the fashion with us; others are curled to the top of their heads, we had a little Princess Saprike from Poland that wore a Turkish habit and head French .... '[48] Lady Sarah, now Lady Sarah Bunbury, was at Spa herself three years later and according to Lady Mary Coke wore 'the polish dress which is very becoming, but would be very particular anywhere but here, where all sorts of dresses are permitted.'[49] Mary Hamilton, at Spa in 1776, returned on foot from a country expedition, suitably equipped for the walk, each lady with 'her Spa cane and riding greatcoat, tied her white handkerchief round her throat and proceeded in regular procession.' They ended their walk by going into the Rooms in the same dress: 'We went into the Rooms in the same procession looking like strolling Gipsies.'[50]

The English spas were also part of fashionable life, and at the same time places of escape from the normal social routine and its conventions. They were places where, through the routine of spa life, people from different groups in society, away from their own backgrounds, mixed with those from groups normally closed to them. Tunbridge Wells was, in the early years of the century, 'the Rendezvous of all the Gentry of the neighbouring Country and of the best Citizen Families in London during the summer season.' There ladies and gentlemen went out in the morning to drink the water in 'dishabille' and then went home to dress. At Epsom 'In the Morning Gentlemen saunter about in their Gowns at the Wells, as at Tunbridge.'[51] It was the same at Bath: 'The Bath countenances the Men of Dress in showing themselves at the Pump in their Indian Night-Gowns, without the least indecorum.'[52] Over fifty years later Smollett in *Humphrey Clinker* described this first social gathering of the day: 'At eight in the morning we go in dishabille to the Pump room; which is crowded like a Welsh fair; and there you see the highest quality and the lowest trades folk jostling each other, without ceremony, hail-fellow-well met.'[53]

The dress worn by those who actually immersed themselves in the waters was described by Celia Fiennes, a connoisseur of spas, who visited Bath both before and after 1700:

> 'The Ladyes goes into the bath with garments made of a fine yellow canvas, which is stiff and made large with great sleeves like a parsons gown, the water fills it up so that it is borne off that your shape is not seen, it does not cling as close as other lining ... the Gentlemen have drawers and waistcoats of the same sort of canvas, this is the best linning for the bath water will change any other yellow.'

As the lady rose out of the water up a flight of steps another garment of 'Flannel made like a nightgown with great sleeves' was slipped on as the other was removed.[54] By the 1770s the gown had become a jacket and petticoat of brown linen 'with chip hats, in which they fix their handkerchiefs to wipe the sweat off their faces.'[55] Not all visitors to Bath subjected themselves to public appearance in this uniform. Evelina, in Fanny Burney's novel, no doubt spoke for many who were 'amazed at the public exhibition of the ladies in the bath: it is true their heads are covered with bonnets, but the idea of being seen in such a situation by whoever pleases to look is indelicate.'[56]

In the second half of the century another type of dress began to appear. At Epsom riding on the downs had always been part of spa life. In 1774 Elizabeth Noel wrote from Bath: 'I have asked for a Cloak which I am to have and Pattens and Stick and then I shall be properly equipped to sally forth.'[57] Mrs Montagu very much disliked what she saw of this kind of dress in Bath in 1780 and the way of life which went with it:

> 'Misses who strut about in morning in Riding dresses and uniforms and the Maccaronis who trip in pumps and with Parasols over their heads . . . . If the sun is so powerfull as to be dangerous to Misses beauty she does not retire to her Chamber till the fervour of the noon is over, but takes her Umbrella; if dripping rains, snow or hail threaten to impair the gloss of her apparel and spot her shoes, she adds a pair of pattens to her equipment, and if the North-East wind rages she takes shelter in a Man's surtout coat . . . short great coats like my pit men's wives in the North.'[58]

This comparison, disparaging the Bath fashion, reveals that, consciously or unconsciously, items of common dress were entering fashionable wear. In the wearing of pattens there was conscious kinship; Betsy Sheridan wrote of hers in 1789: 'We ladies here trot about in Pattens, a privilege granted no where else to genteel women.'[59] They were a Bath fashion, worn in the street of the city,

*Or we walk about in pattins*
*Buying gauzes, cheapening satins*[60]

In spite of Betsy Sheridan's claim for Bath, they were also worn at other spas, and some places had greater practical need of them, as Lady Newdigate found at Buxton in 1781: 'we have had right Buxton weather ... the way to the well was almost impassable ... we have been forced to get high Pattins and with them we do vastly well.' Her sister wrote: 'We do not lose a single glass of water if it rains dogs and cats the Pattins great Coat and large Umbrellas are sufficient security.'[61] Umbrellas and walking-sticks for women were part of 'a course of the waters' and so were available in variety at the spas. The Marchioness Grey wrote to her elder daughter, who was at Tunbridge Wells in 1777: 'Your sister would be glad to have from Tunbridge a Genteel Umbrella and Walking Stick together.' In 1782 she was herself at Margate and wrote from there: 'As to Dress Nothing seems required, Riding habits, Nightgowns and Hats are all that appear.'[62] Margate, now popular for its sea-bathing, was not one of the most fashionable resorts. Scarborough, which had both spa and sea-bathing, maintained the rituals of dressing and undressing adapted to its activities and idleness. 'These watering-places are the idlest in the World and one is perpetually busy without doing anything. For instance the dressing to bathe, re-dressing to ride, riding, and dressing a third time for dinner, occupy a whole morning.'[63]

The spas and watering places showed a great range of dress, fashionable, exaggerated and eccentric; varying degrees of formality and informality, often with a touch of rural masquerade. As nobility and fashionable gentry tried first one then another spa or watering place as they searched for better health or new scenes and recreation they created a network of small centres of fashion over the countryside and around the coast. Samuel Curwen at Sidmouth in 1776 thought the ladies he saw on the beach 'the most brilliant appearance of well-dressed Ladies I have yet seen.'[64] Lady Jane Coke wrote of Tunbridge Wells in 1750:

> 'If anybody has a mind to learne new fashions, I would advise their going to Tunbridge where they abound, and I don't think even Blowzabella in her flounces came up to some figures I saw in a morning, and I was told that at the balls they outdid their usual outdoings. Skeleton caps without number (which I conclude you have seen) made of colours . . . . '

Blowzabella was the name used for the current patroness of the Derby Ladies Assembly by Lady Jane and her friend Mrs Eyre.[65] Lady Margaret Heathcote at Tunbridge in 1763 was amazed at the number of milliners: 'Last night there arrived a cargo of French milliners to the great disturbance of the English ones, who say they should not be allowed to set up a Shop at Spa if they went there.'[66] When she was at Brighton in 1790 Lady Newdigate found there was great choice of muslin there, 'very beautiful and real India.'[67]

It was not only fashionable people and country gentry who went to the spas. Many prosperous London families, whose homes as well as their businesses were still in the city, went to the spas and watering places for fresh air and recreation during the summer months. Tunbridge Wells was particularly convenient for them: 'Illustrious Tunbridge! Healthy in thy water, rich in thy Toy-shops and distinguished in thy Inhabitants .... A fat Lady from Lombard St. shall dance as nimbly, sit up as late, and drink Eau de Barbade as chearfully as if She had been bred all her Life-time in the Courtly Air of St James's.'[68] Some, like Matthew Bramble, the middle-aged country gentleman from Gloucestershire in Smollett's *Humphrey Clinker,* saw Bath as a place of social chaos:

> 'Every upstart of fortune, harnessed in the trappings of the mode presents himself at Bath because here, without further qualification they can mingle with the princes and nobles of the land ... such is the composition of what is called the fashionable company at Bath where a very considerable proportion of genteel people are lost in a mob of impudent plebeians.'[69]

*The London Magazine* of July 1772 also published a lament: 'The lower orders ... of the people (if there are any for distinctions now are confounded) ... very often the most brilliant dress and equipage at these summer retreats is equalled by an inhabitant of Cheapside or Mincing Lane.'

For those outside fashionable society the spas and sea-side resorts were places to see the fashions and to wear clothes as fashionable as they could afford. For people of fashion they were places to relax from fashion and the conventions of dress. The spas produced their own conventions, shared by all visitors, peculiar to the place and way of life, not to a particular social rank.

# IV

# *Servants*

Between the nobility and gentry, the prosperous merchant and professional families and the common people there was a group set apart by occupation, the servants. When de la Rochefoucauld came to England in 1784 he was struck by their numbers compared with the number employed in France and thought that they were needed to maintain the high standards of cleanliness in English houses, which had also struck Per Kalm in 1748. Unfortunately, de la Rochefoucauld noted, this did not extend to the kitchen and the preparing of food. He noticed that women were employed in the cooking and housework, in the work which was not seen, but that men-servants were employed for duties performed in the presence of guests.[1]

In the great houses of the nobility small armies worked, indoors and outdoors, in many occupations. De la Rochefoucauld mentioned thirty or forty men-servants in the houses of certain noblemen. In 1753 the Duke of Bedford had forty servants at Bedford House, London, with a skeleton staff at Woburn. In 1771 there were forty-two.[2] In gentlemen's houses there were smaller teams. John Becher, squire of Renhold, Bedfordshire, had ten servants in 1713. In the village of Renhold at this time sixty people out of a population of 300 were described as servants.[3] Lesser gentlemen, clergy, merchants, farmers kept three or four. Parson Woodforde often wrote of 'my two maids' and he also employed a man and boy. The dress of these servants, the attitudes to it by employer and employed, the constant contact of servants with groups socially above them and in different degrees fashionable, helped to carry fashion and habits of dress from the leisured, fashion-creating classes into their own working class, into common wear.

The employment of servants was a measure of social standing, but the keeping of men-servants was of much greater significance than the number of women servants. The difference appears in the different pattern of dress. All servants when at work in their special occupations wore garments which were functional for the work they were doing (Fig. 55). The coachman exposed to all weathers on the box of his coach needed his triple-caped coat. If he also had to rub the horses down afterwards, as he would in a small household, his clothes were protected

with a linen frock. But the dress of men-servants showed more than occupation. It was a uniform—livery—to mark them not only as servants, but also more precisely as servants of a particular person or family. In Lovelace's schemes against Clarissa he is very careful about the liveries of the various servants he involves, so that by them the impostor may be received as genuine through wearing the right livery, and his own men not recognised either by appearing without livery or wearing that of someone else.[4]

From the Royal Household downwards men-servants, in contact with members of the family they served and its guests, were arrayed in varying degrees of splendour, down to ordinary dress slightly modified into a uniform. The splendour of livery reflected the status of the employer. In 1704 Lady Fermanagh wrote to her stepson, Sir Ralph Verney: 'Sir Ed. Denton has a very rich Leverys a making at your tailor … a whole cloth a laced with Crimson Yellow and Gold, the breadth of your Hand and made full-laced like the Queen's.'[5] In the household of the fourth Duke of Bedford bills for liveries might amount to £150 a year. They were of the orange cloth used since the seventeenth century, of which sixty or seventy yards, at ten shillings a yard, were bought at least every half year. This was enriched with gold lace and many gilt buttons. A postillion's suit, 'richly laced with gold and velvet lace', cost £4. 16. 11½ in 1757.[6] The expression of rank was to some extent transferred to the accompanying servant. Fanny Burney was sharply critical of the way the Duchess of Devonshire was dressed when she saw her walking in the Park on a Sunday morning in 1776: 'Two of her curls came quite unpinned, and fell lank on one of her shoulders; one shoe was down at heel, the trimming of her jacket and coat was in some places unsown; her cap was awry; and her cloak which was rusty and powdered, was flung half on and half off.' She added, significantly: 'Had she not had a servant in a superb livery behind her, she would certainly have been affronted.' Nor did the Duke make any better impression: 'She had hold of the Duke's arm, who is the reverse of herself, for he is ugly, tidy and grave. He looks like a very mean shopkeeper's journeyman.'[7]

The range of livery-wearing servants also extended from those of personal service to estate servants. In 1698 John Verney refused to allow a new livery every year to his keeper: 'I gave him one last year, there is no reason which I should give one a livery that doth not wait on me or my wife ten times in a year.'[8] The dress of the invisible servants was not important, but as soon as they became visible and visibly connected with their employers, their appearance had to match their employer's state.

The servants of the country gentry had more general duties, carrying out the work of the farm and in charge of the horses at the plough as well as at the coach. Yet Joseph Mawde, who in 1704 was hired for a year by Sir Walter Calverley in Yorkshire, man-of-all-work though he was, had a livery. He was paid £5 for the year and 20s to buy him a frock for

55 *Girl Plucking a Turkey. This is a working dress showing the wearing of the bedgown, lilac spotted white, over a greenish blue petticoat, with a blue checked apron, cotton or linen. The gown and the petticoat could also be cotton or linen, or wool or linsey-woolsey. The cap with a pink ribbon is in the fashion of the 1770s.* H. Walton

brewing, and given a livery of coat, waistcoat, breeches, hat and stockings. For this he had to

'Look to all the stables, and horses, and mares, both in the house and pastures, to keep the fold clean, and also the pheasant garden and little garden within the pales in the fold, and see the trees be therein nailed any time as occasion, and also to keep the court before the hall door clean, and grass places in good order and also to brew master all his drink, to keep the jack in order, to take care of the calash and drive it, to keep the boat carefully locked, cleaned and dressed, to wait at table when occasion and if he does not his best but neglects these things to have no wages.'[9]

Here is the reality of Scrub, the servant of Squire Sullen in Farquhar's *The Beaux Stratagem*: 'Of a Monday I drive the coach, of a Tuesday I drive the plough, on Wednesday I follow the hounds, a Thursday I dun the tenants, on Friday I go to market, on Saturdays I draw warrants, and a Sunday, I draw beer.' The Lancashire squire Nicholas Blundell of Crosby employed Henry Sumner as coachman, groom and ploughman in 1706, but his servants were in livery, grey cloth, faced with blue serge, blue serge waistcoats, blue stockings and silver-laced hats.[10] Grey and blue seem to have been a popular choice of livery colours amongst country squires of this time, so general that in Mrs Centlivre's play, *Love's Contrivance,* Sir Toby is advised to alter his livery, 'and give a laced one, for grey turned up with blue looks so like a Country Squire.'

The Purefoys of Shalstone, Buckinghamshire, kept or tried to keep, for servants came and went in rapid succession, three men-servants, a coachman who had to be able to drive four horses, but also had to understand husbandry and cattle, 'for I shall have some Ploughing to do', a footman, and a servant to look after the garden. The footman was also expected to work in the garden and 'go to cart with Thomas', the coachman of the time. There were three maid-servants, a cookmaid, a dairymaid and chambermaid, each with a rather wide range of duties, re-divided according to the skills available,—'she must milk 3 or 4 cows and understand how to manage that dairy as well as the cooking.' The Purefoy livery was yellow serge, described as serge Padua soi in 1738, yellow Padua serge in 1740, and more specifically in 1743, for Mrs Purefoy was particular about colour and quality,

'I desire you will make the coachman a frock the same coloured cloath to the pattern as near as you can & a gold coloured serge paduaSa waistcoat. Pray let the serge paduaSa be better than the last was. It must not be a lemon colour but a gold colour, & the lining of the frock must be of the same colour; and let me have it within a week or as soon as you can.'

The servants' hats were laced with gold lace and had gold loops and buttons; the lace gold 'of both sides & not a gaws lace.'[11]

The father of the Rev. William Cole of Bletchley had given 'no livery at all, or a very slight one', but his son decided to create a livery for his servant, and chose 'Mr Bromley's after Lord Mountfort as my Father had married into his Family.' This was a 'white cloth turned up with yellow and with gilt buttons and yellow plush breeches and his postillion's coat all yellow.' In 1766 he said that he had given this 'above 30 yrs.' Tom's new suit not only marked him as Mr. Cole's servant, but paid homage to the feudal tradition.[12] Parson Woodforde seems to have been rather more casual about his livery. He provided one for Briton, his man-servant in 1785 and another in 1793, but he noted only that the greatcoat of 1785 was of brown cloth with a red cape, that is, a red collar. In 1800 Briton had a new frock of brown velveret, 'which I had by me.'[13]

John Macdonald, a footman who served many masters, published an account of his places and travels in 1790. In seeking a place he often found it difficult to know how plainly or how finely to be dressed. One place he lost for dressing too plainly: 'Is he dressed like a person for my place or like an interpreter?'; another for dressing too finely: 'I am sorry you went dressed in a gold-laced waistcoat ... she said you were too grand for a family servant.' But with or without gold lace most of his employers had a livery, except two gentlemen he worked for in 1764:

> 'I was hired for twenty guineas a year and two suits of clothes: they told me they did not want me to wear a livery. I went to their tailor, and was measured for one of fustian to do my work in, and another of blue Yorkshire cloth: I did not want to be fine. I wanted to be like a servant.'[14]

As blue cloth had been traditional as the colour for serving men's dress from the sixteenth century it alone would have suggested the servant.

Livery garments, unless they were as plain as this, were recognised for what they were. Their materials were mainly cloth, serge and plush, with trimmings of silver or gold lace and many buttons, silver, gilt or brass. There were usually two colours in the coat, its collar and facing or lining contrasting with the main colour and matching the colour of the waistcoat. The hats were laced. The coat sometimes kept the shoulder knot, worn in fashionable dress in the second half of the seventeenth century. Its gold or silver lace also preserved decoration fashionable in the first half of the century which then passed out of wear. Livery was a conservative form of dress in some of its detail, developing into a uniform to mark a man as a servant, but giving him something of the splendour and fineness of dress and grooming which belonged to the fashionable world. Even those who wore the plainer liveries probably had better clothing than they would have done in other occupations open to them.

The number of liveried servants increased as more families showed their prosperity by employing them. Matthew Bramble's tirade in *Humphrey Clinker* expressed the prevailing displeasure of those who saw this as pretentious and demoralising:

> 'The poorest squire as well as the richest peer, must have his house in

town, and make a figure with an extraordinary number of domestics. The ploughboys, cow-herds and lower hinds are debauched and seduced by the appearance and discourse of those coxcombs in livery when they make their summer excursions. They desert their dirt and drudgery and swarm up to London in hopes of getting into service, where they can live luxuriously and wear fine clothes.'[15]

The employing classes, driven by their own social aspirations needed the finery and numbers of their servants to express their social position, but by this indulgence they were helping to break down the established idea of dress according to station. The splendour of the man-servant did not conceal the fact that he was a servant, but it accustomed him to a richer and more decorative style of dress than most working men wore.

Livery suits were generally the property of the employer. Parson Woodforde made the position quite clear to Briton: 'I told Briton that I gave neither to him but only to wear them during his service with me.'[16] But it is not surprising to find that departing servants did not always conform. Mrs Purefoy lost a livery in 1741 when a footman left, taking frock and waistcoat with him. There were sometimes other agreements which gave the servant the right to his livery: 'To Charles in consideration wearing on his old livery and for what he might have sold it for £1. 1s. od.'[16] Nicholas Blundell's servants seem sometimes to have paid part of the cost of a livery themselves.[18]

Because servants either had the right to keep old livery or took it away with them whether they had the right or not, individual livery garments often re-appeared in other dress, worn by the servant, a member of his family, or more widely distributed through the second-hand clothes shops. Lists of missing persons published in the newspapers give descriptions of clothing which reveal what happened to cast-off liveries: a missing farmer of 1759 was said to be wearing 'a dark-coloured fustian frock, blue livery waistcoat, buckskin breeches, brown cut wig.'[19]

Apart from his livery the servant might receive his master's cast-off clothing as a perquisite. John Macdonald felt himself ill-used when the employer, who had told him on engaging him, 'I shall give you my old clothes if you please me', fifteen months later offered him only a few things of little value.[20] Humphrey Clinker's predecessor was sulky because 'squire gave away an ould coat to a poor man; and John says as how 'tis robbing him of his parquisites.'[21] Servants received mourning suits at the time of a death in the family, and they also received bequests of garments: 'If any man servant or men servants shall have lived with me so long [two years] that all my Linnen and wearing apparel (except the best) be divided between such servant or servants . . . .'[22] This cast-off clothing, even if the best was excepted, was of greater value than the livery in bringing them closer in dress to the class they served.

However grand the livery, it was a rise in status for a servant to leave it off. One of John Macdonald's employers promised him, 'If you were to stay I would soon put you out of livery.'[23] As soon as Humphrey

Clinker's birth was discovered he was put 'out of livery and wares ruffles.'[24] Lord Sheffield's sister, Serena Holroyd, wrote of her servant: 'William Foley gave me to understand that being in a livery was unbecoming his future hopes of being raised in the World by some fair one falling in love with him.'[25] From the employer's point of view the dressing of those serving as gentlemen, with the implication that they were served by gentlemen, was a refinement of display beyond the most splendid livery. When Count Kielmansegge was in England in 1761-2 and was entertained by the Duke of Newcastle, he found that 'At least ten to twelve servants out of livery waited upon us, of whom the majority wore long wigs, which would naturally make it difficult for a stranger to distinguish between guests and servants. Now all these people, in spite of their fine clothing, expect their tips when you leave, but to a gold-laced coat you cannot offer a solitary shilling.'[26]

Unlike men-servants, women wore no uniform at all, and some people, Defoe amongst them, thought they should. In 1725 he published a pamphlet on the servant problem as he saw it, *Everybody's Business is Nobody's Business,* and writes of the servant girl becoming a servant in London:

> 'Her neat's leathern shoes are now transformed into laced ones with high heels; her yarn stockings are now turned into fine woollen ones with silk clocks and her high wooden pattens are kicked away for leather clogs; she must have a hoop too as well as her mistress and her poor scanty linsey-woolsey petticoat is changed into a good silk one, four or five yards wide at least. In short, plain country Joan is now turned into a fine London madam.'

And of the social embarrassment this fine madam dress could cause:

> 'I remember I was put very much to the Blush being at a Friend's House and by him required to salute the Ladies, and I kiss'd the chamber jade into the bargain for she was as well dressed as the best. Things of this nature would be easily avoided if Servant Maids were to wear Liveries, as Footmen do; or obliged to go into a Dress suitable to their Station. Our Charity Children are distinguished by their Dresses, why then may not our Women Servants?'[27]

The well-dressed serving-maid remained the whipping girl for vague social ills throughout the century: 'Luxury in the dress of our female servants and the daughters of farmers and many others in inferior stations who think a well-chose cotton gown shall entitle them to the appellation of young ladies is highly prejudicial both to the landowner, the farmer and the public.'[28] (Fig. 56). More specifically, a writer in 1785 thought the fine dress of servant girls a cause of prostitution, although he did not put the whole blame on the servants: 'Mrs Becky was not a whit inferior to her mistress; the cloathes of the latter might probably be more costly, but they were both made after the same fashion, and the soiled cap sat as smartly on the powdered head of the former as it could

56 *The Modern Harlot's Progress;*
*Harriot Heedless at Statute Hall,*
*1780.*
*Carrington Bowles*

have done some weeks before on that of its pristine wearer.' This servant was paid

'No more than usual eight guineas a year, her tea and a few cast-off cloaths, which she deserves for the ingenuity she shows in trimming them to the best advantage .... I am sure there is more pleasure in being attended by a girl that had pride enough to keep herself fit to be seen than by a dirty slattern who pays no regard to her person.'[29]

The mistress defended her servant's right to dress as well as she could, and encouraged her to do so, because a well-dressed servant was as important to her as being well-dressed herself, a reflection of her own fashionable status.

The remark. 'It is a hard matter to know the mistress from the maid, nay very often the maid shall be the finer of the two', made by Defoe in his pamphlet, was repeated throughout the century. Foreign visitors continue to echo Defoe: 'Very few women wear woollen gowns, even servants wear silk on Sundays or holidays.'[30] A visitor of 1765 noticed mistress and maid walking in the streets and public walks: 'The servants and maids of citizens' wives, the waiting women of ladies of first quality and of middling quality attend their ladies in the street and in the public walks in such a dress that if the mistress be not known it is no easy matter

to distinguish her from the maid.'[31] Von Archenholz said much the same of London servants, 'usually well clad in gowns well adapted to their shape, their hats adorned with ribbands. There are some who even wear silk and satin when they are dressed .... As to a Lady's maid ... the eye of the most skilful connoisseur can scarcely distinguish her from her mistress.'[32]

The personal maid, waiting-woman or lady's maid was particularly difficult to distinguish because such maids were themselves often drawn from the ranks of the smaller gentry and clergymen (Fig. 57). Jenny, Charlotte Grandison's maid in Richardson's *The History of Sir Charles Grandison,* was 'a sensible young woman, a clergyman's daughter, well-educated and very obliging.'[33] When Lady Cowper's maid, Godwin was married in 1768, she was dressed in 'a new white satin nightgown and petticoat, a white spotted satin cloak, and bonnet trimmed with blond, new lace handkerchief and ruffles upon gauze, a clear apron, and I gave her a very handsome pair of stone shoe-buckles.'[34] On one occasion at least, in 1792, a maid was actually mistaken, or allowed to pass for, a lady of quality. This was Betty Eden, maid to Mary Noel, who

'was at Court, and somehow by her Ignorance which did as well as impudence contrived, being very well drest to make her way, not

*57 English Family at Tea, c. 1730. The men all wear versions of the long or full-bottom wig and long coats to the knee, covering the breeches. The quilted petticoat is partly revealed, beneath the black gown of the lady making tea, so too are her red shoes. But it is the figure of the maid which takes centre of the stage and it is her dress which is the most interesting. The gown is yellowish green with white stripes; it meets at centre front where it is folded back to show a white lining and the sleeve turned up in the same way makes a white cuff. Her apron is a large, plain working apron, but her cap with pinned-up lappets has the same pleated frill, lying flat on the head, as that of the lady at the tea-table.*
*J. van Aken*

knowing where she went till she actually arrived at the Door of the Drawing Room, on one side of which she actually stood the whole time .... It seems she follow'd some Ladies who were very well drest but not in Court dresses till she came to the Bar where they gave tickets but she was overlook'd and so pass'd in with them.'[35]

Mrs Lybbe Powys's comment on a Norfolk household in 1756 shows how unusual any uniformity of dress amongst the maid-servants was:

'I was surprised to see them all except on Sundays in green stuff gowns, and on my enquiring of Miss Jackson how they all happened to fix so on one particular colour, she told me a green camblet used for many years to be an annual present of her mother's to those servants who behaved well, and had been so many years in her family, and that now indeed as they all behaved well and had lived there so much longer than the limited term this was constantly their old master's New Year gift.'[36]

The giving of dresses to servants by their employer might end in creating a uniform, but from the writer's surprise here, this does not generally seem to have happened. Gifts of clothing were made, but not usually the same material year after year. Parson Woodforde sensibly bought the same material each time he made a gift to both maids: pea-green stuff in 1783, and early in 1801 a pink and white cotton gown for each of them at 2s 6d a yard, a price which suggests a Sunday gown rather than a working one. They had a 'cotton gown apiece' from London in 1789 and a gown each of cotton at 2s 3d a yard in 1795 at the same time as Nancy had cotton for a gown at 2s 6d.[37] In some households dresses for maids, like liveries for men-servants seem to have been provided as an agreed allowance. Elizabeth Strutt, taking over the housekeeping after her mother's death in 1774, at once had a problem about a maid's dress allowance:

'Besides her wages there are two new gowns owing her. When her wages were raised which is 4 years since my Mother promised her a new gown every year that she took no veils [*sic*] and she has had only two of them. She will look upon the crape one as a third unless we choose to take that for another servant and then she will expect two—she has one of our cotton.'

The crape dress was perhaps a mourning dress for Mrs Strutt, and 'our cotton' refers to the Strutt business of cotton manufacture. A year later Elizabeth was still having trouble with the militant Molly, who waged her battle with some skill:

'Molly has two old petticoats, one I gave her today and a bedgown, but I suppose she thinks she deserves a new gown, for she has bought herself a new gown lately to wear every day and she tells me the neighbours say I have not forgotten my Mama's rules, for they see I have given her a new gown.'[38]

The right of the maid to the cast-off clothes of her mistress was well established. Mrs Ann Cook, author of *Professed Cookery,* added to the third edition of her book in 1760, the life story of a friend, another cook who became housekeeper and personal maid. In this post 'castings' were added to the allowances she had previously received as cook. Her mistress, noting the neat appearance of all the maids on Sunday at the chapel, saw that they were dressed in the gowns and linen which she had given to the housekeeper, and asked the chambermaid what she had paid for the gown and linen she was wearing:

'"Nothing at all" answered she, "the Housekeeper said you lent them to her to give to us: But whatever she gives us of yours, she bids us look on as sacred; nor do we wear any Thing that was yours in any other Place but the Church, and as soon as Divine Service is over, we all undress ourselves, and put on our Homespun Gowns, so folds up our Clothes, which she very diligently observes; for no Maid in the Family she allows above one Gown washed in a Quarter of the Year. So everyone of us endeavours which shall keep their Gown cleanest." All this I told your Master, which pleased him so well, that the first Chapman that came with a Horse-pack he bought me three Webs of the best Chintz Cottons; and said, "Make plenty of these Gowns, wear them a while in the Morning, and cast them to your Maid, who very well deserves to have the Distribution of them."'[39]

Everyone in this story sounds a little too good to be true, but it shows castings as the allowance of the upper servant; the freedom to sell to fellow servants; the use of such clothes for Sunday or best wear only; and that it was morning gowns of printed cotton which passed from mistress to maid for this distribution. This distinction was not always made and finer clothing was often included in castings, and often a whole wardrobe in a bequest. When Lady Bristol died, her husband wrote to his son:

'I am glad to find that you have delivered to Williams all the things which were your poor mother's and which by a customary sort of right are now due to every common servant in her place; but as her merit and services for near 18 years have been of the most uncommon kind, that consideration alone would have entitled her to any favour out of the ordinary course of proceedings between executors and residuary legatees.'[40]

Mrs Mary Williams, 'of a good family in Wales', continued in the family of Lord Bristol after Lady Bristol's death. Grace Ridley, waiting-woman to Sarah, Duchess of Marlborough, who left her £15,000 and an annuity of £300, also received half her wearing apparel; the remaining half was divided between two other maids. Lady Mary Wortley Montagu left her maid, Mari Anna Fromenta, 'all my wearing apparel either made or not made and all my Linen either for the Bed, Table or my person' in 1763.[41] In families of this rank clothing, except fine lace or embroidery, was now rarely left to relatives. When Lady Heathcote died in 1764 her husband wished Mary Yorke, her sister-in-law, to have

'3 little Parcels of Dresden Work & blond not made up . . . . I thanked him but declined accepting of them, as I thought tho' they were not made, yet they must have been intended for ware and therefore desired they might go with the Cloaths to the Maid. He said he was particularly desired to give them to me he had always kept them separate—and accordingly sent them without my knowledge . . . they are of some value.'[42]

Her care about this gift, the implication that what was intended for wear, even if not actually worn or even made up, should go with the clothes to Lady Heathcote's maid, shows how well established this right was. Mrs Delany was careful in her will, made in 1778, to distinguish between her wearing apparel and body linen, 'that had been washed and once worn', which she left to her own maid, and certain embroideries and lace and the work of friends and 'all her fur and feather muffs and tippets', which she bequeathed to her niece.[43] Many of these, too, were of her own making or had been made by her friends. A good deal of fine clothing of considerable value was involved in these bequests, much of which must have been sold, either privately or to the second-hand clothes shops. Where there was no formal bequest, the customary right, as the Earl of Bristol implied, could mean that a large quantity of personal belongings fell into undeserving hands. Smollett's story of Mr Baynard in *Humphrey Clinker* shows this happening:

'The aunt ... did not leave the house, however, without giving Mr Baynard to understand that the wardrobe of her niece was the perquisite of her woman; accordingly that worthless drab received all the clothes, laces and linen of her deceased mistress, to the value of five hundred pounds, at a moderate computation.'[44]

The clothing of a master as well as of a mistress might go to a maid. Richard Antonie, who had been apprenticed to a London linen draper but who succeeded to the Colworth estate in Bedfordshire when his elder brother John died in 1760, left his housekeeper, in addition to an annuity and household linen, a share of his linen and wearing apparel with any men-servants who had lived with him for two years before his death; if there were none who had been in his service so long, 'I give the same wholly to the said Jane Clarkson.' It was a common practice to leave a servant money to buy mourning. Mrs Clarkson also had ten guineas for this purpose and a guinea for a mourning ring and a scarf and hood.[45]

As well as these regular perquisites of dress by allowance, castings and bequests from their employers, servants received occasional presents of clothes. When garments pass from employer to servant it is not always clear whether they are extra gifts—'Gave my maid Sally Gunton for sitting up with me when ill 2 yds of black silk being a hatband sent to me by John Manners on the death of his Mother'[46]—or part of an agreed allowance. Guests also made gifts to servants, perhaps in lieu of 'vails' or tips. Parson Woodforde's maid Betty was given a silk bonnet by Mrs

Davie after she had stayed at the parsonage in 1781 and Mr de Quesne gave each maid a muslin apron after a visit in 1789. Dress was also used to reward or bribe other people's servants for various reasons and not surprisingly this is recorded more often in fiction and drama than in factual records. In *Humphrey Clinker* Lydia Melford gives her aunt's maid, Win Jenkins, a gown in the hope that she will say nothing to Miss Bramble which might reveal Lydia's love for 'Mr Wilson'.[47] Lucy, Lydia Languish's maid, in the same situation kept an account of her gains:

> 'For abetting Miss Lydia Languish in a design of running away ... gowns five, hats, ruffles, caps, etc. numberless! Item from Mrs Malaprop for betraying the young people to her when I found matters were likely to be discovered—two guineas and a black paduasoy.'[48]

Although the waiting gentlewomen and many maids were no doubt discriminating in what they selected for their own wear and in the way they wore their castings, gifts and bequests, it is unlikely that all servants used their gifts wisely. Molly Seagrim, appearing in church in a sack-back gown given to her mother by Sophia Western, 'though indeed, that young lady had little apprehension that the poor woman would have been weak enough to let any of her daughters wear it in that form' did not; nor did Win Jenkins in her yellow trollopee, 'which Mrs Drab, the manty maker, says will look very well when it is scowered and smoaked with silfur—You know as how, yallow fitts my fizzogmony. God he knows that havock I shall make among the mail sex, when I make my first appearance in this killing collar.' Win Jenkins is a comic study of the servant who apes the tastes and habits of her employer, but she still emerges as an individual and rather endearing character, 'she dresses and endeavours to look like her mistress, although her own looks are much more engaging.'[49]

Clarissa, in Richardson's novel, like the mistress of Ann Cook's friend, was careful in gift and bequest. She gives her gown of brown lustring to a servant, but employs the mantua-maker's journeywoman to alter it: 'the gown I will give directions about, because the dress, and the robings and facings must be altered for your wear, being, I believe above your station.' This was part of a plan of escape, so that the maid would take off her own 'hood, short cloak and apron' and give Clarissa the chance to take them, put them on as a disguise and slip out of the house as the servant; but the action is also beautifully in character. In her will she shows the same thought:

> 'To Katherine the honest maidservant of Mrs Smith ... ten guineas more in lieu of a suit of my wearing apparel, which once with some linen, I thought of leaving to her. With this she may purchase what may be more suitable to her liking and degree.'[50]

One of the best-known servants in fiction, Richardson's Pamela, has

*58 Pamela and Mr B. in the summer-house. Pamela here is still wearing the clothes she wore as the personal maid of her late mistress, a silk gown, white shot with pink. Mr B.'s brown coat and white waistcoat are laced with gold and his breeches are scarlet.*

*J. Highmore (eng. 1745)*

much to say about her clothes. The passages about dress in this novel, detailed accounts of the dress of a country girl of humble parents who becomes a favoured personal maid, are skilfully used by Richardson. Pamela's dress and her attitudes to it reveal the subtle social messages of dress at this time. Her first alarm was not at Mr B's fine gifts—there was nothing unusual in her receiving his mother's clothes—but at the manner of their giving. She then evokes that symbol of rustic innocence and simplicity since the sixteenth century, the russet gown: 'O how I wished for my gray russet again, and my poor dress with which you fitted me out.' She, unlike Molly Seagrim, realises the effect of wearing garments grander than those of the village community, to which she now wishes to return, and of the mingling of finery with common dress:

> 'For how would your poor daughter look with a silk nightgown, silken petticoats, cambric head-clothes, fine Holland linen, laced shoes, that were my lady's, and fine stockings! And how in a little while, must these have looked, like old cast-offs, and I looked so for wearing them!... And how should I look even if I could purchase homespun clothes, to dwindle into them, one by one as I got them?—May be, an old silk gown, and linsey woolsey petticoat and the like.'

Dressed for return she presents the idealised picture of the pretty, modest country girl—Defoe's serving maid before she succumbed to London ways—

> 'I dressed myself in my new garb, and put on my round-eared ordinary cap, but with a green knot, my home-spun gown and petticoat, and plain leather shoes ... and my ordinary hose ... though I should think good yarn may do very well for every day when I come home. A plain muslin tucker I put on, and my black silk necklace, instead of the French necklace my lady gave me; and put the ear-rings out of my ears. When I was quite equipped, I took my straw hat in my hand, with its two blue strings, and looked in the glass, as proud as anything.'

She then made up three bundles of clothing and took them to the housekeeper. The first was of the things given her by her mistress during the three or four years of her service:

> 'Those things there of my lady's, I can have no claim to, so as to take them away; for she gave them me, supposing I was to wear them in her service .... I cannot wear them at my poor father's for I should bring all the little village upon my back.' (Fig. 58).

The second was of the recent presents of her master: 'I have far less right to these ... for you see what was his intention in giving them me.' The third contained the things she was taking with her and, with the clothes she was wearing, made up her wardrobe for village life:

> 'A calico nightgown, that I used to wear o' mornings. 'Twill be rather too good for me when I get home; but I must have something. Then there is a quilted calimanco coat, a pair of stockings I bought of the pedlar, my

straw hat with blue strings; and a remnant of Scotch cloth which will make two shirts and two shifts, the same I have on for my poor father and mother. And here are four other shifts, one the fellow to that I have on; another pretty good one, and the other two old fine ones, that will serve me to turn and wind with at home, for they are not worth leaving behind me; and here are two pair of shoes; I have taken the lace off, which I will burn, and may-be will fetch me some little matter at a pinch, with an old silver buckle or two ... here's a cotton handkerchief I bought of a pedlar; there should be another somewhere. O here it is; and here are my new-bought mittens; this is my new flannel coat, the fellow to that I have on; and in this parcel pinned together are several pieces of printed calico, remnants of silk and such like... would serve for robings and facings and such-like uses. Here are a pair of pockets; they are too fine for me, but I have no worse.'

Later, immediately before her marriage to Mr B. and in response to his wish that she 'should dress as you used to do, for now, at least, you may call your two bundles your own', she once more puts on the dress of the maid in attendance on her mistress, in her best clothes:

'Fine linen, silk shoes, and fine white cotton stockings, a fine quilted coat, a delicate green Mantua silk gown, and coat, a French necklace, a laced cambric handkerchief, and clean gloves; and taking my fan, I, like a proud little hussy, looked in the glass, and thought myself a gentlewoman once more.'[51]

Pamela shows how the maid, serving the gentlewoman and dressing like her, takes on the way of dress of the class above her. So long as she has a sense of identity and relationship with her employer, she accepts this way of dress and it is generally accepted by society. But until she marries Mr B. she is still her parents' daughter, in her own village one of many village daughters. She realises that the two aspects of her life need different styles of dress. Yet it is one person who wears the two styles, making the link through which fashion may pass from group to group.

The one gown which passed from Pamela's gentlewoman's wardrobe to her wardrobe as a village girl was 'the calico nightgown that I used to wear o' mornings.' Gowns of printed linen or cotton, plain versions of contemporary dress for morning wear, like those of the mistress in Ann Cook's story, were common to the wardrobe of mistress and maid, the working dress of the one becoming the best dress of the other. Even Pamela in her change from silk to homespun wool allowed herself a calico gown for best wear as a village girl. In 1744 Elizabeth Hurst of Luton left members of her family gowns of damask, cherry derry and speckled crape in her will, but to her servant, 'my new printed Linen Gown, a black petticoat, cap, handkerchief and Apron.'[52] Nancy Woodforde gave one of the maids at the parsonage a linen gown which later the girl was married in.[53] Sophie von la Roche saw them in the streets of London:

'. . . the maids, women of the middle class and the children. The former almost all wear black taminy petticoats rather stiff and heavily stitched, and over these, long English calico or linen frocks, though not so long and close-fitting to the body as our tailors and taste cut and point them. Further they mostly wear white aprons; though the servants and working women often appear in striped linen aprons.'[54]

It was not so much the cast-off finery as this simple version of fashionable dress worn by both mistress and maid, although for different occasions, which brought the dress of servants within the fashionable style. It was a simple version which could be passed on and accepted by their own social group. Contact with well-dressed women developed the eye and taste of many serving maids and helped them to dress with understanding of the fashion they followed. The absence of any uniform, on or off duty, left them free to follow fashions according to their own taste and means. If they dressed too finely for their station they might be censured, but the readiness of women to pass on their own clothes to their servants shows there was no sharp division of dress, nor even a social convention against servants occasionally buying the same garment at the same time as the mistress: 'Nancy bought of Bagshaw this morning . . . a very genteel Shawl at 10 shillings. Both my Maids bought 2 Shawls the same as Nancy.'[55] Parson Woodforde records this as a fact, without any judgment, or comment.

# V

# *The Common People*

## Farming People and the Country Towns

At the beginning of the century there was a recognisable group ranking below the gentry, the yeomen who worked their own land, or sometimes land they rented, but were their own masters. Prosperous yeomen, by continued acquisition of land, often rose to the rank of gentry. This social movement was a ready source of comedy in the theatre of the early eighteenth century: 'the Yeoman of Kent, that's half Farmer and half Gentleman, his Horses go to Plow all the week and are put in the coach o' Sunday.' The two ways of life were also emphasised by the dress of the daughter of the 'half Farmer and half Gentleman', for 'notwithstanding he allows her all the Gaiety of Body he obliges her to the Ancient custom of wearing a High-Crown Hat.'[1] The hat kept her among the country housewives; fashion would have taken over completely if she had worn a silk hood. During the century there was a great building-up of large estates. As these absorbed other properties, large and small, yeomen often became tenant farmers, but did not necessarily lose their economic position. The term yeoman was gradually replaced by the term farmer, which covered both these tenant farmers and those who still farmed their own lands as the class itself disintegrated into large farmers, surviving small farmers and a growing number, now without land of their own, who worked as farm servants or day labourers on the larger farms.

The way of life of the large farmers whose wealth increased in the second half of the century approached that of the neighbouring country gentry. Smollett's romantic squire, Launcelot Greaves, disliked the changing ways of the rich yeomen: 'They kept their footmen, their saddle-horses and chaises; their wives and daughters appeared in their jewels, their silks and their satins, their negligees and trollopees; their clumsy shanks like so many shins of beef, new cased in silk hose and embroidered slippers', compared with the 'buxom country lasses' assembled on May Day to dance before Squire Launcelot, 'in their best apparel dight, their white hose and clean short dimity petticoats, their gaudy gowns of printed cotton; their top-knots, kissing strings and stomachers, bedizened with bunches of ribbons of various colours, green, pink and yellow.'[2] In the 1770s Lady Newdigate appeared for the

120

*Sunday Morning,* A Cottage Family Going to Church. *One woman wears the red hooded cloak with bound edges, over a blue gown and red quilted petticoat, and the black silk hat with soft crown and peaked brim, the other a straw hat and long gloves.*
W. R. Bigg *(Reproduced by Courtesy of The Trustees of The British Museum)*

*Morning Employments, 1785-8. The morning dresses here show a plain version of the changing style
of the 1780s, the long-sleeved gown with rising waistline but the skirts still full, and an alternative
informal style of the 1780s and 1790s – a jacket and petticoat. The woman at the embroidery frame is
working with a hook for chain stitch or tambour work and appears to be working a gown. Trousers are
now the established wear for young boys.*
*Engraved 1789 by P. M. Tomkins, after H. W. Bunbury.*
*(Victoria and Albert Museum, Crown Copyright)*

first time at Kirkby church after her marriage 'very genteely dressed I thought but she was greatly outdone in height of Head and Ruffles by the young Ladies of the village.'[3] Parson Woodforde noted Mrs Howlett, wife of a farmer, at church in August 1796, with a black veil over her face and neck and added in his diary: 'Mem. Times must be good for Farmers when their Wives can dress in such a stile.'[4] Lady Jerningham, writing to her daughter in 1802 about their 'tenants' uproar', an annual gathering of tenants and their families, said: 'The Miss Taylors, quite fine young ladies—in deep mourning, no Cap, no handkerchief, long trains, in short might have been at any London assembly; the Mother in a good old-fashioned mob, relating to me how she went out to service at Norwich at eleven years.'[5]

Some farming families still kept their own way of life. In his *Rural Economy of Norfolk* (1795) William Marshall described three different types of farmer within the country:

'Many of them have been and some of them still are rich; this has led them to mix in a greater or a less degree with what is called the world .... The lower class of Norfolk farmers, however, are the same plain men which farmers in general are, living in great measure with their servants. Another class live in the kitchen with their servants, but eat at a separate table; while the upper classes have their "keeping" rooms and other commodious apartments.'[6]

Kalm, the Swedish botanist who was in England in 1748, had found that even then farmers in the Gaddesden district of Hertfordshire kept few farm servants; almost all were day labourers; that the farmers' wives rarely troubled themselves with the work of the farm, but spent their time looking after their houses, 'for about cleanliness they are very careful', and cooking. He was surprised that 'they never take the trouble to bake, because there is a baker in every parish or village .... Weaving and spinning is also in most houses a more than rare thing, because their many manufacturers save them from the necessity of such.' He wrote of the dress of the women of farming families:

'When Englishwomen in the country are going to pay their compliments to each other, they commonly wear a red cloak. They also wear pattens under ordinary shoes when they go out to prevent the dirt on the roads and streets soiling their ordinary shoes. All go laced, and use for everyday a sort of Manteau, made commonly of brownish Camlot. The same headdress as in London. Here it is not unusual to see a farmer or other small personage's wife clad on Sundays like a lady of "quality" at other places in the world and her everyday attire in proportion. When they go out they always wear straw hats which they have made themselves from wheat straw and are pretty enough. On high days they have ruffles.'[7]

They wore stays to give the fashionable shape, but not hoops, that is, they wore the style of fashionable undress or walking dress. They wore two styles: their best dress, Sunday dress or the dress of high days brought them close to fashionable dress, in its less formal version; their everyday dress showed certain divergences from it, the red cloak, the straw hat and the pattens, which appear constantly in references to countrywomen, although not all these were exclusively country wear.

The wealthier farmers in part drew away as they mixed with local gentry and followed their way of dress, but even as they did so they helped to bring fashion nearer to their country neighbours. Some of the gentry were conscious of their responsibility as an influence on the dress of their humbler country neighbours. In 1777 Mrs Delany wrote a letter for her great-niece on *Propriety* which included a paragraph on the subject of dress:

'In the country nothing is more absurd than to dress fantastically, and turn the brains of your humbler neighbours; who will pique themselves in apeing the squire's daughter! And believe me this can't be innocently done, as (such an example) will certainly interfere with their station in life and make them less willing to submit to the duties of it. Dress ought always to be suited to the situation and circumstances of the person ... moderation is always genteel.'[8]

John Byng would have agreed with Mrs Delany. Travelling near Atherstone in 1789 he noted with disapproval a lady too finely dressed for the country, and then described how he thought she should have been dressed: 'A neat short gown with a chip hat, tied with a rose-coloured ribband, strong shoes and easy stays (if stays be necessary at all?) for me a truly ornamental dress for any lady in the country.'[9] He might be describing a well-dressed countrywoman.

Straw or chip hats had been the mark of rural dress since the seventeenth century. In 1667 Samuel Pepys went with his wife and friends to Hatfield and there the women of the party tried on the local straw hats, 'which are much worn in this country', but were obviously strange to these Londoners, living about twenty miles away.[10] Charles Johnson in his play *The Country Lasses* identified them: 'in a straw hat, Kersey Gown and a White Dimity Waistcoat.' Swift saw straw hats in London in 1710: 'Do you know that in our town we are already making hay, and it smells so sweet as we walk through the flowry meads; but the haymaking nymphs are perfect drabs, nothing so clean and pretty as further in the country. There is a mighty increase of dirty wenches in straw hats since I knew London.'[11] Does his comment refer to the country girls who had come into London, not only for haymaking, or does it mean that this country fashion had moved into town, taken up by its 'dirty wenches'? When a few years later, the Prince and Princess of Wales arrived from Hanover, they dined in public at Hampton Court and

'all sorts of people have free admission to see them even of the lowest sort and rank in the common habits .... One day they interested themselves seeing the country folks come in their straw hats and because one came without her straw hat the Princess sent her back again to fetch it. Upon this several of the gentry came with straw hats very fine with footmen attending.'[12]

In various paintings of Covent Garden Market in the 1720s and 1730s, by Van Aken, Angelis and Nebot, women sit with their baskets of country produce, many of them wearing wide-brimmed, flat-crowned hats which appear to be made of straw or chip. Many of their customers wear hoods, but in the Nebot painting a similar though more elegant hat can be seen worn with plain but more fashionable dress (Fig. 59b). A painting of Lady Irwin, at Temple Newsam, Leeds shows her in a garden setting, plainly dressed, and holding a large straw hat very like those of the market women. In the Nebot painting another type of hat is worn by one of the sellers of vegetables, a black hat with pointed crown, the 'witches'' hat of popular tradition. The high-crowned hat of beaver or felt seen in Hollar's engravings of the mid-seventeenth century survived into the 1670s, as can be seen in a painting of the Tichborne Dole, by G. Van Tilborgh. It was then a slightly different shape with a more tapering crown, the type which is still preserved in the uniform of the

*59 (a) and (b)  Two details from B. Nebot's painting of Covent Garden, 1737. The market woman seated on the left in detail (a) wears a black, high-crowned hat, tapering to a point; near her another wears a wide-brimmed, flat-crowned hat of straw or chip. A more fashionable, but still plain version of this form can be seen on the woman with the child in detail (b). She also wears a gown similar to that of the maid in fig. 57 with its front edges and sleeves turned back to make decorative use of contrasting lining.*

(a)

(b)

61  *Whitefield Preaching, 1742. The woman in a pale straw-coloured gown listening earnestly to the preacher wears the straw hat and cap of common wear.*
*J. Wollaston*

61  *Whitefield Preaching, 1742. The woman in a pale straw-coloured gown listening earnestly to the preacher wears the straw hat and cap of common wear.*
*J. Wollaston*

60  *Windsor Castle, the Terrace. The woman with the child has falling cuffs to her gown, worn with a dark petticoat beneath a white apron. Her flat-crowned hat is trimmed round the crown and worn with a fashionable tilt. The baby wears a 'pudding', a padded cap to protect its head.*
*P. Sandby*

bedeswomen of Trinity Hospital, Castle Rising, Norfolk. The crown of the hat in the painting of Covent Garden is much lower but keeps the pointed form. It was probably a hat with this smaller crown which was still worn by the Kentish farmer's daughter, and which Macky saw at Tunbridge Wells: 'The Sussex fresh-coloured Lasses, in the high-crowned hats are no small Ornament to the Place.'[13] There was a fashionable revival of this style which *The Gentleman's Magazine* noted in 1731: 'It seems to be a kind of masquerade; it would insinuate an idea of innocence and rusticity tho' the park is not the likeliest scene of either.' This style appears worn by ladies of the Ashley and Popple families, who were painted by Hogarth in the same year, but it was a short-lived revival in fashionable wear. It was the flat-crowned straw hat, given shape and elegance, which persisted throughout the middle years of the century in fashionable undress wear. During this time fashionable and unfashionable women alike wear a flat-crowned wide-brimmed straw hat (Fig. 60). The distinction of the fashionable hat was that it was usually of the fine straw-plaiting imported from Leghorn; English wheat straw, the material of common hats, produced a much coarser plait. Kalm noted that the hats he saw in Hertfordshire: 'they have made themselves from wheat straw.' This was already a small industry in this district: 'several women who were very busy in making straw hats which they afterwards sent hither and thither to be sold.'[14] Although straw hats were fashionably worn, straw hats and country girls were almost synonymous. The Marchioness Grey visited Stourbridge Fair in 1748, 'where one meets with a Number of clean tight countrymen and maidens tricked out with their Ribbands and

*62  The Haymakers, 1785. One of the women wears a wrapping bedgown secured by her apron. All wear the black hats of 1780s' fashion. The men work in wide-brimmed round hats, and only one has a waistcoat on over a full-sleeved shirt. G. Stubbs*

straw hats to whom this is really a happy, jolly day.' A few years later, at her husband's home at Wimpole, she and her sister-in-law were 'enticed' by the Lord Chancellor to 'a country Fair or Statute in a little Village close to his Park' where they met 'a crowd of people, spruce straw Hats and Linnen Gowns.'[15]

Chip, fine shavings of willow or poplar, was used as well as straw for plaiting or weaving into hats. In fashionable ones the hat was often shaped in chip and then covered with silk. In common wear the straw or chip was worn plain except for a ribbon band and strings and sometimes a lined underbrim (Fig. 61). The flat hats were also made in black felt for common wear. The strings were often tied under the chin, bringing the brim down, bonnet-like over the face. The heroine of Charlotte Smith's *The Old Manor House,* written in 1793 but set in the 1770s, set out in her best dress, a white gown, 'with a little straw hat tied under her chin with blue ribband.' At the end of the century this style re-appeared in fashion as a 'gipsy' hat. In common dress the wearing of the style continued until the end of the century and beyond, but in the 1780s it was joined by another type of hat, of black silk with a large soft crown and stiff brim. When Sophie von la Roche wrote of the caps and black taffeta hats she

saw worn by women in London, noting that 'the milkmaids wear black taffeta hats like the town maids', she said that the caps really resembled those seen in English engravings 'and simple black taffeta hats beside with black ribbons fitting right down the head.'[16] It is not clear whether these were wide-brimmed, flat-crowned hats tied down or a form of soft-crowned hat with a peaked brim tilted over the face. A painting of country people going to church, *Sunday Morning* (1793) by W. R. Bigg, shows the two styles worn by different members of a cottage group (colour plate 3). The crown of the straw hat is back to medium height, moving with the fashionable high-crowned styles of the late 1780s; the black one follows the general shape of the balloon hats of the 1780s. The Stubbs paintings of *Haymakers* and *Reapers* also show these black hats, fashionably large though worn with working dress (Figs 62, 63). There is a slightly later example of the black silk hat with peaked brim in front but no brim at the back and smaller crown in Exeter Museum. By the 1780s this black bonnet was seen as a characteristic of common dress, ' 'tis as unsuitable as linsey woolsy or a black bonnet at the opera.'[17] (Fig. 80). Yet what struck most foreign visitors was the universal wearing of hats by women of all classes. C. P. Moritz, who explored England more

*63  The Reapers, 1785. The two women wear protective mittens on their forearms; the farmer's round hat and those of the men are in the same general style.*
*G. Stubbs*

64 *Joseph Andrews and his Friends at the Inn. This later illustration of Henry Fielding's novel,* Joseph Andrews, *shows Fanny with her gown pinned back, a working woman's habit, not looped up as in a polonaise; but she is wearing her small hat in the fashion of the 1770s.* T. Hearne

65 *Beggars on the Road to Stanmore, c. 1770. The clothing of all of them is little more than a covering, but the woman shows a fashionable shoe and wears the inevitable straw or chip hat.* J. Zoffany

widely than most foreign visitors, and often on foot, was impressed by the hats he saw in Oxfordshire in 1782: 'Women, in general, from the highest to the lowest wear hats, which differ from each other less in fashion than they do in fineness.'[18] (Fig. 64). Archenholz, who was in London at about the same time, wrote: 'No female of whatever rank dares to appear in the streets of London on foot without one of these; the very beggars wear them.'[19] (Fig. 65).

Linen or cotton caps were worn indoors and under the hat out-of-doors. They followed the fashionable shape as this changed. Walton's painting *Girl Plucking a Turkey* (1776) shows a cap, clearly in the style of the 1770s, worn at work with the plainest of working dress (Fig. 55). When Sir John Hawkins, in his life of Johnson published in 1787, compared the period of *The Rambler*, that is the middle period of the century, with the time of *The Tatler, The Spectator* and *The Guardian* fifty years before, he gave the instant spread of fashion as one of the main changes, mentioning particularly the cap of the farmer's wife:

'The convenience of turnpike roads has destroyed the distinction between town and country manners and the maid of honour and the farmer's wife put on a cap of the latest form almost at the same instant. I mention this, because it may have escaped the observations of many that a new fashion

128

pervades the whole of our island almost as instantaneously as a spark of fire illuminates a mass of gunpowder.'[20]

The red cloak seen by Kalm in 1748 is of all garments the one which from its widespread use and long survival might be seen as a traditional garment of the English countrywoman. But it must also be seen within its contemporary context. The cloak was the general outdoor garment for all women; the hooded form was at the beginning of the century usually called a riding-hood. There were many variations of cloaks and hoods, from hoods with short capes to the full-length hooded cloak; cloaks without hoods of all lengths, the shorter ones often with scarf ends. The common cloak also varied in length, and in having, or not having, a hood. Although in the country cloth cloaks might be fashionably worn in winter, silk was the usual fabric of fashionable cloaks made warm by being lined with fur or thickly wadded. Kalm saw red cloaks in Hertfordshire, Madame du Bocage in Oxfordshire in 1750 where she visited the cottages of shepherds and farmers: 'People of this class have their houses well furnished, are well-dressed and eat well; the poorest country girls drink tea, have bodices of chintz, straw hats on their heads and scarlet cloaks upon their shoulders.'[21] More than thirty years later Moritz also saw them in Oxfordshire: 'The women of the lower class here, wear a short kind of cloak made of red cloth.'[22] Sarah Hutchinson saw them in Westmorland in 1811: 'I wish you saw the number of scarlet cloaks and silk pelisses assembled in the churchyard.'[23] Samuel Bamford, recalling in 1850 the dress of the end of the eighteenth century in the Pennine villages of south Lancashire, described the wearing of the cloak for church or chapel on Sunday:

'An ample crimson or scarlet cloak of finest wool, double-milled, and of an intense dye that threw a glimmer wherever it moved, was put on, the hood being thrown over the head, cap and handkerchief and all and drawn closely and comfortably round the face or left open as the wearer chose.'[24]

A cloak from the village of Mobberley in Cheshire is now in the Gallery of English Costume, Manchester. It is of bright scarlet woollen cloth, in three sections, a full-width back section and two half-width front sections, pleated on to a neck-band together with the collar and hood. The collar lies inside the hood so that this cannot be worn over the head without turning up the collar to make exactly the close, weatherproof covering described by Samuel Bamford. The hood is in two sections seamed from back to front and is shaped by pleating to a point at the centre back, which is the way the fashionable silk hoods are also shaped. The hood is lined with matching and brown silk and the collar is quilted with matching silk on cloth so that the silk shows when collar and hood are down and is against the face when both are up. It is 46 inches long, so unless worn by a short woman it would not have been quite full-length, and is 96 inches round the lower edge. By family tradition it was worn as a wedding cloak about 1800. It is well made and had obviously been kept for best wear. There is another red cloak at Hartlebury Museum, Worcestershire, said to have been worn by a donkey woman of Malvern Wells in the early nineteenth century. This is shorter, 42 inches at the back, 29 inches at the front and 135 inches at the lower edge, sewn to a black silk band at the neck to which the hood is also gathered; the front edges are bound with black ribbon, the bottom edge raw, similar in appearance with this binding and neck-band to the cloak in the W. R. Bigg painting *Sunday Morning* (colour plate 3). Many red cloaks survive in miniature, in the dress of pedlar dolls of the first half of the nineteenth century.

The cloak itself had a long survival. Mary Russell Mitford could still write from her Berkshire village in the 1820s: 'The road is gay now, carts and post chaises and girls in red cloaks', and describe Mrs Sally Mearing: 'Here she is with the hood of her red cloak, pulled over her close black bonnet of that silk which once was fashionable since it is still called mode.'[25] By 1840, according to *The Workwoman's Guide*, it survived only as an elderly fashion, 'Old Woman's Cloak and Hood', generally made of 'scarlet cloth or duffle'.[26]

Throughout the eighteenth century, at least from the 1740s, it was worn all over England, and also in other parts of the British Isles. In Scotland it appeared in the cities; a writer, looking back from the 1780s to the 1760s, said that in Edinburgh in 1763 the maid-servants dressed 'decently in blue or red cloaks, or in plaids, suitable to their station'; Sarah Hutchinson saw it in Glasgow many years later, in 1814, worn with the hood up, without a bonnet, 'on the hottest days'.[27] The wearing of cloaks this way, summer and winter alike, was also mentioned by travellers in Ireland. Not all cloaks were red, many Welsh ones were blue and Irish ones, blue, grey or black as well as red. The red ones, however, seem to have been most popular in the eighteenth and early nineteenth century. A writer on Co. Tyrone just after 1800 found that 'The cloak is generally of some cheap shop-cloth, often grey, though they affect scarlet when they can afford the price.'[28] Samuel Bamford remembered the red cloaks of Lancashire as prized possessions. They were Sunday, church-going dress when Sarah Hutchinson saw them in 1811, making their sharp contrast with the fashionable silk pelisses, a contrast now of form as well as of fabric.

Although pattens had a long survival in country wear, continuing in some places until the end of the nineteenth century, they were in the eighteenth century also worn by working housewives of the towns. Kalm noticed them in London, seeing them as part of the housewife's concern for the clean floors of her house. 'They leave in the passage their pattins, that is a kind of wooden shoe which stands on a high iron ring. Into these wooden shoes they thrust their ordinary leather or stuff shoes (when they go out) and so go by that means quite free from all dirt into the room.'[29] Monconys had seen and described them in London in 1663

and Mrs Pepys wore them there.[30] Gay wrote of them in *Trivia,* his
poem of the London streets:

> *Good Housewives all the Winter's Rage despise*
> *Defended by the Riding-hood's disguise*
> *Or underneath the Umbrella's oily shed*
> *Safe through the wet on clinking Pattens tread,*

pointing out that they were not quite so useful in snow,

> *Let not the Virgin tread these slippery Roads*
> *The gathering Fleece the hollow Patten loads.*

Clogs, leather undershoes which fastened on over the instep, were the
fashionable alternative to pattens; they were more elegant and more
comfortable to wear, but gave less clearance from the wet and dirt of
roads or street. In 1742 Mrs Bracegirdle, Congreve's original
Millamant, then an old lady, visited Horace Walpole. When she was
about to leave and asked for her clogs, she recalled her early days in the
theatre: 'I remember at the playhouse they used to call Mrs Oldfield's
chair! Mrs Barry's clogs! and—Mrs Bracegirdle's pattens!'[31]
Gentlewomen might still wear pattens in the mid-eighteenth century, as
Mrs Russel did, for in 1769 she found she had 'a Blister as big as a Hazel
Nut at the side of my foot where the iron of the patten goes', but they
were disappearing from wear at this level.[31] Mrs Bracegirdle's story
neatly placed them—with herself—in a social hierarachy.

Kalm's description of the gowns of the Hertfordshire women, 'a sort
of manteau of brownish camlot', makes it clear that their everyday
gowns were of wool, although the implication is that for Sunday or best
wear a silk gown and petticoat might be worn. Defoe had written in the
1720s of a country grocer's wife, 'not dressed over fine', but he gave her
a silk gown and petticoat of Spitalfields silk for best wear, for 'she must
have something decent being new married too, and especially as times
go, when the burghers wives of Horsham or any other town go as fine as
they do in any other place; allow her then to have a silk gown.' She also
had a quilted petticoat of black calimanco and a wrapper or morning
gown of printed Irish linen, the petticoat serving as an underpetticoat for
the silk, but probably worn as the upper petticoat beneath the linen
gown. Beneath the calimanco there were inner petticoats of flannel and
swanskin, like Pamela's underpetticoats.[32]

Towns like Horsham were part of the countryside, the centres for the
surrounding villages and farms, with movement and family links
between them. Hannah Wainwright, a widow, was living in the small
market town of Ampthill, Bedfordshire, when she died in 1734; her
stepson was a farmer in a neighbouring village. She left clothes and
personal possessions mainly to her nieces. Her best gown was a woollen
one, calimanco, but it was lined with silk and had a silk petticoat
'belonging to it' so that it was probably worn turned back to show this

silk lining, in the mantua form, which was then passing out of fashion; or the lining could, more fashionably, have been folded back to appear as robings down the opening of the gown (Figs 57, 59). Pamela, in Richardson's novel, put facings of calico on a stuff gown for this purpose. Hannah Wainwright also possessed at the time of her death a 'gown with green Ribbands' which she bequeathed with a watered petticoat, another 'old Calamanca Gown' and an 'old Sattin Gown'. She left petticoats of brown damask, red tammy and a striped quilted petticoat. She also had a set of mourning clothes which she left as a single bequest, a black and white gown and a black silk apron. There were a number of aprons, one of flowered muslin, laced handkerchiefs, shifts, two gold rings, two silver thimbles, a purse 'wrought with silver', a fan and 'my hood and cloak'.[33] The satin and damask may have been silk materials, but could have been wool.

In another part of the country, in 1756, Jane Youngs, a member of a land-owning yeoman or farming family in Hampshire, made a will distributing her clothes and personal possessions. Her best suit of clothes with the linen belonging to it were left to a cousin who also had her mourning suit of clothes and a black hat. These were matching gowns and petticoats, but she did not mention what the material of her best suit was. She left also a dark-coloured damask gown and two other gowns, one 'robed' with grey silk, the other with green, and with the green silk one she left a pair of green worsted gloves. As she mentioned the silk of the robings but not the material of the gowns, it is likely that these were of wool and the silk robings would appear with the same contrasting effect as the calico on Pamela's stuff gown, a feature not generally seen on fashionable gowns. The best gown and petticoat were probably silk if the other damask gown was also silk, but this, like Hannah Wainwright's damask, could be of wool. There were three quilted petticoats, two of unspecified material, one 'covered with linen'; a fourth petticoat had 'three borders to the tail', which suggests the petticoats of the early years of the century. She had several suits of linen, one laced, several handkerchiefs and aprons, wash-leather mittens and four gold rings. She left to the same person her 'best short Rokett and a straw hat.' The rocket was a cloak; the term was becoming obsolete but survived as a local dialect term in several parts of the country. These were her best clothes left mainly to relatives. As a final bequest she left 'all my old Close everything that I do wear every day to Mary Heppen.'[34] This suggests that Mary Heppen was a servant or a poorer person and that the best clothes remain with the same social group while the everyday ones are passed on to the group below, making once again an overlap of dress between two levels of society.

Both these women sign with a mark not a signature. They appear to have had a reasonable quantity and range of clothes with a special suit of clothes for mourning wear and no lack of linen. They were middling people; their lists make it possible to compare the clothes two women actually possessed with general comment and give some idea of the gradations of dress which may lie within common dress, the dress of people outside fashionable society.

In the eyes of foreign visitors the most striking thing about the dress of English countrymen was their wearing of good cloth. As early as 1685 Misson was surprised to find that 'the very peasants are generally dressed in cloth.'[35] A Swiss traveller in the early years of the century wrote: 'je connois les Paisans Anglois que par un endroit. Je les vois tous a cheval, en juste au corp du drap et en culottes de peluche, bottez et toujours au galop.'[36] De Saussure said much the same: 'A farmer never travels far from home except on horseback, this being the reason you see so many of them booted, spurred and in riding coats.'[37]

John Blundell of Meppershall, Bedfordshire, was a small farmer, owning his land, and selling wheat, barley and malt in local markets. He was a bachelor and paid Betty Sharp 'for doing for me' £2. 12s a year. He kept a notebook in which, amongst details of sales of malt and money paid to blacksmith and saddler, are notes of what he spent on clothes between 1762 and 1772. His most expensive item during these years was a cloth suit, coat, waistcoat and breeches, which cost £4. 8s in 1764. He bought fustian for breeches, three yards at 22d a yard and paid 1s 6d for their making. In December he had a new cloth greatcoat which cost £1. 11. 7. In 1765 there was a pair of buckskin breeches and a cloth coat and waistcoat, and in the next year another pair of fustian breeches; in 1767 there was a buff-coloured cloth waistcoat and cloth breeches and in 1770 a cloth coat. He had a striped linen waistcoat in 1762 which cost 10s and 2s for making, a flannel waistcoat in 1766 and a flowered waistcoat, 3s in 1772. Coats and waistcoats were turned in 1763, 1767 and 1771. In 1762 he bought a frock, the material £1. 11s, wadding 6d and making 5s and also cloth for shirts, and after this had two shirts in 1764, 1766, 1767, 1768, 1770, 1772. The price varied between 6s 4d and 8s 6d, but the making was always 2s a shirt; the material is generally noted just as cloth, but in 1772 it is '6 Ells of Irish for 2 shirts 16s 3d.' He bought worsted in 11 or 12 ounce lots for stockings, noting once that it was grey, another time speckled; he paid his sister for knitting them. Sometimes they were re-footed and others were bought ready-made; a pair of ribbed hose at Shillington Statute fair were 5s 6d, which was about the same price as the knitted ones. He noted four pairs of gloves in ten years, one of washed leathern' at 1s 2d; three wigs, at £1, £1. 1s and the third, for which he found the hair, 10s; two hats each at 10s 6d. There were a pair of boots and three pairs of shoes and several records of soling or soling and heeling and also the buying of 'a ball to black shoes.' He also had a pair of plated spurs. Cloth was bought to make 'neckings', dimity to make nightcaps, muslin to make neckcloths. When he left his house for a while in 1763 he took with him eight shirts, five pairs of hose, eight 'neckings', three wigs and three hats.[38]

As John Blundell used the word cloth in the general sense of material, it cannot be assumed that the cloth of his coats, waistcoats and breeches was always broadcloth, but the price of his complete suit of 1764 is comparable with the 'superfine blue suit of cloathes, very good cloth' which James Woodforde had in 1758 when he was at Oxford, and which cost £4. 10s, and the price of the separate items of cloth coat, waistcoat or breeches are in proportion. The clothes of this Bedfordshire farmer seem to confirm what Grosley said of the men he saw on his way from Dover to London in 1765: 'A considerable number of carriages loaded with corn and hay. Each of the drivers (who were all either labourers or husbandmen) dressed in good cloth, a warm greatcoat upon his back and good boots on his legs, rode upon a little nag.'[39] The eight shirts he took with him from home also showed his care for clean linen. John Byng, calling on a tenant farmer on the Southill estate in the 1770s, recalled the man's father, 'who wore the same coloured coarse cloth all the year round and tied his shoes with thongs',[40] seeing great change in his own generation of farmers. Some years later C. P. Moritz, spending Sunday in an Oxfordshire village, saw farmers there dressed, 'not as ours are in coarse frocks, but with some taste, in fine good cloth; and were to be distinguished from people of the town not so much by their dress as by the greater simplicity and modesty of their behaviour.'[41]

Kalm was surprised in 1748 to find that wigs were worn by all classes of men: 'I had to look around a long time in a church or other gathering of people, before I saw anyone with his own hair' and he noticed that in the country at work men still wore wigs, 'farm servants, clodhoppers, day labourers, farmers, in a word all labouring folk go through their usual everyday duties all with Peruques on the head.'[42] These would probably have been short wigs, some form of the bob wig, which also appeared in fashionable undress wear.

The countryside had its highly specialised occupations (Fig. 66): William Poulton of Eversholt in Bedfordshire was described as falconer in his will of 1754, but he also left some small properties in the district. He left clothing to his three sons. One had a new suit, coat, waistcoat and breeches in shag, a long-piled woollen material. The coat and waistcoat and the pair of shag breeches 'belonging thereto', which went to another son, probably made a second complete suit in plush, but the more important part of this bequest seems to have been the buttons of the coat and waistcoat, as he left his 'best set of plate Buttons, both Coat Buttons and Wastcoat Buttons and the Coat and Wastcoat the said Buttons are on.' A gold laced hat also went to this son. The third bequest was of new buckskin breeches, another set of buttons, 'square plate Buttons' for coat and waistcoat, silver shoe- and knee-buckles and silver spurs.[43] The shag worn by the falconer was also used for breeches by at least one country vicar: 'I carried down to Mr Porter's some shagg, for a pair of breeches for Mr Porter.'[44] (Fig. 67).

66  *William Millward, woodcutter
to the Duke of Kent, Wrest Park, in
the early eighteenth century. His
coat is a plain basic form of the
collarless coat of the time over a good
linen shirt with thread button
fastenings; its plain slit cuff is the
main variant for a working coat and
the added belt; the thongs tying the
breeches are also a feature of common
wear, and the large brimmed hat,
cocked at random.*

67  *Red plush waistcoat, double-
breasted with metal buttons, linen
back and lining, 1780–1800.*

In the 1720s Defoe listed the clothes of 'the poorest countryman' with
the object of showing the number of manufactures involved in clothing
someone who spent the minimum amount of money on clothes:

'If his coat be of woollen cloth, he has that from Yorkshire
The lining of shaloon from Berkshire
The waistcoat is of calimanco from Norwich
The breeches of a strong drugget, from Devizes, Wiltshire
The stockings being of yarn, from Westmorland
The hat is a felt from Leicester
The gloves of leather, from Somersetshire
The shoes from Northampton
The buttons from Macclesfield in Cheshire; or if they are of metal they
come from Birmingham, or Warwickshire
His garters from Manchester
His shirt of home-made linen of Lancashire or Scotland'

He then takes the clothes of the 'middling tradesman', a grocer in a
market town:

*68 Saying Grace, c. 1730. The older man appears to keep to the custom of wearing a hat indoors which he has removed for this grace; he wears a collarless coat, long with the pockets set low, more shaped than that of William Millward (fig. 66), but with heavy shoes painted in all their stiffness. His wig though rather loosely made is in the contemporary style; the younger man is probably wearing his own hair. The young woman wears a cap of contemporary fashion, similar to those of fig. 57. The lacing of her gown from its lining across her handkerchief is clearly shown; the petticoat with a lower section like a deep flounce may still show the influence of the flounced petticoats of the late seventeenth century.*
*J. van Aken*
(Ashmolean Museum, Oxford)

'For his clothing of himself (for we must allow him to have a new suit of clothes when he begins the world) take them to be just as above; for as to quality or quantity, it is much the same; only that instead of buying the cloth from Yorkshire, perhaps he had it a little finer than the poor man above, and so his comes out of Wiltshire; and his stockings are, it may be of worsted, not of yarn; and so they came from Nottingham, not Westmorland.'[45]

Defoe saw little difference between the dress of the countryman and the tradesman in a country town (Fig. 68). The difference between the tradesman of country town and tradesman of London was more marked, but it was one of detail and influence (Fig. 69). When Grosley spoke to the young London shopkeeper who was a Methodist, he saw him in his working dress, 'a young man in white silk stockings, a waistcoat of fine cloth, and an apron about his waist.'[46] The white silk stockings are the mark of the Londoner, a fashionable achievement of the trading people, which was not followed in the country and which set them apart just as, at a different level, John Howard set himself apart from the neighbouring country gentry when he wore them as everyday dress in the country. Stockings were a carefully graded item of dress, the grading based partly but not entirely on practical considerations. There was no simple distinction between wool and silk, but a progression from coarse yarn to finer worsted and silk. In the country even among the gentry the silk ones were generally limited to dress wear. The London tradesmen who had contact with people of fashion had a different version of fashionable dress as their model.

Foreign travellers might note the good cloth of the countryman's clothing, but the fashionable Englishman noticed other points of dress. In 1779 a clergyman friend of George Selwyn wrote of the countrymen at Leicester races: the 'clodpated yeoman's son in his Sunday clothes; his drab coat and red waistcoat, tight leather breeches and light grey worsted stockings, with one strap of the shoe coming out from under the buckle upon the foot; his lank hair and silk handkerchief, new for *Reace-time* about his neck.'[47] In 1709 *The Tatler* had given a character sketch of 'a Dapper', adding that 'the true place of residence of this species' was in the country: 'The habit of a Dapper when he is at home, is a light broadcloth, with calamanca or red waistcoat and breeches and it is remarkable that their wigs seldom hide the collar of their coats.'[48] This was, of course, at the time of the long, full-bottomed wigs. Calimanco for the waistcoat of the countryman appeared in Defoe's list. Although leather breeches were worn fashionably for riding, they were seen as the mark of the farmer and countryman. John Blundell had breeches of cloth, fustian and leather. The lank hair suggests that the wearing of wigs by all countrymen, which surprised Kalm in 1748, was no longer followed by the younger men.

The young men who, dressed like coachmen and grooms in the 1730s and 1740s in 'a narrow-edged Hat flapped down, a plain shirt, Buckskin Breeches and an Indian Handkerchief round the neck', were rejecting either the cravat, a narrow white muslin scarf loosely tied in front, which was worn until the 1730s or its successor, a pleated band of muslin held tightly round the neck by a buckle at the back. In men's dress the neck has been a sensitive point of status, and fineness of neck-linen and its constant renewal essential in good dressing. The countryman's tied neck-cloth was a simple version of the earlier cravat form, and the silk India handkerchief was adopted for its best or Sunday version. In 1795 Parson Woodforde bought '2 Silk Handkerchiefs from Spittal Fields,

Chocolate Ground and Yellow Spots, pd. 11.0. One of which I gave to Ben and the other to Boy, Tim.'[49] This remained a feature of common dress still worn by the village beau of Mary Russell Mitford's *Our Village*, a carter, 'silk handkerchief, tied very loosely round his neck, a shirt collar open so as to show his throat as you commonly see in the portraits of artists.'[50] It was later still a prized item of dress amongst the London costermongers, and in its plainer, everyday cotton, continued in working wear throughout the nineteenth century, when the achievement of a collar instead of a tied handkerchief became a matter of great social significance to those involved.

*69 John Cuff, an optician of Fleet Street with his assistant, 1772. He is working in a jacket or sleeved waistcoat without a wig, wearing a cap; his assistant has tie-on sleeves to a sleeveless waistcoat and a leather working apron.*
*J. Zoffany*
*(Reproduced by Gracious Permission of Her Majesty the Queen)*

## Labourers and Small Tradesmen

Between the prosperous farmers with many acres, those who were just able to make a living by farming their own land, or what they were able to rent, and the landless cottagers employed as day labourers, there were several shallow gradations of decreasing prosperity and so of money available to spend on clothing. Beside the agricultural workers in the villages were the craftsmen who served agriculture, the blacksmiths and saddlers, the tradesmen who served the farms and village, shopkeepers and shoemakers. There were also men and women who worked at some craft, often a textile craft, either in their own homes or in small workshops which grew up in some parts of the country, and by the end of the century were expanding into larger mills and factories. The dress of the prosperous farmers and the landless countrymen was different in quality and quantity, in the fabrics of which it was made, but it consisted of the same garments in the same general style. There was the contrast of coarse woollen cloth with fine broadcloth at the beginning of the century, and by the second half of the century heavy cotton fabrics, fustian and corduroy made another contrast. For some, fustian was the material of the working suit and wool of the best suit. When John Macdonald was in a position as footman where he was not required to wear livery, in the 1760s, but was given two suits of clothes, he had a fustian one made 'to do my work in' and another of blue Yorkshire cloth —'I wanted to be like a servant—for other duties of waiting on his employer.[51] All those who could afford it would have a cloth suit for best wear.

In the last quarter of the century a new garment came into use amongst agricultural workers, worn for both everyday and best wear. This was another form of frock, known as the round frock or smock frock. In 1774 Mary Yorke, travelling between Rochester and Chatham, passed 'three or four tidy lads with silk handkerchiefs round their necks, some in clean white Frocks, others in Fustian Sutes, perhaps as many lasses in straw hats and clean linen gowns.'[52] Loose-fitting linen frocks had been used since the early years of the century as working garments. Henry Purefoy ordered one for his coachman in 1746 'to put over his clothes when he rubs the horses down.'[53] This was probably in the coat form and differed from the frock of normal wear in being of a light washable material and in having little shaping. By the end of the century the word covered another form, sometimes described more exactly as round frock, that is a frock without a front opening. An early example of this, worn by a carter, and so again connected with horses, is shown in Randle Holme's *Academy of Armory,* 1688. It is long with short wide sleeves and is described as 'a linnen or canvas coat'. The drill frocks which labouring men wore during the century—the clean white frocks Mary Yorke saw might have been of this heavy linen, or cotton, material—were still close to the frock in their shaping. Only towards the end of the century does the loose overall-like garment appear, worn first by men at their work on farms, as carters, cowmen and shepherds, and then more generally. In 1797, Marianne Thornton came from Yorkshire into Sussex, and seeing these garments wrote: 'I have never seen any peasants dress so picturesque as these; it consists generally of a brown or light blue linen frock (for men) with a straw hat bound with black ribbon.'[54] These could have been either the coat or the round form, but Thomas Pennant, who also saw them in Sussex, used the term smock frock in 1801, which leaves no doubt that he saw the closed type: 'We . . . continued our journey to Chichester. At this time it was enlivened by crowds of well-dressed female peasants, the young in grey or coloured petticoats, the elder in sober black. The men had chiefly smock frocks over their clothes and were mounted on pretty ponies.'[55] The 'pretty ponies' suggest that these were fairly prosperous people. The ornament which developed in the smock frocks of the nineteenth century does not appear in the illustrations of the early examples. What gathering there is, is functional, to hold the fullness back and front, by a gathered, stitched-down panel centre back and front, or in the coat form at each side of the front opening. The smock, already seen as picturesque peasant wear in 1797, was during the last years of the century becoming established as the dress of the agricultural worker over much of southern England, and it was to remain so for the first half of the nineteenth century, with survival into the twentieth century.

In common dress, instead of fashionable variations there is the basic division between working or everyday dress and best or Sunday dress. This division was, however, carefully maintained, and abandoned only in extreme poverty. In working dress the needs of the occupation to some extent determine the garments worn and show dress at its most functional. The horseman's linen frock to put over his clothes when he rubbed down the horses was dress of this kind. At the same time garments worn for a particular occupation reveal that occupation and through it the wearer's place in society. Sunday dress could be free from any statement of this kind. The linen frock, in both forms, was originally a protective working garment (Figs 70, 71). What happened during the

*70 Labourers at Southill, Bedfordshire, 1781. Coats, a short jacket and a sleeveless waistcoat, all in shades of brown, with blackish hats and one conspicuous white shirt, show, within its narrow limits, the variety of labouring dress at the same task. (Detail)*
*G. Stubbs*

71 'Ye Generous Britons, Venerate the Plough,' 1801. Most of this dress suggests the countryman's best wear: the hat, the knotted handkerchief, the red waistcoat with the fob at the waist and brooch on the shirt; but the short flexible boots, laced with a single thong, were a working style, though occasionally seen on fashionable sportsmen. He appears to be wearing a type of smock, rolled up round the waist, unusually close in fit and cut with the collar and front-opening of the shirt. It does not, however, show the shirt construction which Stubbs clearly records in figs. 62, 63 and 70 and James Ward in fig. 88, nor the loose construction of the later smock. A painting by Wheatley, dated 1794, of a cottage interior shows a man wearing a similar, though looser, garment of the same kind.
Valentine Green

last years of the century was that it passed from a purely working garment to become an everyday garment of more general wear and finally was also worn as Sunday dress. This was a lessening of the distinction between working dress and best dress, which suggests a fall in standards. The growth of elaborate ornament on the smocks of the nineteenth century, which makes them now appear as picturesque country survivals, may be the way of re-creating this distinction, between working smock and Sunday smock. As an alternative to this, mainly in Surrey and Sussex, the smocks remained lightly gathered, but were often made of fine linen, almost as fine as the linen of a shirt. In 1823 Cobbett wrote of the wearing of the smock: 'When country people do not they always look dirty and comfortless.'[56] The smock, which could be worn to protect good clothing, could also conceal poor clothing.

In certain occupations, in the retail trades, where the working appearance is part of the necessary civility towards the customer, working dress moves towards fashionable dress, or towards best dress

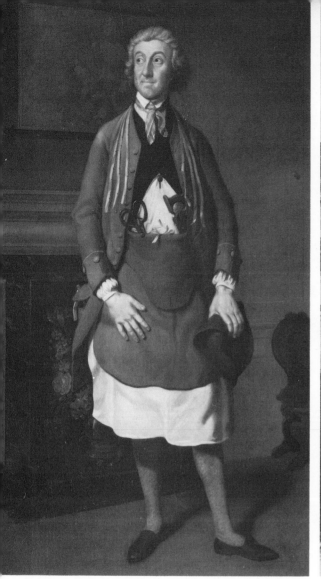

(Figs 72, 73). Robert Owen, a shop assistant in a drapery business on old London Bridge at the end of the century, wrote that 'Boy as I was then I had to wait my turn for the hairdresser to powder and pomatum and curl my hair, for I had two large curls on each side, and a stiff pigtail, and until all this was very nicely and systematically done, no one would think of appearing before a customer.'[57]

Much of the work of women was of this kind, or based on domestic occupations, but some were employed in work where the practical features imposed by the work on the dress led to the maximum divergence between working dress and best dress (Figs 74, 75). Fanny Burney was amazed at what she described as 'the barbarous dress' of the fisherwomen of Teignmouth:

'They have stays, half laced and something by way of handkerchief about their necks; they wear a single coloured flannel or stuff petticoat; no shoes or stockings notwithstanding the hard pebbles and stones all along the

72 *Richard Suett as Dicky Gossip, 1797, in Prince Hoare's farce,* My Grandmother *(1793), a barber, apothecary, tailor and coffin-maker, with the equipment of his various trades about him over a collarless coat with curving-back front and small cuffs, the knotted handkerchief of common neckwear, and speckled stockings with his low-heeled, tied shoes.*
S. de Wilde
(Ashmolean Museum, Oxford)

73 *Thomas Gregory of Toddington (1742–1816), parish clerk, schoolmaster and sexton.*

74 *The Milkmaids' Garland,
c. 1745. This Mayday frolic of
London milkmaids and chimney-
sweeps was noted by many
travellers, from Misson at the end of
the seventeenth century to Samuel
Curwen in 1776. The scene shown
here was part of the decorations at
Ranelagh and is probably a rather
theatrical interpretation, but the back
view of the milkmaid shows clearly
the construction of her gown, an
early version of fig. 14, and both
wear over their caps the common
hats of straw or chip, trimmed with
ribbon or flowers.*
F. Hayman

75 *At the Inn Door. The woman's
cap is in the fashion of the late 1780s
and her shoes also have the look of
fashion of this date. Instead of a
bedgown she wears the much less
common fitted jacket, which here is
worn with cuffs fitted over the
elbow, a type of cuff which also
appears in fashionable dress in the
1770s and 1780s. The traveller is in
the fashion of the 1780s with the
large buttons of his coat, but his
garters and the loosely knotted
spotted handkerchief are features of
common dress.*
H. Singleton

beach; and their coat is pinned up in the shape of a pair of trousers, leaving them wholly naked to the knee.'[58]

If she had seen the same women on a Sunday she would probably have seen nothing 'barbarous' about them. Their working dress showed a greater difference from their best dress than this did from fashionable wear.

A garment peculiar to women's working dress was the bedgown (Fig. 76). This was a short loose gown with a wrap-over front, often held in place by the apron tied over it. It can be seen in many paintings and engravings from Hogarth's *The Harlot's Progress* to Stubbs' *The Haymakers* (Fig. 62). The girl in Walton's *Girl Plucking a Turkey* is wearing one of check material (Fig. 55). The sleeves shown here and in the Stubbs' painting are fairly tight and long, a fashionable point even in this garment, whereas earlier examples show a shorter, wider sleeve. George Eliot's description of Adam Bede's mother in *Adam Bede,* set at the end of the century, was no doubt drawn from the recollections of the older generation:

> 'Her gray hair is turned neatly back under a pure linen cap with a black bow round it; her broad chest is covered with a buff handkerchief and below this you see a sort of short bedgown made of blue checkered linen, tied round the waist and descending to the hips from whence there is a considerable length of linsey-woolsey petticoat.'[59]

Samuel Bamford, a Lancashire radical who was born in 1788, remembered his mother in her everyday dress in the 1790s, a dress that closely resembled that described by George Eliot: 'Her dark hair was combed over a roll before and behind and confined by a mob cap as white as bleached linen could be made, her neck covered with a

76  *A bedgown of linen and cotton, printed in dark purple, red, blue and lilac, 1775–90.*

handkerchief, over which she wore a bedgown; and a clean checked apron with black hose and shoes completed her everyday attire.'[60] The wearing of the bedgown continued well into the nineteenth century. Examples of it can be seen amongst the figures of Pyne's *Microcosm* and in Walker's *Costume of Yorkshire*.

A working woman when actually working might appear without either gown or bedgown, in her stays, worn over a short-sleeved shift, with a handkerchief over neck and shoulders and a petticoat. In a painting of Covent Garden by Pieter Angelis, 1725–30, there is a woman wearing high, back-lacing stays without a gown, The women in a kitchen in Paul Sandby's drawing, *At Sandpit Gate, Washing Day,* c. 1750, are working in the same degree of undress. The girl working with the sheep-shearers in G. Robertson's *Summer, Sheep-shearing* also appears without a gown in short, tabbed stays (Fig. 89); and one of the returning gleaners in James Ward's *The Gleaners Returned*, in short-tabbed stays over a red petticoat, with a handkerchief placed loosely over neck and shoulders, but revealing white shift sleeves. The stays were still regarded as boned bodices without sleeves, rather than the undergarment they had become when shaping and stiffening was no longer inserted into the bodice of the gown itself. The stiff-bodied gown of royal ceremonial was one survival of this earlier form; the other was in this extreme of working dress. Women wearing their stays in this way felt no more undressed than a man who had removed his coat to work (Fig. 77).

## The Northern Counties

Sir Frederick Eden, writing of dress in Cumberland in the 1790s, saw a clear division between the dress of labouring people in the midlands and southern countries and dress in the north:

'In the midland and southern counties of England the labourer, in general, purchases a very considerable portion, if not the whole, of his clothes from the shopkeeper .... In the vicinity of the metropolis working people seldom buy new clothes; they content themselves with a cast-off coat, which may usually be purchased for about 5s and secondhand waistcoat and breeches .... In the north, on the contrary, almost every article of dress, worn by farmers, mechanics and labourers, is manufactured at home, shoes and hats excepted—that is the linen thread is spun from the lint and the yarn from the wool, and sent to the weavers and dyers so that almost every family has its web of linen cloth annually and often one of woollen also, which is either dyed for coats or made into flannel, etc .... Although broadcloth purchased in the shops begins now to be worn by opulent farmers, and others, on Sundays, yet there are many respectable persons, at this day, who never wore a bought pair of stockings, coat or waistcoat in their lives; and within these past twenty years a coat bought at a shop was considered as a mark of extravagance and pride, if the buyer was not possessed of an independent fortune.'

This kind of clothing, made from home-grown flax and wool, had

earlier in the century been prepared in the homes of the gentry, as
Nicholas Blundell recorded in 1712. Eden realised that by the 1790s this
was changing even in the north; many labourers were too poor to
purchase the raw material to spin thread or yarn at home and wait for its
return in the long process from raw material to garment. It was not only
the opulent farmers who now bought clothes, for 'articles of clothing
can be purchased in the shops at a much lower price than those who
make them at home can afford to sell them for', although in wear the
home-made clothing was much more lasting. Eden listed the dress of
working men and women in Cumberland:

77 *Gleaners near Stevenage,
Hertfordshire, 1788.
S. H. Grimm*

> 'the usual price of a hat worn by labourers is about 2s 6d; a coat purchased
> (four yards) costs about 2s 6d a yard; a waistcoat takes a yard and a half; a
> pair of leather breeches costs 3s 6d; labourers somethimes wear breeches
> of flannel or coloured cloth. A tailor charges 5s. for making a whole suit.
> A linen shirt takes about 3¼ yards at 17d a yard; this is strong and wears
> well. About 11 oz of wool at 8d the lb will make a pair of stockings. They
> are almost invariably spun and knit at home.'

For women's dress he lists:

> 'a black stuff hat, of the price of 1s 8d; a linen bed-gown (stamped with
> blue) mostly of the home manufacture—this usually costs in the shops
> about 5s 6d; a cotton or linen neckcloth, price about 1s 6d; two petticoats
> of flannel, the upper one dyed blue, value of the two about 11s 6d; coarse
> woollen stockings, home manufacture, value about 1s 8d; linen shift,
> home manufacture, 2½ yards at 1s 3d the yard. Women generally wear
> stays, or rather bodices of various prices. Their gowns are sometimes
> made of woollen stuff at 1s 6d the yard. The women, however, generally
> wear black silk hats and cotton gowns on Sundays and holidays.'[61]

So on Sundays and holidays the women of Cumberland dressed much as
women elsewhere.

Samuel Bamford wrote in 1850 of the dress of women of the late eighteenth century in South Lancashire, of both their working and best dress, dress of a period partly beyond his own recollection. Their working dress:

'almost invariably consisted of a blue flannel bedgown, which left the arm bare below the elbow; a petticoat of the same material and colour, and an apron to match, except that sometimes the apron would be of blue linen instead of flannel. . . . The married females wore, on their heads, mob caps of a thorough clear whiteness, whilst their hose as well as those of the younger females were generally of white or black woollen yarn, of their own knitting; and their shoes were strong, well fastened with leathern thongs, and of a weight which would footlock a modern dandy. Their appearance on Sundays or other holidays was more varied than when in their working day attire; in addition, on such occasions to a clean cap, they would generally wear a smart bedgown of white or blue cotton, prints not being then in general use. A pair of lighter shoes raised at the heels would be donned; and if they went a short distance from home they would put on a silk handkerchief, generally of a brown chocolate colour with spots which they threw over their caps and tied under the chin. If their visit was to church or chapel on a Sunday . . . they would make themselves very smart in their stuff gown or a garment much similar but known as "a rocket" would probably satisfy the vanity of one of the younger class: instead of bonnets they wore a low-crowned broad-brimmed gypsy hat of felt, or chip, covered with silk.'[62]

He then adds the red cloak for winter wear. Elsewhere he notes that cotton bedgowns were worn instead of flannel ones if the area was a cotton-working area. In a wage book of Burr's Mill, a spinning mill near Bury, some women workers had money deducted for a bedgown, always 4s 6d in 1800-2.[63] Samuel Bamford makes three divisions of dress: working dress, Sunday or holiday dress and a third for actual church-going. His rocket is a gown, not a cloak, but what the exact difference was between a gown and a rocket is lost. His picture is a composite one, and some details may go back to the middle of the century (for instance the lack of printed cottons), while others, like the wearing of the red cloak, seem to be what he had himself seen. This dress gives a much less fashionable impression than the dress of the southern and midland counties, but the full-dress version comes closer to it, with the fine hooded cloak and the flat silk-covered or felt hat over a stuff gown.

John Collier, who lived in south Lancashire in the eighteenth century, was an eye-witness of holiday dress at Milnrow. In a letter to his wife in 1781 he gave a different, more fashionable picture:

'Many hobbletehoys with silk bands about their hats, fastened with fine shining bright buckles. New leather breeches and large square buckles glittering at their shoes; all as proud as Major-generals. The lasses standing in the market in white aprons, silk or washing gowns, small hats placed over the nose; so that all was incog. but the screwed mouth and the chin, with as many doubled ribbands as you generally see at a country marling.'[64]

Samuel Bamford does not describe the best dress of the men of the district, but he gives their working dress:

'A low-crowned hat with broad brims, a blue or drab short coat, or rather jacket, of coarse woollen or fustian; a waistcoat without neck collar, and with long flapping pockets; a pair of breeches buttoned at the knees, and generally of a strong fustian or sheep-skin leather; brown or blue hose, home knitted and of strong home-made yarn, and very strong shoes, nailed with clinkers and fastened by straps and buckles. In the flannel districts, the men also generally wore a striped flannel apron, which when at the loom hung down, and when in the fields, or on a journey would be wrapped round the waist.'[65]

A jacket or short coat often replaced the longer coat in working wear. In form it was similar to a sleeved waistcoat, but was, as here, worn as a coat over a waistcoat. The shoes are similar to the ones Kalm saw in 1748:

'The shoes which the labouring men commonly used were strongly armed with iron. Under the heel was set an iron which followed the shape of the heel and somewhat resembled a horseshoe. Round about the soles were nails knocked in quite close beside each other. It was also knocked full of nails under the middle of the sole. ... They had sometimes gaiters.'[66]

Samuel Pepys had seen these nailed shoes in 1667 worn by a shepherd at Epsom. In the northwest of England a different type of shoe was worn, with a wooden sole; these were known as clogs, completely different from the fashionable leather clogs. They were worn throughout Cumberland and in the surrounding counties. In 1750, Dr Pococke, travelling there, wrote: 'In these counties of Westmorland, Cumberland and the north part of Lancashire they wear shoes with wooden soles.'[67] The clogs had irons round the soles too, but Bamford, writing in the 1850s, either took clogs so much for granted in the working wear that he did not refer to the wooden soles of the shoes he described or else they were not yet generally worn in south Lancashire. It was not until the nineteenth century that they became the general wear of the working women in the industrial districts of southern Lancashire and Yorkshire. Most of the references to them during the eighteenth century are to their wearing by men, but there are a few to their use by women. Although mainly worn by working people, they were also worn by others for their practical qualities for walking in a wet countryside.

## Wales

The way the dress of the common people in England was drawn into the main stream of fashion appears in sharp contrast to dress in contemporary Wales, where in 1774 Mary Yorke, because of this, thought that she was 'cast up on some Foreign Coast.'[68] Macky at the beginning of the century was at Shrewsbury on a market day and was 'particularly pleased to see the Welsh Ladies come to Market in their Laced Hats, their own Hair hanging round their Shoulders and blue and scarlet cloaks like our Amazons.'[69] The laced hats and the flowing hair and the comparison to Amazons may mean that the laced hats were like the riding hats worn by women at that time, that is like men's hats. In 1774 Mary Yorke noticed particularly that women wore hats like men's hats and no cap beneath them: 'a nasty handkerchief instead of a cap appear truly masculine.' At a service in St David's cathedral she noticed fashionable women side by side with an old woman with this head-dress and over her shoulders a square piece of flannel, 'fastened before with a Thorn', a detail linking her with a very distant past.[70]

Catherine Hutton, who travelled to Aberystwyth in 1787, also noted the masculine appearance of women in their hats: 'The women universally wear a petticoat and jacket fitting close to the waist of striped woollen and a man's hat. A blue cloak many of them have, but it is reserved for dress and in common they wear a long piece of woollen cloth wrapped round the waist.'[71] This hat and the wearing of a handkerchief, not a cap beneath it, was one of the distinctive features of Welsh dress to Pyne when he published *The Costume of Great Britain* in 1808: 'The women are accustomed to wrap their heads in handkerchiefs over which they wear men's hats.' The other was the difference in the fabric of the dress: 'the dress worn by the Welsh peasants are very different from the English, being principally of woollen, striped, checked, etc.'[72] This shape of hat was not, however, completely confined to Wales. The hats worn by the Wensleydale knitters in Walker's *Costume of Yorkshire* are rather nondescript in shape, but resemble a man's round hat as then worn; they too have a headcloth or hood beneath them, not a cap. These hats could be seen as a survival of the seventeenth-century high-crowned hat, with its crown much diminished, surviving strongly in Wales, although in England long dispersed by fashion to a sparse and limited wear. Or it may show a form shared by men and women, a breaking down of a division of dress by sex, just as some working women at the end of the nineteenth century, in everyday dress, wore a man's cap. A painting by Ibbetson of a group of women at Newcastle Emlyn in 1792 shows them all wearing these hats (Fig. 78). One woman has the long piece of woollen cloth wrapped round her waist as Miss Hutton described; another is wearing it over one shoulder, perhaps using it as a carrying shawl. There are short cloaks, red and blue, though some of these may be the cloth worn in yet a third way, over both shoulders. There is one long blue cloak with a hood. All the women appear to be wearing bedgowns in striped or checked materials, and none the fitted jacket which Catherine Hutton saw in 1787 around Aberystwyth.

In England in 1750 Madame du Bocage mentioned chintz bodices

worn by country women in Oxfordshire, which also suggests short jackets rather than gowns, but this garment seems to have been little worn compared with the longer gown, just as in fashionable dress, short jacket forms for undress wear were less general than the nightgown, at least until the late 1770s.

Catherine Hutton travelled again in Wales in 1796 and saw a wedding in the mountains above Llanberis where 'not a female appeared in anything but woollen or without a man's hat, except the mother of the bride who was cook.' Then she saw another wedding of a shoemaker's daughter and a sailor at Caernarvon:

'The town ladies were clad, not like the mountaineers in woollen, but in printed cotton gowns, white petticoats and white stockings; but they retained the beaver hat, and as the morning was cloudy, the blue cloak, which nothing but the hottest sunshine and sometimes not even that could persuade them to lay aside.'[73]

The changes of fabric, already established in England, were now visible in Caernarvon, but in the mountains dress still came from the sheep of the country (Fig. 79). It was the difference of fabric, the unshaped cloth, worn in various ways, the men's hats over headcloths not caps, which struck English travellers in the second half of the century.

*78 Women at Newcastle Emlyn, 1792, wearing round hats like men's hats and gowns and aprons of striped and checked materials; some have lengths of cloth wound round the waist, or worn over the shoulders as shawls, others short cloaks and one a long blue hooded cloak.*
*J. C. Ibbetson*
*(By permission of The National Museum of Wales)*

## The Poor

79 *A Market Place, 1792–5. Most of the women here also wear the same round hats as those in fig. 78 but mixing with them is a woman with a rather more fashionable hat, worn with a hooded blue cloak and one woman, in complete contrast, in fashionable style.*
J. C. Ibbetson

80 *Cottage Interior, 1793. The woman wears a wrapping bedgown and neck handkerchief and one of the black, full-crowned, peaked hats over her cap. It is probably her cloak which hangs over the back of the chair.*
W. R. Bigg

Many labouring people, through agricultural and technical changes, the changing levels of prices and wages, the influence of changing fashions or personal misfortune, suffered a lowering of their standards of dress during the century, while others were able to raise them a little nearer to the class immediately above them. Some parts of the country appeared to be better clothed than others. Sylas Neville in 1781, having travelled through Derbyshire and then southwestwards, remarked that 'the girls of Wiltshire look better and are better clothed than those of Derbyshire.'[74] An occupation or district might suffer in a time of prosperity or maintain itself when there was depression around it. The lace-making industry of the East Midlands, for instance, had a bad period at the time of the American War: 'I am an eyewitness of their poverty and do know that hundreds in this little town are upon the point of starving and that the most unremitting industry is but barely sufficient to keep them from it.'[75] Yet at the end of the century the lace-makers were comparatively prosperous: 'The women who are mostly lacemakers, can, if expert, maintain themselves even in the present dear times.'[76]

152

Times had become very dear, with rising prices at the end of the century for the bare necessities of life (Fig. 80). When Eden wrote of clothes in *The State of the Poor* he was less concerned with the clothes themselves than with clothing as a necessary expense. He lists the prices in 'a slop-shop in the neighbourhood of London' for a single outfit for men and women. For men there is coat, waistcoat, breeches, shirt, stockings, shoes and hat: for women, gown, petticoat, shift, coarse apron and check apron—the coarse one worn over the other for working—stockings, hat, neckerchief, cap, stays, cloak. He quotes a gown of stuff and a linsey-woolsey petticoat and gives a six-year life to the stays, so he is taking a very poor degree of dress. If the cost of the items not bought every year are spread over the period of wear, the lists give an annual cost of £1. 10.11 for men and £1. 8s for women.[77] In 1771 Arthur Young took one budget in Lincolnshire, in which the man spent £2. 3s a year on a coat, waistcoat and breeches, three shirts, hat, two pairs of shoes and three pairs of stockings. The clothing of the wife and two children together was £4. 6s, a better situation than Eden's later estimate from the London Area.[78]

In 1787 David Davies, a Berkshire rector, started to collect information about the earnings and expenses of labouring families in his parish. Later he tried to get similar information from other parishes, and published the results in *The Case of the Labourers in Husbandry* (1795). For his own parish he estimated the annual outgoings for clothing for a family of husband, wife and three children as £3. 10s: for the man: wear of a suit per annum, 5s., wear of a working jacket and breeches, 4s., two shirts, 8s., one pair of stout shoes, nailed, 7s., two pair of stockings, 4s, hat, handkerchief, etc., 2s., amounting to £1. 10s; for the wife: wear of gown and petticoats, 4s., one shift, 3s 6d., one pair of strong shoes, 4s., one pair of stockings, 1s 6d., two aprons, 3s., handkerchiefs, caps, etc., 4s., amounting to £1; the children's clothing was partly and usually made up of the parents' old clothes or bought second-hand, but what was bought he reckoned for three children at £1. The man's clothing has the distinction of a suit, separate from the working jacket and breeches; the wife's distinction, from what is stated here, could only have been a new gown and petticoat worn first for best wear and then taken into everyday use. His correspondents from Wales note that most poor families buy wool and manufacture their own clothing from it.[79]

The eighteenth-century idea of a basic minimum of dress can be seen in the dress supplied to its poor, that is the dress supplied by the parish overseers to the impoverished and to the parish apprentices. Elizabeth Hillersden, a Luton widow, who died in 1723 and is, in the entry of her burial, described as 'poor', was able to make a will in which she bequeathed a number of garments. These may have been the garments which she had kept from better days:

'Two white hoods, my best white apron, my best blue apron, my best Straw Hatt, my best Gown and Petticoat, four best Laced Caps, my best

Neckhandkerchief, my two best pockett handkerchiefs and my riding hood . . . my black and white gown and petticoat . . . my best pair of shoes . . . my black silk hood and my Red petticoate . . . the rest of my wearing apparel not herein before bequeathed.'[80]

She too had a suit of clothes for mourning, her black and white gown and petticoat.

Overseers of the poor made allowances of clothing in direct relief in the early years of the century, until the workhouse system brought the poor together in workhouses; then the clothing issued became the uniform of an institution. There were also many charitable foundations for young and old which provided their own particular dress, a subject which has been fully dealt with in *Charity Costumes* by P. Cunnington and C. Lucas (1978). The aim of the overseers was to supply the basic needs in as cheap and lasting a form as possible, leather breeches for men, leather stays for women, but from time to time entries appear which suggest occasional generosity, until the problem of poor relief became overwhelming at the end of the century. Clothing was generally given out, garment by garment, as need arose, but for boys and girls sent out as apprentices the overseers recognised the need for two sets of clothing, one for everyday and one for Sunday. At the end of the term of apprenticeship the master or mistress usually agreed to make the same provision when the apprentice was sent out into the world. In 1698 Ann Castleman was to leave her apprenticeship with 'two new gowns, two new petticoats, one paire of boddyes, two paire of stockings, one pair of shoes, two new shifts, two new Aprons, one straw hatt, two suites of head Cloathes and two handkerchiefs.'[81] In 1730 the overseers of Eaton Socon, Bedfordshire, provided Mary Hewatt with 'two sutes of cloathes the one fit and decent for weekdays and the other for Sundays', and the phrases, 'the parish is to double suit him out with apparel both for Holyday and Working day' or 'the parish is to double cloathe her' occur several times in the records of this parish between 1706 and 1718 while the overseers administered direct relief.[82] Whether there was any difference in the two sets of clothing, or whether one was worn everyday and the other kept in better condition by being worn only on Sundays and then taken into everyday wear as the everyday one wore out, is not revealed.

# VI

## *Buying and Making Clothes*

### Shopping In Europe

Some fashionable shopping was done in Europe, particularly in Paris. Those who travelled not only bought for themselves but were often given commissions to buy clothes for others and asked to carry back purchases which friends and relatives in France had made for friends and relatives in England. Lady Mary Wortley Montagu's sister, Lady Mar, was living in Paris in 1722, when Lady Mary sent over money for lutestring as she was 'in terrible want of linings'; she suggested it should be sent eight yards at a time. There seemed to be some difficulty in getting it or sending it, so she decided to have a nightgown instead: 'There can be no difficulty in sending that by the first person that comes over—I shall like it the better for your having worn it one day, and then it may be answered for that 'tis not new.' Two years later she asked for a made-up mantua and petticoat: 'It will be no trouble to you to send such a thing of that nature by the first travelling lady.'[1] Lady Lansdowne, who had been the 'travelling lady' who had brought Lady Mary's nightgown back to England in 1722, was active for her friends in this way. She sent a manteau for Mrs Howard from Paris in 1721, 'the choice of a lady that is famous for a good fancy and the pattern is the newest' (that is most likely, the pattern of the silk). When Mrs Howard wrote to thank her, she replied, 'I hope you will employ me in anything you have a mind to in these parts of the world.'[2]

It was much easier to bring back made-up garments, which could pass the customs as personal clothing, than lengths of material. So the material was sometimes made up, only to be re-made later. Frederick Robinson asked his brother to send vicuna cloth from Spain, as he found this superior to what passed for the same cloth in France or England: 'Whenever my baggage comes I shall desire you to send me four livres and half of Vicuna made into the shape of a suit of cloathes of the natural colour, it is for Mr Langlois and is to be made up to avoid the Custom house.' He added in a later letter that it was to be made up 'without lining or buttonholes.'[3] A suit sent from Paris for Lord Riverstone, together with the bill for it, which includes carriage and customs dues is preserved in Birmingham Museum (Fig. 81).

There were frequent commissions for lace. Lady Mary Coke in

156

81 *Suit made for Lord Riverstone in Paris, 1763. A note preserved with it records that £27.10.3 was paid for a 'Suit of Scarlet Velvit' and that for bringing it from Paris, and landing it, duty free, Capt. Cheny was paid £2.5.6. Matching breeches, not shown here, complete the suit.* (By courtesy of Birmingham Museums and Art Gallery)

Brussels in 1767 bought ruffles for Lord Strafford, part of a suit of lace for Lady Strafford and a complete suit for Lady Dalkeith which cost 'three and thirty guineas and a crown, but a finer lace you never saw.' In 1773, again in Brussels, she bespoke a suit of lace for Lady Greenwich. The next year in Paris she bought ribbon for her sister, Lady Strafford, although this was a commission she was surprised to receive, 'as plain ribbons of all colours are better in England.'[4]

## London Shops

Most fashionable shopping was done in London and the most important shops were those of the mercers who imported silks from France and Italy and also bought from the weavers of Spitalfields. According to Defoe, the mercers of the late seventeenth century had been

'few in number but great dealers. Paternoster Row was the centre of their trade; the street was built for them; the spacious shops, back-warehouses, skylights and other conveniences made on purpose for their trade are still to be seen ... we saw the outlying mercers set up about Aldgate, the east end of Lombard Street and around Covent Garden; in a few years more Covent Garden began to get a name and at length, by degrees intercepted the quality so much, the streets being also large and commodious for coaches, that the court came no more to the city to buy clothes ... within ten years more the trade shifted again; Covent Garden began to decline and the mercers went back to the city.'[5]

De Saussure saw Ludgate Hill, 'entirely occupied by merchants' wares, silken tissues of beautiful and costly kinds being sold there' and admired the Royal Exchange in the middle of Cornhill, with its 'four galleries or wide passages, with booths along either side covered with rich merchandise, jewellery and other tempting wares. These four streets,— the Strand, Fleet Street, Cheapside and Cornhill—are, I imagine, the finest in Europe.'[6] The decline of Covent Garden was temporary; fashionable people went there for their silks—and sometimes to the City—for the rest of the century. The trade also moved still further west, to Charing Cross, St James's and Oxford Street. In 1771 Mrs Russel went 'to every Mercer and peace broker from Charing Cross, all round Covent Garden, Strand, behind St Clements, Fleet Street, up to Cheapside to match the green Lutestring I am to make up. ... I got better than I expected in Pall Mall.'[7] Sophie von la Roche in 1786 admired Oxford Street in the evening, with its street lighting, its brightly-lit shop fronts and glimpses of living and workrooms through the illuminated showrooms. She admired the displays of silks, chintzes and muslins hanging down in folds in the large, high windows, so that the effect in the folds of a dress could be seen, and how one colour looked with others, but 'the linen shops are the loveliest; every kind of white wear, from swaddling clothes to shrouds, and any species of linen, can be had. Night-caps for ladies and children trimmed with muslin and various kinds of Brussels lace, more exquisitely stitched than I ever saw before.'[8]

One of the mercers patronised by the nobility in the early years of the century was John Vickers, or Vickers and Eyre. The Earl of Bristol bought the damask for his nightgowns from them between 1720 and 1735; and the Duke of Kent the wedding silks for his daughter, Lady Jemima Grey in 1724, at a total cost of £90. 11. 5. Her sister's bill for a gown of pink and silver paduasoy and white satin, with pink persian for lining was £22. 17s. Another fashionable mercer, also patronised by Lord Bristol, was Thomas Hinchcliffe who sold him velvet for coronation robes in 1714 and gold and silver fabric for a manteau and petticoat for one of his daughters, costing £56. 10s in 1725.[9] The same firm, now Hinchcliffe and Croft, supplied silks to Lady Mary Coke in 1772: 'I've made two summer sacks ... one a plain white lutestring trimmed with white gauze the other I bespoke of Mr Hinchcliffe white lutestring also, with a small silver spot all over it, it is trimmed with silver.' This firm was in Henrietta Street, Covent Garden. Silks were often bespoke, that is woven to order from a chosen pattern. Lady Mary had sent for King, another mercer, of Bedford Street, to bespeak a silk in 1766.[10] The mercers were not always very quick to see that contrasting materials in gown and petticoat should harmonise. Lady Anson's whole scheme of dress was upset 'by the Mercers not making the new Stuff for a gown of a Color that could be worn with that proposed for a Petticoat.'[11] They thought of the fabrics, not the dress. Although the chief mercers kept to silk fabrics, some also sold camlet and calimancos, and other worsted stuffs of the Norwich manufacturers, including the crapes and bombazines of mourning wear. Some also sold ready-made silk hoods and short cloaks, men's morning gowns and quilted petticoats and hoops. 'The quilted coat was the handsomest she could get, 'tis lined with stuff, but there was no such thing to be had as one with silk ready made, it cost £2. 12. 6.'[12] The woollen drapers sold broadcloths and other cloths of the West Country and Yorkshire. Linen and cottons were sold by linen drapers. Lady Mary Gregory in 1756, having tried all Covent Garden, went to French in New Bond Street and 'found his the prittiest.'[13]

The letters of the Marchioness Grey and her daughters from the 1740s to the 1780s, reveal not only the changing fashions but a good deal about the buying and making-up of dresses. During these years they also bought silks, or tried to buy them, from Hinchcliffe and King, and from another fashionable mercer, Carr; occasionally from Allanson or Swann; or from Vansommer, who was a designer as well as partner in a weaving firm. Sometimes they visited the shops, sometimes they were waited on at their homes by the shopmen. In 1753 Lady Anson in looking for a silk for herself and for her sister-in-law, the Marchioness Grey, 'turned over all Carr's and Swann's shops two or three times.' In the end Lady Grey's silk came from Mr Hinchcliffe, who 'says he must have 3 guineas pr. yard, I say 3 £.' When her daughters were grown up, married and in the country, Lady Grey was kept busy helping to buy silks for them in London, still from the same shops. In 1774 she was looking for silk for her elder daughter, for a birthday court:

'I have been at two Mercers this week and can give you little satisfaction on the subject. . . . The Flowered Silks at Carrs I cannot recommend, at Kings there are much greater variety and prettier, but then the best of them and these not looking Rich are from 30s and 38s a yard, an enormous price, some very neat, but in appearance slight styles there are at 14s and 16s. The Flowered Tabbies from Carrs I thought pretty but fitter for sacks than gowns and petticoats.'

She sent a package of patterns with the letter. It is interesting that she now finds silks of 30s an enormous price, half the price of silks being discussed for her own court gowns in the 1750s, but the silks of the 1770s were by comparison, as they seemed to her, slight.[14]

When a suitable silk had been found, it went to the dressmaker, who was called the mantua-maker. The name came from the division of work between men and women in the making of women's clothes, which in the seventeenth century had been in the hands of tailors. Women, who were the seamstresses of underwear and accessories, then took over the making of the loose morning gowns, and when stiff-bodied gowns ceased to be made, took over the making of all gowns. The stays, now separate from the bodice of the gown, continued to be made by men in the first half of the century, although as their construction became lighter in the second half, women also became staymakers. Fashionable stays were always made to measure and the gowns shaped to them. Riding habits for women remained with the tailors. Although the sewing on linen underwear and muslin accessories is usually of high quality, the sewing in the construction of many gowns, particularly those of the first half of the century, shows a certain disregard of fine finish. It seems as if as little stitching as possible was done so that the expensive material could more easily be unpicked to make up again. The cost of making gowns at this time was a very small proportion of the whole cost, particularly when rich silks were used. The eighteen yards of white and silver stuff which was the most expensive item amongst the wedding silks of Lady Jemima Grey in 1724 was made into a 'manto and petty' by Elizabeth Ackers. The silk cost £45; its making-up, 16s. Elizabeth Ackers received the same amount for making up the less expensive white satin into another mantua and petticoat, and 8s for making a satin nightgown.[15]

Mrs Lafare was one of the fashionable mantua-makers of the 1750s and 1760s. She was patronised by the Marchioness Grey and Lady Anson, who in 1759 referred to her as *Madame la Marquise*. Lady Anson was a fashionable woman who saw the fashion dolls from France, and had at least one dress made and sent from there. Her taste was much respected by her sister-in-law. The directions she sent to her mantua-maker, the formidable Mrs Lafare, show the part played by the fashionable client in setting the details of fashion. She and Lady Grey were having gowns of the same material, a blossom and silver silk, 'the ground what they call *Pluye d'argent*: (silver mixed with blossom like a frosting)' which had come from Mr Carr and cost £3. 10s a yard. This time it was Lady Grey who was in London and Lady Anson writing from the country:

> 'if Mrs La Fare thinks more silk necessary, she will please get ½ yd of silk of the colour and *corded* if she can find it at Mr Carr's to put in the Breadth behind. I am very sorry and indeed ashamed to give your Ladyship this impertinent trouble ... and I must add so much more trouble as to beg you will be so good as to direct her to turn it round the bottom with a handsome Net Silver Lace of reasonable breadth (not a narrow one) and to trim the Robing, Ruffles, Pockets with a narrower suitable, and also to put *a little* on the pinning up of the Gown behind, as I think I do not love

to see the trimming stop short there. If the Pettycoat *must* be gored it must be trimmed up the sides of the Hoop, but I think that may very well be spared.'[16]

The corded breadth behind would not show beneath the skirt of the gown; the trimming of the pockets means the pocket slits at the top of the side seams.

Lady Mary Coke, by the entries in her journals, gives an account of the buying and making of a gown in 1767, from the loom to her wearing it at court: 'At half an hour after two the Mercer sent me word the silk would not be out of the Loom till the next day. . . . The Mercer brought my silk. I paid him seventy pounds.' She then, on 13 January, sent for the laceman to choose some silver lace to trim the gown. On 16 January she tried the gown on and thought it 'extremely pretty.' The next day it came home, finished and 'my sute of point finished; both very fine.' On 19 January she wore it and Lady Powis 'took my gown for imbroidery, 'twas indeed a beautiful silk.'[17]

In the second half of the century the mantua-makers' techniques show greater skill and finish. At the same time the interest and expense of the gown was passing from fabric to trimmings, and now it was the trimming on which time and care was spent: 'Lady Charles bespoke a most elegant Trimming for the Birthday.' The milliner from this time took a more important place in the making of gowns, supplying the ribbons, laces, gauzes, flowers, fringes, used in the making-up of trimmings as well as made up ruffles, caps and head-dresses. In 1774 the Marchioness Grey wrote to her elder daughter, Lady Polwarth: 'The Mantua-makers you know furnish everything if you chuse it. Mrs Callion tells me she intends to set up for a Gown Trimmer this winter and has provided material and patterns from Paris for that purpose.' In 1780 her younger daughter, Mary, about to marry Lord Grantham, was buying wedding clothes. There was trouble about the silks:

'We proceeded to Mr Kings with an intention to get a slight white and silver, to be trimmed with all the usual appurtenances; but behold! no such thing could we find that was ready at present; patterns there were, but they could not be finished under a fortnight. Mr Vansommer's Shop was ransacked with no better success and at last after a 2nd jaunt to Kings he promised to try if a slight white and gold could be ready for the beginning of next week; if not I must take a white satin to be trimmed.'

A few days later she wrote to her mother:

'Mr King has promised that enough of the Silk for the Petticoat shall go to Mrs Smith tomorrow Night and the rest on Monday Night, the latter has promised that Mrs Beauvais' people should have the Petticoat Tuesday morning; they assure me that the whole shall be ready in good time but did not keep their word in shewing me any trimmings put together; so all I could do this morning was to fix in a general on a Crape with Gold Spangles and intermixed here and there with Green and Pink Foils in the shape of very small Roses and some of that Silver Chain you saw to be introduced also with some light Gold and Silver Tassels but I limited the price to 20 and 30£. I fixed on the Suit of Point for 56£ thinking it on the whole rather finer looking than the other with the Ruffles in an intire piece.'[18]

This was the suit of lace for court wear.

Mrs Beauvais was a fashionable milliner of the 1770s and 1780s, making up the elaborate caps and head-dresses of the time and the equally elaborate trimmings for gowns, which were often more costly now than the silk itself and certainly more costly than the work of the mantua-maker. Mrs Beauvais, who made annual journeys for her goods, probably to France, may have been French or simply have adopted a French name, but she seems to have followed the French practice of being mantua-maker as well as milliner, although some of her customers may have kept the two parts of the dressmaking in different hands. Mrs Thrale had a dress made by her in 1777, probably for her presentation at court, a plain white silk bought in Paris, 'of a colour peculiarly elegant—trimmed with pale Purple and Silver by the fine Madame Beauvais and in the newest and highest Fashion.'[19] Madame Beauvais was entrusted by the Queen with making the special ball gowns for the Windsor fête celebrating the King's recovery in 1789.[20]

The milliner sometimes made up caps and head-dresses for a customer, but often these were made up and displayed in her shop as the newest fashions. 'I shall hope to learn from my sister's next letter', wrote Lady Polwarth in 1774, 'whether les nouvelles modes exist but in Mrs Beauvais' shop and head.'[21] Lady Sheffield wrote to her daughter in 1790: 'I sent Maynard this morn. to examine Mrs Coxe's Regiment of Caps, but they are all so fashionable—they were totally useless to me.'[22] Like Mrs Beauvais, several milliners had or adopted French names. Lady Holland sent caps to her sister in Ireland in 1762, two from Mrs Laplace, three from Mlle Laborde.[23]

The embroideresses of dress were individual craftswomen with small workrooms. Embroidered dresses, which were costly, were the finest of all fine dresses. Lady Mary Coke was delighted when her dress of woven silk was taken for embroidery. Mrs Wright with her nieces, Mrs Pawsey and Mrs Wilton, was a well-known embroideress under royal patronage. Jenny Glegg's work was much admired by Mrs Delany.

Although the milliner sold lace there were also specialist lace shops. Like the mercers they had first gathered in the St Paul's area, but in the eighteenth century were also in Covent Garden and the Strand. There were two groups of lacemen. The dealers in gold and silver lace, which was costly and much used in the dress of men and women in the first half of the century, were lacemen 'who by their fortunes are in the first class of tradesmen' and 'keep very handsome shops.' Lace shops or chambers were also kept by those who 'import Brussels and Mechlin lace also those who sell Bone Lace made in Buckinghamshire.'[24] They were dealers importing lace or buying in the English lacemaking districts. Sometimes the lace chambers were part of a linen draper's shop, and the selling of lace was combined with selling the fine linens that were used in its making-up into caps, ruffles and neck handkerchiefs. Mrs Delany bought her fine new-fashioned suit of Brussels lace, which cost nearly £50 in 1743, from Mrs Carter.[25] Mrs Chancellor of Duke Street was a fashionable lacewoman of the 1760s and 1770s. Boswell, charmed by her sales talk about her fashionable customers, was 'catched in her Mechlin toils' in 1775 and bought a suit of lace for his wife for thirty guineas, which was a higher price than he had originally intended.[26] Mrs Giberne was another well-known dealer of the 1750s and 1760s. She moved from Old Jewry to Parliament Street in 1756. Lady Yarmouth and Horace Walpole's friend Mrs Leneve were among her customers and according to her husband she made 'in keeping a Lace and Linen Warehouse about £400 a year.'[27]

Lace could also be bought amongst the many goods sold by haberdashers, who dealt, as the milliners did, in ruffles, aprons and trimmings, but they did not make up caps and head-dresses and they also sold gloves, stockings and hats, although there were also specialist hatters. They were in competition with some mercers in selling silk hoods and cloaks, men's nightgowns and quilted petticoats. The making of hoop petticoats had become a specialised trade in the first half of the century; the hoops were made for individual customers or supplied to shops which kept stock of them. Early in the century Thomas Hawksworth, a poor boy, after an apprenticeship with a tailor in Yorkshire, went to London and set up a shop there selling 'riding-hoods and hoops for petticoats and Norwich stuffs and has got considerable estate.'[28] The bespoke hoop petticoat maker often made the whole petticoat: 'Yesterday I bespoke a hoop petticoat of the exact dimensions of my old one; the fashionable hoops are made of the richest damask, trimmed with gold and silver, fourteen guineas a hoop.'[29]

There were a large number of tailors in London, in large and small establishments of master tailor, journeyman, apprentices. Campbell, in *The London Tradesman*, 1747, sets out the difference between the fashionable tailor and the rest:

'He ought to have a quick Eye to steal the Cut of a Sleeve, the Pattern of a Flap, or the shape of a good Trimming at a Glance; any Bungler may cut out a Shape when he has a Pattern before him, but a good Workman takes it by his Eye in the passing of a Chariot or in the Space between Door and Coach. He must be able, not only to cut for the Handsome and Well-shaped, but to bestow a good shape where Nature had not designed it .... His hand and his head must go together. He must be a nice Cutter and finish his work with Elegancy ... they make a handsome Penny and would raise Estates soon were it not for the Delays in Payment among the Quality.'[30]

Andrew Regnier was a tailor who served the nobility and gentry in the first half of the century. He was one of several who made clothes for the Earl of Bristol in the 1720s.[31] Mrs Boscawen sent for him in 1747 to make a mourning frock for her husband.[32] In 1759 Thomas Robinson, afterwards Lord Grantham, wrote from Cambridge to his father: 'We think it necessary for me to have some Cloaths against I come to you and they make them so badly here that I should by rights have them ready for me in London ... if you approve from Renier .... The Note only contains Directions to make me a plain suit of cloaths.'[33]

The tailor gave his customers advice on points of fashion. In 1704 Lady Fermanagh wrote to her step-son, Ralph Verney, about a suit he was having made by Mr Bedford: 'He tells me that nobody has such a thing as Silk Buttons to a Silk wascoat, and that if you have it done with Silver it will be very handsome, and my Lord thinks so too.' Lord Fermanagh had a coloured cloth suit from Katharine Barradell and Samuel Palmer in 1719, which together with buttons, linings, wadding and stiffening, ribbons and silk twist cost £2. 8. 3. which did not please Lady Fermanagh: 'I'me sadly vexed for your clothes, I think Mr Palmer spoyls all he makes.'[34] Henry Purefoy also had trouble with his clothes from a London tailor, John Boyce, in 1736. He wrote for patterns on 5 May, which John Boyce sent off the following day. On 11 May Mr Purefoy returned the pattern of the cloth he had chosen and gave directions for lining, buttons and trimmings, referring to his order of the previous year and sending a pair of breeches, by carrier, for a pattern. He said he was 'the same bigness as I was when in Town last, but you made the last cloaths a little too streight.' The clothes arrived sometime before 6 June, when a disappointed Henry Purefoy wrote that he found they were a tolerable fit, but had to have an inch off the coat at the bottom and the breeches were too short. The coat sleeves were longer than last year's, but he wondered whether this might now be fashionable. He also thought the silk of the waistcoat poorer than it should be. This unsatisfactory suit cost £13.15s.[35] As tailors often had to work without proper measurements and fittings, relying on earlier measurements, specimen garments and directions set out in a letter, it is not surprising that suits often did not please the customer. At least they usually worked quickly. Nicholas Blundell, in London again in 1716, chose 'out Side and Lining for a Surtute at that Shop in the Strand as is now called Doyleys' on 2 January. On 5 January 'Nailer the Taylor brought my Camblet Sertute.'[36] (Fig. 82).

By the 1770s breeches-making had become a separate trade. Mr Finney of Dean Street, who was the London tailor of John Baker, formerly Solicitor-General of the Leeward Islands, who lived in Sussex in the early 1770s and then in London, generally supplied coat and waistcoat only. [37] The makers of leather breeches, because of the material they worked in, were grouped as a separate craft. Francis Place was apprenticed to a leather breeches-maker in 1785 and became an

82 *Tailor's bill, 1772. Robert
Johnson, tailor, a bill for alterations,
cleaning and renewing, sponging and
pressing as well as for making new
garments.*

expert in cutting, which was the master's job and the most important part of the operation. Place found that the trade in leather breeches was declining as gentlemen were then wearing cloth breeches and even corduroy for riding, while at the cheaper end of the trade (the making of 'rag-fair' breeches, that is the ready-made ones from damaged or poorer skins) leather was giving way to the hard-wearing cottons, velveteens and corduroys. To keep their trade going the leather breeches-makers turned to the making of cloth breeches. Place claimed that in 1795 the tailors could not themselves make breeches to fit as the breeches-makers did.[38]

Throughout the century tailors made riding habits for women as well as suits for men. In 1785 Lord Wentworth was asked to order a habit for his sister from Scampelain, a fashionable tailor of the second half of the century, and he had to report to her:

'I have blundered that business in a manner which I am ashamed of. There is a fashionable and I think good colour called *Cheval d'Henri quatre* which I took for granted Scampelain knew, and I ordered it— but he sent your habit made of the ugliest colour he could possibly find. I had a great mind not to have sent it and if I should be rich enough . . . I will make up for my sins by giving you another.'

His sister also found the habit 'diabolically ugly' and, determined he should be kept to his offer, sent him the body of a habit for a pattern and instructions that the petticoat must be a yard and seven inches. He made full amends with 'a most elegant and most fashionable habit.'[39]

There were in the City and Covent Garden a number of shops called warehouses which often carried on both wholesale and retail trade. They sold fabrics and trimmings and the things sold by haberdashers. They also sold a number of ready-made items such as greatcoats, cloaks, riding hoods, wrappers, bedgowns, hats, chip and silk-covered, morning gowns for men and masquerade habits. One warehouse, in Gracechurch Street, advertised itself as 'Packer's Cheap Warehouse for Gentlemen, Readymade Clothes', selling greatcoats, coats, waistcoats, breeches for men as well as greatcoats, cloaks and the ubiquitous quilted petticoats for women.[40] James Lackington bought his first greatcoat ready-made in 1773: 'My landlord showed me one made of a coarse kind of Bath coating which he purchased at a shop in Rosemary Lane for ten shillings and sixpence.'[41] Rosemary Lane was also a centre for second-hand clothes. The shopkeeper tried unsuccessfully to charge James Lackington a higher price for a similar coat. Some of the warehouses specialised in a particular type of garment. Samuel Curwen went to 'Rogers shop in Fleet street, the great silk waistcoat store to exchange a black mohair shag for a black moleskin or long-piled velvet.' This shop seems to have made up the waistcoats to order, as he goes on to say that the tailor

'is about to make me one of the same colour and fashion for 16/- in lieu of that returned stuff $1\frac{3}{4}$ of which of the same quality cost me without making 14/-. The reason of which is this, the wholesale salesman procuring the various stuffs they make up at so much easier rate than a common buyer, can afford a garment at very near the price that their stuff alone would cost.'

M. Russell had a ready-made shirt warehouse in the Strand, in 1790. Samuel Curwen had his made by a seamstress, Miss Nebit, from a pattern shirt supplied by him. [42]

## Wigs and Hairdressing

The wig was so important a part of a man's appearance that wig-makers abounded. Many of them, like the milliners, were of French origin or adopted French names and called themselves perruquiers, or at least peruke-makers. However, Mr Cole, after his return from France sent his two French wigs 'to my London barber to alter them, they being made so miserably I could not wear them.' His barber was Mr Matthews of

Bishopsgate Street. [43] Peruke-makers also made 'Ladies Tates', as William Johnson of the Royal Exchange advertised in the 1750s. Thomas Gibbons of Rosemary Lane, true to his area, also sold 'left-off wigs'. [44] According to Campbell, the peruke-makers generally also dressed wigs and shaved, that is were also barbers, but some kept the two branches distinct. [45]

The best wigs were made of human hair, cheaper ones of horsehair; other materials had brief periods of experiment or fashion. Wigs needed constant dressing and gave regular work to barbers, combing, covering with pomatum to keep the curls, and later the toupee, in good order and then dusting with powder. The powder was pulverised rice starch, scented, put on with a large puff or blower, and a powdering gown was worn during the operation (Fig. 83). Hair powder could be a domestic problem. Dr Morris in 1710 contrived a hoop 'for my Peruke stand to keep the Hair powder from fouling the Chamber.' [46] In Bickerstaffe's *Lionel and Clarissa* (1768), the young fop, Mr Jessamy, exclaims: 'Not a dust of powder left in my hair, and the frissure as flat as the fore-top of an attorney's clerk—get your comb and pomatum; you must borrow some powder; I suppose there's such a thing as a dressing room in the house?' Lady Polwarth wrote in 1780 that a relative looked 'as like a pretty Master as ever with his brown and perfumed Powder.' [47] John Cater, a young man of twenty-three, wrote from Bedfordshire in 1777 to ask Mrs Williamson if she would get him 'a pot of Warren's best scented Jessamine soft pomatum and a rowl of hard' and in the following year asked for two rolls of hard and another pot of soft. This time his mother protested: 'I think the pomatum most extravagantly dear.' [48] Warren was a perfumer in Marylebone [Regent] Street and Cheapside who 'Imports Makes and Sells all sorts of Richest Perfumery Goods in all its branches in greatest perfection Wholesale Retail and for Export.' [49]

*83 Caricature, 1770, showing the powder puff in use.*

Although some styles of women's hairdressing in the first half of the century needed puffs, rolls and wires and sometimes added hair, wigs were not generally worn. Even in the second half of the century, when hairdressing grew elaborate, culminating in the extravagances of the 1770s and 1780s, it was the skill of the hairdresser rather than the wig-maker which was in demand. Mrs Thrale, however, wore a wig in the early days of her marriage, for an interesting reason, which she revealed in a letter in 1777:

> 'Did I tell you that my Master grew ashamed of his Wife's Peruke since we came here and made me pull it off and dress my own hair which looks so well now it is dressed that he begins innocently to wonder why he ever let me wear a Wig. I remember well, however, the why, the when, and the where. My Mother thought it a good scheme to keep young married women at home.'[50]

London hairdressers, like peruke-makers were often French. Lady Sarah Lennox went to Mr Montes in 1759, 'the hair cutter' and in 1762, to 'dear Mr L'Estoret' who dressed her hair *'en perfection'*.[51] The demand for the hairdresser's skill grew in the 1770s: 'These coiffures on one side quite alarm me', Lady Polwarth wrote in 1774 'as they would make a hairdresser necessary almost every day and therefore bode evil both to my time and purse.'[52] In Smollett's *Humphrey Clinker,* Lydia Melford, when she came to London could 'hardly find patience to be put in a condition to appear, yet as I was not above six hours under the hands of the hairdresser, who stuffed my head with as much black wool as would have made a quilted petticoat; and after all, it was the smallest head in the assembly except my aunt's.'[53] Mary Hamilton several times mentioned the dressing of her hair in the 1780s. Her maid gave it daily attention which took 'an hour and sometimes longer' and from time to time, Mrs Harman came to dress it, a much longer process: 'Under Mrs Harman's hands near 3 hours. What a waste of time! however I always read so I need not say that. She has been putting my hair into fashionable order, cutting, curling, dressing it.' Miss Hamilton always had a book 'for Hair-dressing reading.'[54] Mrs Papendiek, who often had to economise by remaking her clothes, had her hair dressed and her cap arranged by a hairdresser for special occasions. Mary Frampton, a child of the 1770s, had a vivid recollection of the process of dressing her sister's hair in 1780:

> 'At that time everybody wore powder and pomatum; a large triangular thing called a cushion to which the hair was frizzed up with three or four enormous curls on each side; the higher the pyramid of hair, gauze, feathers and other ornaments was carried the more fashionable it was thought, and such was the labour employed to rear the fabric that night caps were made in proportion to it and covered over the hair, immensely long black pins, double and single, powder and pomatum and all, ready for the next day.'[55]

The hairdresser waited on fashionable women in their own homes, but a lady's maid was expected to be skilled in the daily care and dressing of even the more complicated styles of the 1770s and 1780s. When Mrs Box became Lady Polwarth's maid in 1772, 'She only wanted to be taught the art of hairdressing to make a good servant, and now I think under such a Master she must be perfectly skilled in the art of frizing and pining, etc. . . .' Tuition was not wasted on Mrs Box, for later Lady Polwarth wrote: 'Mrs Box is admired for her Hairdressing.'[56] Yet some fashionable women did not allow themselves to become dependent. Lord Sheffield's sister wrote to her niece, then fifteen years old, in 1780:

'Might I advise if she [Lady Sheffield] does not disapprove of it, that you should learn to dress your hair a little yourself? I do not mean you should not have a hair dresser as often as you please: but I mean that you should know how to do it when occasion may require . . . . I know girls of the very first fashion who are taught to dress themselves entirely—to pack up even and take care of all their clothes.'[57]

## Provincial Shopping

When Sophie von la Roche came to England she travelled to London via Colchester and there, even before she saw the London shops which later delighted her, she 'enjoyed the fine shops . . . having large window panes behind which wares are displayed, so that these shops look far more elegant than those in Paris.'[58] Fashionable people did their shopping for more important clothes in London and many of the country gentry as well as fashionable people shopped there by proxy. Those who normally bought clothes at the nearest city or market town might buy in London for special occasions, though they lived at a distance, as Nicholas Blundell did, and Mrs Morris, whose husband was a physician in Wells. She got two suits of clothes from London to give her daughter as a wedding gift in 1718.[59]

Although fashionable shopping was mostly done in London, some was done locally in the provincial centres, the cities and large towns, particularly in those which were also social centres. Lord Bristol had a suit made for his son by Temple, a Bury St Edmunds tailor in 1725, 'a brown suit trimmed with silver' which cost £17, and he bought one of his many wigs from Daniel Crosman in Bury, a bob wig at £3. 3s.[60] Robert Owen, in his autobiography, described a shop at Stamford, where he had worked in the 1780s:

'The articles dealt in were of the best, finest and most choice qualities that could be procured from all the markets of the world; for many of the customers of the establishment were among the highest nobility in the kingdom . . . among the frequenters of the house as customers were the families of Burleigh, Westmoreland, Lowther, Ancaster, Browton, Noel, Trollope and many others whose names I have forgotten.'

According to Robert Owen, Mr McGuffog went frequently to London to make purchases of fine materials to satisfy his customers. After a period at Flint and Palmers in London, Owen went to Mr Satterfields in Manchester: 'His establishment was then first in his line in the retail department, but not much to boast of as a wholesale warehouse.' Mr Satterfield's customers were generally 'well to do manufacturers and merchants wives and families—a class intermediate between Mr McGuffogs and Messrs Flint and Palmer.' Owen had described Flint and Palmers on London Bridge as an old established house; he thought it was the first shop to sell at a small profit with a fixed price for everything, and for ready money only. The customers he described as 'of an inferior class.'[61]

Nicholas Blundell shopped mainly at Liverpool, sometimes at Ormskirk. In 1703 he had a black coat made by Edward Pates of Liverpool, for his journey to Heythrop before his marriage. He dealt chiefly with Mr Hurst at Liverpool for his materials, but had several tailors, among them Nicholas Johnson who 'came with two men to look at a Cloak and a Riding Coat' and who then made him a riding coat from a camlet cloak. Johnson continued to work for him till 1708, but a tailor from Ormskirk, William Holme, made mourning clothes for Mrs Blundell in 1705, and in 1708 Holme with his man Thomas 'came to lodge here they are tomorrow to begin to make a black and white callico sute for my wife.' William Holme seems to have worked mainly on clothes for Mrs Blundell and her two young daughters, and Johnson for Mr Blundell, although it was Holme who made 'a pair of breeches for me of Norway leather' in 1709. Holme made Mrs Blundell a 'callico Mantew' again in 1711, showing that here the mantua-maker had not yet taken over from the tailor. There was also a James Holme, tailor, who made stays for Mrs Blundell in 1710, and was perhaps the 'taylor from Leverpole' who came to mend a pair for her in 1708.[62]

From the evidence of published letters the Purefoys bought more clothes in London than they did from local drapers in Buckinghamshire, but they had a shoemaker at Buckingham, bought cloth from three different shops in Brackley and silk from a mercer at Bicester. They also bought lace from Miss Barrett at Buckingham; this must have been bone or thread lace, not the gold or silver lace which always came from London. Henry Purefoy seems to have given up his London tailor after 1736 and had his clothes made by Edward and Francis Fell of Chipping Norton. The Fells did not always come on the appointed date to take measurements: 'The Rev Mr Haws our Rector would have a suit of cloathes of you and stayed at home on purpose on the Thursday I desired you to come on.' Nor did they always deliver as promised: 'you said in your last I should have them Tuesday or Wednesday se'nnight.' When he did get them they were sometimes of poor fit: 'I despair of your altering them they are so unfit as you will see by them I send, so fancy you must make another pair.' Another tailor, Mr Johnson of Tingewick, seems to have done mainly alterations and repairs.[63] Tailors and mantua-makers worked at the homes of their customers as well as on their own premises. In January 1766 Tom Allen was at the Bletchley rectory making a warm waistcoat for Mr Cole and again in July to make him a 'Nankeen thin waistcoat', although Mr Cole seems to have had the tailors there more often for his man, Tom, than for himself.[64]

The shopping facilities at Norwich at the end of the century are clearly revealed in Mr Woodforde's diary. He and Nancy went to two mercers: Smith, who sold cloth as well as silks, and Brownsmith, who was specifically referred to on one occasion as a silk mercer and from whom they bought only silk. They bought linens and cottons from Lewis, household linen sometimes from Thwaites. Corbold and Wilmot both supplied hats to Mr Woodforde, Nancy's riding hats came from Oxley, a hatter in the Market Place. A haberdasher, Graham, supplied stockings and ribbons; Nosworthy, who was Nancy's hairdresser, sold not only shaving-soap and pomatum, but also umbrellas. Mr Baker sold perfume, wig combs, combs for 'craping hair', 'a machine for Paste' which cost 1s, Clay's Patent Paper Buttons, and a habit brush with a looking-glass at the back of it. Mr Woodforde bought several of his wigs from Mr Brown usually described as barber, but also as peruke-maker. Mr Brown shaved him and dressed his wigs, but before 1786 and after 1791 Mr Woodforde went to other barbers and also had a wig from London in 1791. While he was at Oxford he made a contract with Mr Owen 'to shave me and dress 2 wiggs each time, twice a week, at 3s a quarter.' This was a little more expensive than John Salusbury's contract at Leighton Buzzard, also made in the 1760s. Nancy had her hair dressed in Norwich, the barber or 'frizeur' attending her at an inn, the King's Head. In her diary she records going there in May 1792, 'where I desired Mr Nosworthy to come and dress my Hair, which he did and I paid him for cutting and dressing, 2s.' This operation was repeated in July. In 1782 she spent the day at Weston Hall having her hair dressed with Mrs Custance, by 'Brown, the best Ladies Frisseur in Norwich.' In 1786 she had her hair 'full dressed' in London.

Mr Woodforde's tailor was Mr Clarke of Norwich, but towards the end of his life, from 1797, he had clothes made by a tailor in Weston: 'Had a New Coat brought home this Morning by Robert Cary of this Parish, Taylor.' This coat, of black second-cloth, cost 7s for making out of a total cost of £2. 5s. He had a breeches-maker, Mr Scott, who also supplied him with gloves. The first riding habit Nancy had in 1782 was made by her uncle's tailor, the next, in 1793 by Barth, Stay and Habit-maker of Norwich. Barth also made her stays at this date, and re-lined a pair in 1792 for 2s. Soon after her arrival at Weston another Norwich staymaker, Mottram, had come to Weston to measure her. For this journey she paid him 2s 6d and £1. 11. 6. for the stays. She paid the same amount for a pair from Adcock in 1783. Both Nancy and her uncle had shoes from Mr Doughty, a Bungay shoemaker, but Nancy also had shoes from Mr Newstead of Norwich, who in 1792 supplied her with a pair of the newly fashionable 'sandle shoes' in black and yellow. At the end of the year she paid him 13s for two pairs of shoes and two bows.

Nancy had a mantua-maker in Norwich, Miss Bell, later Mrs Clarke; in 1792 Miss Tooke of Norwich received 3s for making a blue muslin gown and 2s for providing the lining for it. Nancy also had gowns made by Mrs Batchelor of Reepham and in 1799 Betty Burroughs of Mattishall Burgh, also described as a mantua-maker, came to the parsonage and worked for three days there. For this she received 2s and her three days' board. Nancy had gowns occasionally from Miss Ryder of Chancery Lane, London, who was also a milliner, and dealt with another London milliner, Miss Stevenson of Greek Street, on a visit there. It was, however, Miss Browne, the Norwich milliner, who supplied not only fashionable hats, trimmings and accessories, but also the news of new fashions. Nancy and her uncle went to Miss Browne's in 1794 'to see the fashions.' On 25 July 1792 Nancy ordered a bonnet from her, straw colour, with straw-colour and purple gauze ribbon, and bought to go with it a matching pair of straw-coloured gloves. The bonnet came home two days later and pleased not only Nancy but also Mrs Custance, who at once ordered one like it except that it was to be in white. In October Nancy paid a bill of £2. 15. 6 from Miss Browne, which probably included the gloves and a muslin handkerchief and cap which she had also bought during the summer.[65]

The trade of milliners had grown during the second half of the century. With the increased trimming and decoration of dress from the 1750s their importance amongst the dressmaking trades increased, and with the concentration of fashion on the head-dress, caps, bonnets and hats in the 1770s and 1780s, the creation of caps and hats became a major part of the milliner's trade. Mantua-makers and milliners from provincial centres made regular visits to London. Boswell, on one of his coach journeys from London to Scotland, in 1778, had a mantua-maker from Lincoln, on her way home after one of these visits, as a fellow passenger.[66] John Byng, leaving London on the Manchester coach in 1790, 'bodkined and surrounded by high and wide flat caps', was surrounded also by,

> 'elaborate discussions about fashions, feathers, robes, bodies, French backs, etc ... etc ..., and then Miss H. proclaimed herself a mantua-maker, told them for who and for what prices she worked ... they had been up to town to see and study fashions; and to view (as they said) *The Qualaty* going into the birthday, and who walked in St James's Park of a Sunday evening.'[67]

Susanna Towsey, who with her sister ran a drapery and haberdashery shop in Chester in the 1780s, went to London for goods, and, when she entrusted the journey to her assistant, set out instructions in a memorandum book of 1782. There were eight shops to be visited, to settle accounts and to look at silks, gloves and ribbons. 'And be sure to get some white souflee for tippets as we have some bespoke for next week.'[68]

Cities and country towns like Chester and Norwich, which were social and commercial centres, had not only a wide range of shops to supply different kinds of fashionable goods, but also a range of quality which extended from the fashionable establishments supplying the local gentry and merchants to the shops which supplied the common people of city or town and of the surrounding countryside. There was another Elizabeth Browne at Norwich in the 1780s as well as Nancy Woodforde's milliner, who appears to have traded, though not successfully, in a cheaper range of goods. When she went bankrupt in 1785 an inventory of her stock was made, which has survived and has been published in full.[69] Although called a milliner, she might equally well have been called a haberdasher, as she sold flowers, ribbons, trimmings, gloves, stockings, caps, hats, materials for sewing, toilet preparations and some ready-made garments. Most of the goods were low-priced; it may be that some of these were damaged or shop-soiled from remaining for a long time unsold, but there was considerable variety within each class of goods offered. She had Leghorn hats, chip hats, cane hats, Leghorn and horsehair bonnets and hats, cane bonnets, black and white chip hats, chip hats covered in silk and satin and '46 old straw, chip, etc Hats, 4s.' A balloon bonnet in a box at 8s was the most expensive hat in the shop, and was fashionably named. Some of the hats may, however, have been foundations only and would have been made up for a customer or to display in the shop; covered and trimmed they would have been more expensive. In this shop scarlet cloaks could be bought ready-made. There were ten scarlet cardinals left in stock, priced for children at 4s, and 5s, for girls at 5s; for women there was a range of price, 10s, 12s, 15s. There were also white cardinals, a girls', 'napt' at 10s 6d, women's 7s, and 7s 6d, and two, described as 'fine' at 18s each; and two drab cardinals, 4s and 5s. Six scarlet hoods for cardinals and two white ones were listed separately, all at 1s each.

The town of Kirkby Stephen, Westmorland, which had a population of 1,141 in the 1801 census, was in the eighteenth century the commercial centre of a large area. It seems to have been able to support two milliners in 1784, although its linen and woollen drapers were also grocers, and Abraham Dent sold mercery, grocery and stationery. For him the term mercer covered a wide range of fabrics and haberdashery. Some of his business records survive and have been the subject of a study by Dr T. S. Willan, *An Eighteenth-Century Shopkeeper, Abraham Dent, of Kirkby Stephen, 1729–1803*. In the 1760s Abraham Dent was selling a few made-up garments. The scarlet cardinal appears again, at 15s 6d, and a silk cloak at 15s; a stamped linen gown, sold to his servant, was 26s in 1764. He sold forty different kinds of fabric, from harden at 6d a yard to superfine cloth at 16s, mainly woollens and worsteds, linens and cottons. They were bought by a fairly wide range of customer, clergy, small

*84 Inventory of the goods of Edward
Kitchiner, draper of Biggleswade,
Bedfordshire, 1713.*

gentry, lawyers and tradesmen. The attorney and the mason bought
worsted shag of the same price. In a single year Abraham Dent bought
his drapery goods from forty-seven suppliers; little of his stock was
produced locally. Knitting stockings was a local industry. Abraham
Dent dealt in stockings, as a retailer, but very little in the local product.
In 1767 he bought stockings from Nottingham. These were a different
type from the local ones, being woven, that is, machine-knitted, instead
of hand-knitted, as the local stockings were. He did, however, deal in the
local product as manufacturer and wholesaler, selling almost entirely to
two army contractors in London. He bought silk, which he did not sell
in any quantity, from London, and also scarlet and black cloth. Cloth
also came from Yorkshire, Barnard Castle and Penrith; linen of different
kinds also came from Penrith, and gloves. From different suppliers in
Kendal he bought bombazine, calimanco and lace; from Cockermouth,
shalloon. Striped linens and cottons, worsted shag, baize and flannel,
fustian small wares, came from Manchester, stuffs from Norwich. He
made regular visits to London. The transport of goods between London
and Kirkby Stephen took a fortnight; the service was regular and
reliable, but costly. He was one of the many merchants who after a life in
business, holding such public offices as churchwarden and surveyor of
highways, finally acquired the status of gentleman; in Abraham Dent's
case with the aid of property which came with his third marriage.[70]

Many of the drapers in the smaller towns combined the business of
drapery with grocery. Robert Owen's first job, as a boy in Newtown,
was in the shop of two maiden ladies who 'kept a superior shop for the
sale of drapery and haberdashery on one side, and groceries on the
other.'[71] Edward Kitchiner of Biggleswade, who died in 1713, seems to
have sold no other goods, but the quantities of materials in stock at the
time of his death—'200 yards of ordinary stuffs, 400 yards of cantaloons,
115 yards of shalloon'—suggest that he may have been a wholesale as
well as a retail dealer (Fig. 84). Biggleswade was a small market town
about 45 miles north of London on the Great North Road. Its population
at the end of the seventeenth century has been estimated at 642; at the end
of the eighteenth century, the 1801 census recorded 1650. The position
of the town meant that some customers might have been passing
travellers, but he would also have been conveniently placed for the
travelling salesmen to buy supplies from him. The prices of the goods do
not suggest fashionable customers, but they probably supplied a fairly
wide social range, the gentry for part, the local farming, trading and
labouring people for most of their needs. There is a comparatively small
quantity of silk, 40 yards of sattinet and silk Damask valued at £8. 5s
being the most expensive; narrow and broad black silk were 3s a yard
and 3s 6d an ell. There were mixed fabrics of silk and worsted, burdett,
camlet, poplin, crape, probably mourning crape, in two qualities, 1s 3d
and 10d a yard. There were many woollen and worsted fabrics, striped
and black calimanco, serge, shagg, drugget and stuffs; and a great deal of

An Inventory of the Goods and Chattells and
personall Estate of Edward Kitchiner late of
the Town of Bigglefwade in the County of Bedford
deceafed taken and apprized by uf whofe names
are thereunto fett on the fifteenth day of August
Anno dñi one Thousand Seaven hundred and
Thirteene as followeth

## In the Shopp

| | |
|---|---|
| Imprid, Tenn Yards of Tabby | 1:10:00 |
| Eight Remnants of Tabby Perfian | 5:00:00 |
| Nine Yards floured Sattin | 1:07:00 |
| Twenty ffour Yards of Thread Sattin | 0:00:00 |
| Eighteen Yards of Thread Sattin | 1:04:00 |
| ffour Peeces of Burdett Sixty two yards | 5:03:04 |
| ffifty Yards of Spotted Poplin | 4:17:02 |
| ffour whole peeces of Sattinett and Poplin | 7:16:00 |
| Thirty Yards of Poplin | 2:18:00 |
| ffourty Yards of Sattinett & Silk Damafk | 5:05:00 |
| One whole peece of Antezine ffourty Seaven Yards | 2:02:11 |
| Seventy Seaven Yards & Remnants of Antezine | 3:04:02 |
| Two Remnants of Damafk Twenty Yards | 1:00:00 |
| Twenty Yards of Black Ruffell | 1:06:03 |
| ffifty three Yards of Calamancow Stript and Black | 3:10:08 |
| Two peeces of Cambletts Thirty Six Yards | 2:11:00 |
| Two whole peeces of Double Camlott | 4:16:00 |
| ffive Remnants of Double Camlott | 1:03:04 |
| Ninty Seaven Yards of half Silk Ordinary | 4:04:08 |
| One whole peece of Coloured Damafk | 1:00:00 |
| Sixty ffive Yards of Remnants of Colourd Damafk | 2:14:02 |
| ffourty two Yards of Spanifh Poplin | 1:16:01 |
| Some Odd Remnants of Sattinolls | 1:06:03 |
| Three peeces of ffine Crape Sixty ffour Yards | 4:00:00 |
| ffourty one Yards of Ordinary Crape | 1:14:10 |
| Two peeces of Coloured linfoy | 3:08:00 |
| Two Remnants of water Chenoy | 0:12:00 |
| Two whole peeces of ffloured linfoy | 2:08:00 |
| One Dozen of Childrens Shooes | 0:04:00 |
| ffour Hatts | 0:02:00 |
| One Made Gown | 0:02:00 |
| ffourty Eight Yards of Burying Crape | 2:08:00 |
| One peece of Blew linfoy Eighteen Yards | 1:02:00 |

87:10:03

linen, blue linen in different widths and qualities, 'ordinary printed blue and white linen', 21 yards valued at 15s 9d, printed linen, 26 yards at £1. 0. 4, printed linsey, 75 yards at £3. 0. 10. There was white linen and a whole range of linen goods named from their places of origin, Irish cloth, Scotch cloth, Holland, 'Osnerbridge', Doulace, Garlick Holland, Ghenting. There was 74 yards of callicoes at £7. 0. 4, 30 yards of striped flowered Dimity, two whole pieces of flowered linsey, and damask which could be wool, silk or linen. Muslin was one of the more expensive fabrics at 3s a yard, but it is difficult to assess prices and qualities unless the widths of the fabric are known. The stock is considerable and shows both the variety of fabric available and the limits of choice at this level of trading. There were some made-up items of dress, gloves, stockings, men's shirts, children's shoes, caps, handker-chiefs, women's and girls' 'bodyes' and 'leather bodyes', petticoats and one made gown at 2s. There were also shoe-buckles, combs, buttons, pins and needles, 'sweet powder and rolls', which would be for wigs, and 'some silver things and gold rings', valued at £8 which were the only goods outside a drapery business proper. The total value of the stock was about £315. Edward Kitchiner's own wearing apparel together with ready money was valued at only £3. 10s. The house he lived in had kitchen, pantry, buttery, parlour and study, three bedrooms and barn, brewhouse and outbuildings.[72]

## Travelling Salesmen

Where there were no shops, fashion was brought into village and hamlet by travelling salesmen, the hawkers and pedlars. Their customers ranged from gentry to farmers, servants, country tradespeople and labourers. John Steward and his wife 'came with their Packs to sell goods' to Nicholas Blundell in Lancashire several times in the early years of the century; in 1710 he noted what he bought from them: 'my wife and I bought some Handkerchaffs, etc off her.'[73] Thomas Marchant, who lived in Sussex and shopped in Horsham and Lewes, bought edgings and muslin amounting to 15s 9d from a Scotchman in 1719.[74] The Scotchman sold textiles, linen, muslin, lace and later, cotton. The name may have come from the goods sold, for Scotland was the main source of home-produced muslins: 'They make them so good and fine that great quantities are often sent into England and sold there at a good price; they are usually striped, and are very much used for aprons by the ladies, and sometimes in head-clothes by the English women of a meaner sort.'[75] The muslins of fashionable dress were imported mostly from the Netherlands; Defoe allowed his country grocer's wife to have her muslin and linen from 'foreign trade' although her husband's linen was from Lancashire or Scotland. The term Scotchmen may, however, come from their way of business, for they bought and sold on credit.

All those who sold goods by retail, 'going from town to town or to other men's houses', had since 1697 been required by law to hold a licence. The number of country shopkeepers increased during the century and by the 1780s there was opposition to the hawkers from this source, and an attempt was made to repeal the acts licensing hawkers and to make hawking illegal. The Bridgnorth Society of Travelling Scotchmen petitioned against the bill, stating that the Society purchased goods from manufacturers on credit:

> 'Goods in the Silk, Linen, Muslin and Lace way from several Manufacturers therof in different parts of Great Britain and Ireland to furnish the Travelling Scotchmen with goods sold upon credit . . . and the said Travelling Scotchmen have also due to them from their Country Customers the sum of £1,500 upwards.'

Similar petitions were presented by the Travelling Scotchmen of several other districts. There was support for them too from the manufacturers, so the travelling salesman continued on his way.[76] Betty, an under-housemaid in Charlotte Smith's novel *The Old Manor House,* published in 1793 but set in the late 1770s, bought a new gown from a Scotchman: 'I had not enough money without it to buy my new cotton gown when Alexander Macgill the Scotchman called here, and so away went my poor dear crown.'[77] Credit terms were not, it seemed, available to all. In 1798 Jane Austen bought six shifts, that is the linen for them, at 3s 6d a yard and four pairs of stockings from 'the Overton Scotchman.'[78]

Many pedlars or petty chapmen sold a wider range of goods. Pamela in Richardson's novel 'bought of a pedlar two pretty round-eared caps, a little straw hat, a pair of knit mittens, turned up with white calico and two pair of blue worsted hose with white clocks.'[79] Even those people who were able to visit towns for their shopping found the travelling salesmen useful. Master, mistress and maids all bought from the men who called regularly at Weston parsonage. In 1781 'One Mr Alldridge who goes about with a cart with Linen, Cottons, Laces, etc called at the House this morning to know if we wanted anything in his way.' Mr Woodforde bought cotton for a morning gown and chintz for a gown for Nancy. Thereafter Mr Aldridge called regularly 'once in ten weeks' and from 1788 they bought things from him, up to three or four times a year. In 1796 Mr Woodforde revealed that he was William Aldridge of Norwich and that he made visits to London, for on one occasion he was asked to pay a bill for Mr Woodforde when he next sent to London. The goods they bought were mainly printed cottons, linens and muslins, lace, ribbons and stockings. Nancy's chintz gown of 1781 was amongst the more expensive, five and a half yards, costing £1. 14s. The cotton for Mr Woodforde's morning gowns, for other gowns for Nancy and the maids was cheaper and all about the same price, between 2s and 2s 6d a yard. The muslin for stocks and cravats was a comparatively expensive material, three yards of cambric at 7s a yard to make nine stocks, and three yards of muslin at 8s a yard to make six cravats in 1793. 'Waistcoat pieces', that is fabric for the foreparts, could also be bought, 'a marcella waistcoat piece, yellow ground, ¾ yd square for Ben Leggatt' for 8s in 1795, and again in 1801 for Ben and his other man, two pieces of 'woolen but of pretty Pattern, red, green and brown in stripes' which cost 14s and another woollen piece for his boy, 4s. Aldridge also sold silk handkerchiefs, East India and Spitalfields. On one occasion Nancy bought a second-hand scarf-shawl, 'late Miss Stone's as good as New— 3½ yds long and a Yard wide which cost at first Three Guineas and which Miss Woodforde bought of Aldridge for £1. 11. 6.'

Another travelling salesman who made regular visits was 'one Bagshaw, a Derbyshire Man and who carries a Pack with divers things in it to sell.' He sold a slightly different range of goods from Aldridge, although some goods were common to both. It was from him that Mr Woodforde bought his coursing stockings of undressed wool and other stockings of this type, coarse ribbed stockings, 'ash-coloured Welch stockings', and also flannel, black velveret and olive 'Jennett' for breeches. There was a man 'who comes from Windham and carries about stuffs for gowns', probably of Norwich manufacture. Mr and Mrs Burden were 'travelling people' from London who called in February 1792. Nancy bought from them a worked muslin apron for which she paid eleven shillings and sixpence, and a muslin one at six shillings and ninepence. They also left with her 'a very handsome Chintz Gown which I liked very well and which they are to call again for in May if I do not chuse to keep it. I am to give two Guineas and a half for it, as that they declared is the lowest price. I shall buy it as it is a very handsome good Gown.' In May she recorded: 'Paid Mr Burden for my Chintz Gown 2.10.'—not the two and a half guineas quoted in February. In 1796 when Mr Burdon called again Mr Woodforde described him as a Scotchman.[80]

The shops and mantua-makers of the provincial centres were able to supply not only a wide range of goods, but also information on London fashions through their regular visits. In the country districts, even for those unable to visit the larger towns there seems to have been little difficulty in obtaining fabrics, sewing materials and such items as stockings and gloves, provided there was money to buy them. The travelling salesmen were able to offer considerable variety of goods, justifying their claim that they dealt in 'almost every article of Female attire whether for use or ornament.'[81]

## Markets and Fairs

Clothing was also sold in the markets held in market towns and at fairs which were held not only in market towns but in places which had no markets. Many markets and fairs, particularly in the first half of the century, were concerned with wholesale dealing, but they also gathered together goods to tempt the ordinary buyer.

One of the most famous of fairs was at Stourbridge, a village outside Cambridge, held in September, and 'stored with all kinds of wares and commodities which the Londoners take special care to import.'[82] In Mrs Centlivre's *The Man's Bewitched* a young country squire refers to his new suit: 'Father bought the cloth last Stourbrich Fair and the Taylor comes to-morrow.' It was still flourishing in the middle of the century when the Marchioness Grey visited it from her father-in-law's home at Wimpole in 1748. Everyone at this time went to Stourbridge Fair, nobility, gentry and common people: 'One day of it is a sort of general meeting of the gentry in the Neighbourhood .... Here you may furnish yourself with everything that is necessary, convenient or ornamental for your person or Family, for the Fine Lady or the Country Huswife, from a yard of ribbon to a Pad or Cart-horse.'[83]

In the villages there were smaller fairs which were often the statute fairs at which servants gathered when seeking employment, like the one at Shillington, the Bedfordshire village, at which John Blundell bought himself a pair of ribbed stockings in 1764. The goods sold at these fairs were usually small useful or ornamental items, which had their own name, 'fairings':

> *How Pedlars Stalls with Glittering Toys are laid*
> *The various Fairings of the Country Maid*
> *Long silken Laces hang upon the Twine*
> *And rows of Pins and amber Bracelets shine;*
> *How the tight Lass, Knives, Combs, Scissars spys*
> *And looks on Thimbles with desiring Eyes.*[84]

By the end of the century, with the increasing numbers of shops in country towns, the smaller markets and the commercial importance of the fairs declined.

## Second-hand Clothes

The large quantities of good clothing which by 'castings' and bequests came into possession of servants encouraged the development of a flourishing second-hand trade. It was not only servants who supplied the market. A man like Samuel Curwen sold his clothes as he acquired new ones, sometimes to a dealer in second-hand clothes, sometimes to the shopkeeper from whom he bought his new ones. He agreed with his tailor to take the suit on his back in part payment for a new one in 1776.[85] Roderick Random 'disposed of a good part of my apparel to a salesman in Monmouth Street and bought two new suits with the money.'[86] Monmouth Street in the parish of St Giles-in-the-Fields was already synonymous with second-hand finery at the beginning of the century. Lovelace in *Clarissa* sent one of his agents who was to be imposed on her to Monmouth Street to get the clothes to fit the part.[87] Lady Mary Wortley Montagu used Monmouth Street finery to express her scorn of Irish peerages: 'Ever since I knew the World Irish peerages have been hung out to Sale like the laced and embroidered Coats in Monmouth Street and bought up by the same sort of People; I mean those who had rather have shabby Finery than no Finery at all.'[88]

Wendeborn, who had lived in London for twenty years, wrote in the 1780s that in Germany there was a great difference in value between the dress of different ranks of people, but in England this was less marked:

'The clothing manufactured for the poor and common people is in small proportion to their numbers and few or none of them like to wear it. Even in country places it is but little used; and in London, or the great towns, it is seldom or never to be seen. All do their best to wear fine clothes, and those who cannot afford to purchase them buy the old at secondhand that they may at least have the appearance of finery.'[89]

London was a major market in this trade. Eden also stated that 'in the vicinity of the metropolis' working people seldom bought new clothes: 'they content themselves with a cast-off coat, which may usually be purchased for about 5s and second-hand waistcoats and breeches. Their wives seldom make up any article of dress, except making and mending clothes for the children.'[90] But it was not only in London that second-hand clothes were bought. Davies for his own Berkshire parish said that children's clothing was in part made from the parents' old clothing, in part bought second-hand. One of his correspondents from Brington, Northamptonshire, wrote that what clothing was bought there was generally second-hand.[91]

## Making Clothes

The making of clothes was generally left to tailors and mantua-makers, not only by fashionable people and gentry, but by at least the more prosperous of the common people. A few people of fashion amused themselves by occasionally making a gown. Lady Carlow wrote to her sister, Lady Louisa Stuart in 1781: 'My chief amusement since I came from town has been making myself a white polonaise, in which I have succeeded to a miracle, and repent having given one to a famous mantua-maker in Dublin who spoilt it entirely for me.'[92] Lady Heathcote made herself a masquerade dress, a peasant's dress, in 1755.[93] Some references are ambiguous because making a gown may mean embroidering the fabric rather than making it up. Gowns or parts of them were embroidered and so were waistcoat fronts for men, and sent to mantua-maker or tailor for making up as a garment. Or the silk of a gown might be painted. When Lady Heathcote had dealt with her masquerade dress she was able to get on with painting white satin for a sack:

'My painted sack profits by my not having any more Masquerade Dresses to contrive and make: it is nearly all finished except the Flounces and even upon them the little Festoons (your Favourites) are painted; there now

only remains a row of Sprigs along the head of the deepest of them, before
I am quite at a stand for want of Ly Anson's Flounce Sprig.'

Lady Anson 'turned out very good: the Flounce arrived (to a day) at the
time I wanted it.' From the 1780s embroidering the whole fabric of a
gown was a popular, fashionable occupation. The dress worn by
Elizabeth Yorke at court in 1787 was almost certainly an example of her
skill as an embroideress not a dressmaker: 'I hope you'll like her
Birthday Dress as it is her own making, pray observe the petticoat.'[94] In
1790 Maria Josepha Holroyd started to work herself 'a Gown in Spots,
which is a very great undertaking, but I hope the Fashions will have the
complaisance to wait for me; and that Spotted Muslins will not go out.'
In 1793 she embarked again on the working of a gown, 'for Mrs
Woodward, in the Tambour by way of Winter Employment.'[95] Even
the princesses joined in this employment. The Princess Royal worked her
own wedding-dress. Queen Charlotte herself told Fanny Burney about
it, 'and the real labour it had proved, from her steadiness to have no
help, well knowing that 3 stitches done by any other would make it
immediately said it was none of it by herself.'[96]

Dress accessories, aprons, handkerchiefs, ruffles and muffs and men's
waistcoats were embroidered, and from the 1750s to the 1780s there was
the making-up of elaborate trimmings for gowns. Mrs Delany was
noted for her fine embroidery, which was treasured by her family after
her death. Her views about needlework were also preserved: 'The
ornamental work of gentlewomen ought to be superior to bought work
in design and taste and their plain work the model for their maids.' Not
all the work done to ornament dress was, strictly speaking, embroidery.
Special crafts were developed and practised and produced their own
fashions. One of these was the making of tippets and muffs from
feathers. Mrs Delany wrote to her sister in 1728: 'I will send ... a tippet
of my own making and invention', which may be the tippet with long
scarf-ends, made of feathers of the macaw and of the canary which was
still in existence when Lady Llanover published Mrs Delany's letters in
1861. The Duchess of Portland also worked with feathers and wrote to
Mrs Delany in 1737 that she was going to make a muff of jay's feathers.[97]
Feathers were collected and exchanged with enthusiasm. The
Marchioness Grey sent a muff of peacocks' feathers to her elder daughter
in 1780, who was herself collecting feathers, saying it was work of 'Miss
Delane'.[98] Some of the embroidered waistcoats worn by men were
worked by relatives and friends. Horace Walpole was lyrical about a
waistcoat Lady Ossory sent him as a New Year's gift in 1775: 'The
present I saw came from no mortal hand .... Venus had chosen the
pattern, Flora painted the roses after those at Paphos, Minerva worked
the tambour part....'[99] Richardson's Pamela spent part of her time after
the death of her mistress in flowering a waistcoat for her master: 'I work
all hours with my needle upon his linen and the fine linen of the family;

and am besides about flowering him a waistcoat.'[100] The working on linen and the general care of clothes was a usual task for a personal maid, although some entered service after training as milliner or mantua-maker.

Women of the gentry rarely made their own gowns, although they embroidered them. Mrs Papendiek, who altered and re-trimmed gowns and hats, embroidered at least one waistcoat for her husband and made clothes for her children and was able to set down details of them many years afterwards, stated that 'no new gown was ever made at home and the mantua-maker, the term of those days, attended upon dress occasions to see that her work was correct and to assist in having it properly put on.' She helped Miss Jervois embroider a gown she was to wear at a ball at Windsor in 1789, 'a most beautiful Indian jaconet muslin which was to be embroidered in small sprigs and stripes with gold thread ... we worked like slaves.'[101] Sophia and Fanny Cater embroidered their gowns for the Bedford Races ball in 1776, but they always had their gowns made up, with the help of Mrs Williamson, usually by a London mantua-maker, but not always to Mrs Cater's satisfaction: 'I can't help saying that in my opinion Mrs Lenox managed very badly to have so many joynings in the polonese as there was certainly a great quantity of silk for that part.'[102] Both Mrs Custance and Nancy Woodforde embroidered and made many of their dress accessories. In this Nancy appears to have been the more expert. She netted aprons in the 1780s, and in 1787 taught Mrs Custance how 'to make the Diamond edge netting.' In her diary, which survives for the year 1792, there is record of a year's work. She bought herself one worked muslin apron but worked most of her muslin herself, a handkerchief in January, a double handkerchief during April and May, a muslin bonnet in June. On 20 June Mrs Bodham lent her a tucker and ruff all in one for her to take a pattern and she spent the next day making one like it. On the 26th Lady Bacon, Mrs Custance's sister, also lent her a tucker for a pattern of the work on it, and three days later a pattern for working a muslin petticoat. She drew this pattern and returned the petticoat the same day, but put the pattern aside to work during the winter. She showed Lady Bacon and Mrs Custance how to make tuckers out of old ruffles which were now no longer worn. In August she made a handkerchief like her own for Mrs Custance; this took her three days. Mrs Custance then lent her 'a new fashion handkerchief to take the pattern of.' In December the making of a muslin morning cap spread over three days.[103] Patterns for working gowns, aprons, caps and handkerchiefs were published with *The Lady's Magazine* from 1770 onwards (Fig. 85). Before this patterns came from professional pattern-drawers and once bought were circulated amongst friends, or patterns were taken, as Nancy Woodforde took some, from existing work. There were also talented amateur artists who drew patterns for themselves and their friends.

Catherine Hutton, it seems, did actually make some of her own

85  *Pattern for embroidering an apron or handkerchief from* The Lady's Magazine, *1785.*

clothes. In 1788 she had asked her friend in Enfield to send her a description of fashionable cloaks:

'I thank you for your description of the gauze cloak, which would have enabled me to make mine correctly if it had not been made before it arrived; but having waited a fortnight, I consider your milliner very uncertain; that my wanting a cloak to take to Blackpool was very sure, and that if I committed a trifling error there was probably no one who could detect me . . . . It is very full and elegant and when it appears draws all eyes after the wearer. There is nothing like it to be seen in Birmingham.'

In an account she gave towards the end of her life of the work she did she said she made clothes as well as decorating them: 'I have made shirts for my father and brother and all sorts of wearing apparel for myself, with the exception of shoes, stockings and gloves . . . . I have worked embroidery on muslin, satin and canvas and netted upwards of one hundred wallet purses . . . . I net much still.'[104]

Shirt-making by the women of the family for fathers and brothers seems to have been an accepted duty, although shirts were also made by seamstresses and could be bought ready-made. Even daughters of the nobility sometimes undertook this work, or at least the responsibility for it. Lord Sheffield's daughter found in 1794 that her father was 'all in Rags. I want to know what price the Cloth that makes his shirts is? and what Linnen draper you have dealt with last?' Two months later she wrote to her aunt: 'What do you think I have done? An amazing feat indeed! Nothing less than cut out a set of Shirts for Papa, and I am going to make one Shirt myself. I have got a new kind of thing for them, that Mrs Maynard recommends, called Suffolk Hemp. It looks very strong and she says it will wear well.'[105] Jane Austen made shirts for her brothers. In 1796 when she was staying with Edward she wrote that they were 'very busy making Edward's shirts, and I am proud to say that I am the neatest worker of the party.' In 1799 she warned Cassandra: 'When you come home you will have some shirts to make up for Charles, Mrs Davies frightened him into buying a piece of Irish when we were in Basingstoke.'[106]

Clothes were re-fashioned at all levels of society. Even amongst the nobility gowns were altered for a change of fashion or for greater use by changing them from one type of use to another. Mrs Delany had a white tabby altered in 1726.[107] Lady Polwarth in 1777 planned to re-use the silk of a court dress for a sack. There were rather more re-makings of gowns amongst the gentry. Mrs Papendiek, who was wife of a court official, has left a rare record of the life of a gown which she wore over a period of ten years, for her court attendances and other dress occasions. She first acquired it in 1781, her first satin gown, puce, trimmed with white satin over a white satin petticoat; the next year it was re-trimmed. In 1785 she removed the white satin trimming and replaced it with a

new, fashionable, trimming in steel. The next year she trimmed it again
with blonde lace and in 1788 added three broad white satin straps,
buckled with steel buckles and a gauze apron. She also had alternative
straps of puce satin. In 1789 the gown was 'once more put in order for
the winter with gauze capes and satin trimmings.' Finally in 1792 she
decided that the end had come. During these ten years she had other
dress gowns, one white silk, another in a silk called 'Emperor's eye'
which she described as 'knife steel' colour. These seem to have been
replaced in 1789 by a new muslin. These three were summer gowns; the
puce satin seems to have been kept for winter occasions, a garment re-
made for the same occasion to meet changing fashion.[109] Garments were
also re-made into other garments. In 1715 Dudley Ryder went to his
tailor 'about making a pair of breeches out of old silk stockings.'[110]
Nicholas Blundell's tailor made him a riding coat from a cloak in
1705.[111] Jane Austen turned her 'coarse spot gown' into a petticoat in
1798. She also made alterations to her gowns to meet a new fashion, and
sometimes to correct mistakes of her mantua-maker. After a 'dreadful
epoch of mantua-making' in 1798, when she wished that gowns could
be bought ready-made, she had in 1801 to alter one which had just been
made for her by Mrs Mussell of Bath as it was not quite to her liking:
'She does not always succeed with lighter colours. My white one I was
obliged to alter a good deal.'[112]

Although specific bequests of clothing in wills of the gentry appear
less often as the century progressed, dresses still passed by bequest from
one generation to another, like the silk gown Nancy Woodforde had in
1782 which had belonged to her great-aunt. Many surviving dresses
show evidence of alterations, often of complete re-making, with the
fabric a decade or so earlier than the form of the dress. For fashionable
people the changing patterns of silks, particularly in the first half of the
century, were changing fashion, but the less fashionable accepted them
over a much longer period, until there was more complete change. The
second gown, a green silk damask, that Mr Woodforde gave to Nancy
from his Aunt Parr's clothing in 1790, was well out of fashion. This she
did not take to her mantua-maker, but altered herself and wore it at
home, perhaps out of deference to her uncle. The sack gowns so much
worn in the middle years of the century were ideal for re-making, with
their uncut widths of material, and many gowns of the 1770s and 1780s
were originally made in this form. Some of the re-fashionings show skill
and fashionable understanding, others have a more uncertain touch; but
even these suggest an awareness of a new style. The rising waistline of
the 1790s brought many alterations. The turn-over of the skirt as it was
pleated on to the bodice was usually generous enough to allow the skirt
to be raised and make a horizontal line with the bodice at the back. This,
carried out in the cottons and light silks fashionable in the last ten years
or so, could be successful; attempts to carry it out in the stiffer silks of
earlier fashion, like Nancy Woodforde's damask, could not. The altered

dresses show how acceptable the carrying on of something from a previous style into the next one was and the overlapping pattern this made in changing fashion.

Local records show a large number of tailors not only in market towns but in most villages. Unless a tailor made clothing for a fair proportion of people in his village he would not have been able to survive, so their existence in quite small centres of population suggests that amongst the common people all but the poorest had their clothes made by a local tailor. In the market town of Ampthill, Bedfordshire, with an estimated population of 599 in 1671 and of 1234 in the census of 1801, ten men are recorded as tailors between 1700 and 1710. John Blundell of Meppershall had clothes made by three different local men. He also had a coat and later a waistcoat turned by one of them. Mantua-makers do not appear so frequently. It may be that the village tailor at the beginning of the century also made women's clothes, until the mantua-makers were more general, but it is most likely that records of many of them are lost because women's occupations have always been less carefully recorded than those of men. There was a mantua-maker in Ampthill in 1716, but she appears only in the records of apprenticeship, not in parish registers, which at this time meticulously record the occupations of men. Catherine Talbot in 1748 wrote of her 'crimson stuff gown made by a Cuddesden Manteau Maker',[113] the mantua-maker of an Oxfordshire village. Nancy Woodforde had gowns made by a mantua-maker from Reepham as well as by her Norwich mantua-maker, and had a visiting mantua-maker from Mattishall Burgh. Such mantua-makers in the villages formed another fashion link between customers in one social group and those of another. Edward Kitchiner had 'one Made Gown' in his shop as well as petticoats, in 1713. Probably some women made their own gowns, as Pamela did her homespun woollen one, with its facings of calico. Women of the common people must, however, have received a good deal of their clothing second-hand, even if they did not buy it second-hand. The more prosperous of them left bequests of clothing to relatives and friends in their wills, passing on everyday or old clothes to a servant. Many people of quite small means had one servant, so that there could be a constant passing down of clothing. Elizabeth Preston of Cardington, Bedfordshire, who died in 1780, was a widow, her total effects were valued at £100, her son was a labourer, her brother-in-law and nephew wheelwrights. She left to her sister-in-law her crape gown; once again, as often in such wills, this was probably a mourning gown; and 'to her maid a suit of her old cloth.' At the end of the chain the poorest, according to character and ability, would either wear these clothes as they were or alter them to follow what fashion they knew, for best wear.

# VII

# *Fabrics and Wearers*

At the beginning of the century most of the clothing worn in England was supplied by the English woollen industries. The proportion of woollen clothing worn varied according to rank and way of life; some people wore wool in a few garments only, for a particular type of dress; others wore little else. Linen, sometimes mixed with cotton, was also worn by most people, though in varying quality and quantity.

Only one group, the women of fashion, rarely wore woollen fabrics at all, except concealed in linings, for warmth; outwardly it appeared in their riding habits, but even these were often of camlet, a mixture of wool and silk, though later of cloth. Men of fashion, however, had a large proportion of woollen clothing, in their undress wear, in the country, and even, provided the cloth was the finest and suitably trimmed with gold and silver lace, in dress wear. The gentry wore rather more cloth, often keeping to it, with suitably rich trimming of coat and waistcoat, in dress wear, and having only the waistcoats of rich and patterned silks. Women of the gentry wore more silk than wool, although they had stuff gowns for winter, as Catherine Talbot and Barbara Johnson did. So still, at the end of the century, did Jane Austen, who wrote to her sister in December 1798: 'I find great comfort in my stuff gown, but I hope you do not wear yours too often.' She may have meant that she hoped the weather was mild, but more likely she was hoping that Cassandra was having such a gay time that she wore this homely gown less often. In 1801, in January, when Cassandra was again staying with their brother she wrote: 'I begin with the hope . . . that you often wore a white gown in the morning, at the time of all the gay *party's* being with you.'[1] Below this level the clothing of both men and women early in the century was woollen, although for women a silk gown for best wear was not uncommon. Therefore, at one extreme, in the clothes of the fashionable woman, the fabrics were almost entirely imported; other groups wore a decreasing proportion of imported fabrics, until in the lower ranks of the common people clothing was entirely home-produced, that is produced in Great Britain.

This state of dress was not the result of any legal restriction. From the fourteenth century sumptuary laws had been passed, constantly attempting to maintain social distinctions and, on moral grounds, to control 'excess of apparel', the expression of luxury and pride. They had been repeated and added to, making an increasingly complex pattern of status of person and status of fabric until the seventeenth century, but their enforcement was always difficult. No rank wanted to restrict itself, only to restrict the ranks below. There is little evidence of the effectiveness of the laws and few prosecutions have been traced. In England these attempts at legal restriction were abandoned much earlier than they were in most countries of Europe. It was, ironically, the Puritan government of the Commonwealth which finally realised that regulation of dress by acts of Parliament in the interests of the social hierarchy was a lost cause.[2] The need to maintain every outward and visible sign of this hierarchy had been balanced against an urge to increase wealth through the expansion of trade, and the trading interests won. The established social hierarchy, though still firm in structure, was changing, with subdivision of its ranks and a good deal of individual movement between the shallower gradations; and much of the sumptuary legislation already embodied a secondary aim, that of encouraging the English cloth industry.

In the eighteenth century the laws which affected dress were generally enacted to encourage or promote a textile industry or one of the smaller industries supplying parts of clothing; but any interest which conflicted with the interest of the woollen industry, in its export as well as its home trade, was likely to suffer. Woollen industries were long established all over England, making a great variety of woollen and worsted fabrics and mixed fabrics of wool and silk, wool and linen. They had been established in certain districts, each type of cloth produced in one or two particular areas, although industries also moved and changed. There was a great range of quality, of weight and texture of cloth. Already at the beginning of the century the trade was so organised that the different products of each area were available throughout the rest of the country, the cheaper fabrics as well as those for the more fashionable market. 'Suppose the poorest countryman wants to be clothed . . . yet he shall in some part employ every one of the manufacturing counties of England.' Defoe's 'poorest countryman' was dressed, except for shirt, shoes, garters and gloves, entirely in wool, but in four different kinds of woollen fabric; his coat, cloth from Yorkshire, lined with shalloon from Berkshire, his breeches, drugget from Devizes, his waistcoat, calimanco from Norwich. The inventory of Edward Kitchiner's draper's shop shows that all these woollen fabrics and many more besides were available at Biggleswade in 1713: 'Every town in England uses something, not only of one or other, but of all the rest; every sort of goods is wanted everywhere; and where they make one sort of goods and sell them all over England, they at the same time want other goods from almost every part.'[3]

There were still in the early years of the century, even among the gentry, those whose clothes came from wool of their own spinning,

*86  Coat of brown woollen cloth with cloth-covered buttons. The origin of this coat is unknown, but it has all the appearance of a coat of common wear of the mid-eighteenth century.*

which was then woven into a web by a local weaver, scoured and fulled by a fuller and, if required, dyed by a dyer. Nicholas Blundell had two suits made from wool spun at home during 1712; in February, 'I bought Lining Silk, etc at Mr Hursts to make up a Sute of Clothes for myself the Outside was of our own spinning'; and in October he had his second suit. He described both as drugget; his woollen yarn was mixed with a worsted yarn. The following year Mrs Blundell had two pieces of serge dyed at Liverpool, which were 'of our own spinning of Gersey.'[4] The practice of producing homespun cloth with the services of the specialist local craftsmen was no longer general, even amongst farming people, by the middle of the century (Fig. 86). Kalm noticed this in 1748 in Hertfordshire: 'Weaving and spinning is also in most houses a more than rare thing, because their many manufacturers save them from the necessity of such.'[5] It continued only in the more remote and pastoral areas of the country where Eden reported its decline in the northern counties in the 1790s. In Wales it survived longer; and English travellers, seeing the dress which resulted from it, were struck by the contrast this made with the contemporary dress worn by common people in England.

In men's dress the use of fine cloth increased during the century, not so much because it was worn by people who previously had not done so, but because it was worn more often, taking over the whole dress of men of fashion and the gentry at the expense of silk. For common wear, cloth, although not of first quality, was often used, at least in best wear. Other woollen fabrics also had their fine and coarser varieties, so the name of a material does not always indicate exactly the quality of dress. Serge, drugget and kersey, made in Devonshire, Berkshire, Yorkshire, and the long-piled shag were worn. Linen, and linen and cotton mixtures in their heavier qualities were also used for the different garments of the suit. Fustian, a linen or linen and cotton twill, could be as slight a fabric as the sample in Barbara Johnson's album, which she had for a riding-dress in 1757, but it was also a heavy-weight fabric, thickened by a closely shaven pile, with something of the appearance and toughness of leather. This was a Lancashire manufacture and with this Lancashire also developed the new cotton velvet, called Manchester velvet, patent velvet or velveret, to distinguish it from silk velvet. This was the fabric which Talbot Williamson recommended for breeches in 1762, and Parson Woodforde often bought for the same purpose. The heavier ribbed cotton velvet, corduroy, and fustian were both used for working garments; so that during the last quarter of the century cotton was taking the place of woollen fabrics in working men's working dress, and in breeches the place of leather.

The finest silks worn by men and women of fashion during the first half of the century were imported from France and Italy and these either paid heavy duty or were smuggled into the country. An English silk industry was, however, beginning to flourish in London, in Spitalfields, following an influx of Huguenot refugees from France in the late seventeenth century, and profiting from the years of war with France at the beginning of the eighteenth century. This industry was producing high-quality brocaded silks, but light-weight silks and fabrics of silk and worsted were also made there. The fine quality silks were to become serious rivals of the imported French silks and supply much of the fashionable demand from the 1730s. Just before the end of the seventeenth century another fabric entered fashionable dress. Indian chintz had appeared in the 1660s as a furnishing fabric; it was also used for the loose informal gowns of morning and home wear; but it did not at first penetrate further into fashionable dress. The arrival of William and Mary from Holland, where Indian chintz was already fashionable dress wear, probably encouraged a greater use of it in England. The chintzes, with their brilliance and freshness of colour—the dyes were fast—brought a new quality into fashionable dress. As the trade between India and England developed the original Indian patterns had been adapted to Western taste, and as soon as this was successfully achieved the acceptance of Indian chintz was assured. This fashionable material was painted cotton; cheaper, block-printed cottons from India had also found their way to England; but these were only used in the linings of dress, or in common wear. Imports from India also included Indian silks. The silk industry, faced with the competition of French silks on one hand and Indian chintzes and silks on the other, campaigned for prohibition of the Indian imports which they secured in 1701, but as this act contained no prohibition against imports for re-export, nor prohibition of actual use or wear, it was not very effective and fashionable women continued to wear chintz gowns and houses continued to be furnished with chintz.

The prohibition of imported goods had the effect of making them fashionably desirable, for supplies were available through a flourishing smuggling trade. In his play, *The Reformed Wife* (1700), William Burnaby reflects the fashionable passion, not only for the fabrics themselves, but for fabrics because they were prohibited: 'Be sure you get me the Lace', says Lady Dainty to Mrs Pert, her milliner from the Exchange, 'for I'll wear none but what is Prohibited.' In *The Ladies Visiting Day* (1701), Indian goods are included, as two characters express opposing views: Fulvia, who is 'of the unfashionable Humour, to imploy our own People and wear our own Improvements', and Lady Lovetoy, who would be 'as much ashamed to have anything about me that I could not say was right French, right Mechlin or right Indian; as I should be to wear False Diamonds or false teeth.' Prohibition or heavy duties remained on French silks, French lace and Indian chintzes for the rest of the century, but a good deal still entered the country through the many travellers between England and Europe, with their amateur smuggling, as well as through the regular smuggling trade. Lady Caroline Fox was given a painted taffeta for her sister in 1756, which 'being India and unmade, I fear 'twill be seized unless some careful body carries it.'[6] Lady Holderness, called by Horace Walpole 'the Queen of Smugglers', transported goods on the grand scale, and had according to report as many as 114 French gowns and silks seized in 1764.[7] In 1768 she and Lady Mary Coke walked from Walmer Castle to Deal, one of the centres of the smuggling trade, 'where she carried me to three of the Houses that smuggle India goods. I saw several pieces of very pretty silks. I shall certainly buy one before I go.'[8] Other more law-abiding members of the aristocracy did not approve of the activities of Lady Holderness: 'I was I confess not a little pleased at the disappointment Lord and Lady Holderness met with in the seizure of all those very fine things which they had properly no right to as so very open a violation of laws in People of their Rank is particularly harmful.'[9] Smuggled goods were, however, widely available and bought with little concern. Even the Rev. James Woodforde had his supply of smuggled rum. In *Clarissa,* in a letter of Miss Howe's attempting to get help to Clarissa, she introduces Mrs Townsend,

'Who is a great dealer in Indian silks, Brussels and French laces, cambrics, linen and other valuable goods; which she has a way of coming at duty-free; and has a great vend for them... in the private families of the gentry round us. She has her days of being in town and then is at a chamber she rents at an inn in Southwark, where she keeps patterns of all her silks and much of her portable goods, for the convenience of her London customers. But her place of residence and where she has her principal warehouse is at Deptford, for the opportunity of getting her goods on shore .... Now my dear I must own that I do not love to encourage these contraband traders ... she has been aboard and often goes abroad in the way of her business.'[10]

Of all contraband textiles lace was the most portable, and of highest value for its small bulk. High-quality lace was of the greatest importance in fashionable dress, and the lacemaking industry which had developed in two areas of the country in particular, South Devon and the midland counties of Buckinghamshire, Northamptonshire and Bedfordshire, was rarely able to produce a lace of a quality approaching the Flemish laces of Mechlin, Valenciennes and Brussels. An act of 1697 had protected the English industry by the prohibition of all foreign laces, but this at once met the opposition of the English woollen industries, as it had resulted in a counter prohibition of English woollen goods in the Low Countries, and the opposition of the retailers of foreign laces. The act was repealed in so far as laces from the Low Countries were concerned, but French lace was still prohibited, which meant that the needlepoint laces of France were still contraband.[11] Although there were from time to time attempts to raise the quality of the English laces to bring them into competition with the imported lace, the industry from this time concentrated on the less fashionable market. The midlands industry, in particular, produced the narrow laces which were worn by such people as Defoe's country grocer's wife, whose lace and edgings came from 'Stony Stratford the first and Great Marlow the last.' The price range of lace of this area, according to two independent witnesses of the 1760s, was from 2d to £1 a yard; and up to 25s a yard.[12] The lace industry was fully organised to sell its lace all over the country. Local merchants collected it from country workers and sold it in London to milliners and haberdashers or had their own chambers there. They also travelled, as wholesale merchants, selling to the retailers of the principal towns, and buying and selling in the markets and fairs of the lacemaking districts. The Rev. William Cole was the friend of two lace merchants of Bletchley, James and Nathaniel Cartwright, who had their lace chamber at the shop of a draper in Ludgate Street. In 1767 Mr Cole wrote in his diary that Nathaniel set off on 25 July 'for his long Journey into the North and by Gloucester, with above £1,000 of Lace.' He returned in September. One of the brothers regularly attended the lace market which at this time was held weekly at Newport Pagnell, and one was in London while the other remained in Buckinghamshire, 'to attend to their Lace-makers.'[13]

The technical processes of Indian chintz had been studied and were gradually being mastered in Europe, particularly in Holland and England and combined with the European technique of printing on cloth from a wood block. Before the end of the seventeenth century printing establishments had been set up near London. This new industry aroused the combined opposition of both the silk and the wool industries. It had at first aimed at taking the place of the Indian chintzes in the fashionable market, but seeing the possibilities of a wider market turned to the production of less expensive printed cottons. In doing this it was competing not so much with the silk industry of fashionable silks as with the cheaper silks and the mixed silk and worsteds and the light-weight worsteds:

> 'The calicoes painted in India were most used by the richer sort of people while the poor continued to wear and use our woollen goods; the calicoes now painted in England are so very cheap and so much the fashion that persons of all qualities and degrees clothe themselves and furnish their houses in great measure with these.'[14]

So excise duties were levied on printed cottons in 1712, doubled in 1714, and in 1721 another act was passed to strengthen the act of 1701 against Indian imports. This now prohibited not only the import and sale, but also the use and wearing of all printed cottons, not only Indian goods; which meant that English printed cottons were also prohibited, except as goods for export.

The English calico printers, now sure of their market, evaded the 1721 act by printing on linen or on mixed fabrics of linen warp and cotton weft, which were outside the prohibition of the 1721 act. There was still opposition to the industry from the woollen interests, expressed continually in contemporary periodicals and pamphlets:

> 'A manufacture of painted linen, which, touching the particular pride and gay humour of the ordinary sort of people intercepts the woollen manufacture which they would otherwise be clothed with ... the poorer sort of people, the servants and the wives and children of the farmers and country people, and of the labouring poor who wear this new fangle are a vast multitude.'[15]

The new development was a great impetus to the linen industry; Irish and Scottish linen was sent to London for printing. In spite of his championship of the woollen industry, Defoe allowed his country grocer's wife not only her gown of Spitalfields silk, but also 'a wrapper or morning gown of Irish linen, printed at London.' Lancashire, where linens and mixed fabrics of cotton and linen were already made, began to do their own printing in the 1760s. There was also printing in the Carlisle area; the gown which Abraham Dent sold to his servant in 1764, 'stamped linen gown, 26s.', may have been of this local manufacture. By 1774 the British industry achieved an act which lifted the prohibition against the home sale of printed, all-cotton goods, although it still remained on imports of painted or printed cottons. British cottons which were printed had to be distinguished by the weaving of three blue threads in their selvedge; these can be seen in the cottons of many surviving gowns.

Linens also were now printed in their place of origin. In 1785 the Glasgow manufacturers presented a petition against a tax on printed linens, and once again the statement is made that these goods now serve the common people:

> 'A very considerable manufacture of low-priced Printed Goods is carried

on in the City of Glasgow ... when the original duty of three pence per square Yard was first imposed on printed linen by the Tenth and Twelfth of Queen Anne, the Consumption of this Article was principally confined to the higher classes of the People and the Tax as originally laid was only meant to reach the Opulent and the Rich, but by successive improvements and by adapting the Coarse fabrics of Printed Linen to the Circumstances of Common People these Goods have become almost universally a great part of the Cloathing of the middle and lower ranks.'[16]

Irish linen was also from the 1750s printed in Ireland as well as being sent to England for printing. By the 1780s evidence from Manchester on cottons supports that from Glasgow on linens that '3 parts out of 4 of printed goods are consumed by the lower class of people.'[17] There was still, however, a market for the better qualities of printed cottons and linens in fashionable undress. Barbara Johnson regularly inserted patterns of printed fabrics in her album—even a rare printed stuff. Between 1751 and 1763 when fabrics are included for every year, she noted three linen or cotton gowns. From 1764, linen, long lawn, cotton, calico or chintz, with their printed patterns appear more often. She distinguished a blue and white printed linen of 1764 as 'copper-plate' and a purple and white one of 1771 in the same way. She noted one of the four chintzes which she had between 1778 and 1781 as an English chintz. There is a gap in her record until 1789 and then till 1792, but after this silk gowns, satin, sarsnet or taffety are in a minority amongst muslin, cotton, calico and gingham. The patterns of her linens and cottons show designs which link them both with contemporary silks and with their Indian sources.[18] In 1778 Mrs Cater saw a friend wearing 'a most beautiful Linnen Gown which I took for a Chinze and cost no more than 27s; it was bought at your Linnen Draper, Mr Husseys and my Mary has fallen in love with it.' This meant that the long-suffering Mrs Williamson was being asked to buy some for her. Two years earlier Mrs Cater had asked her to get 'one of the *new* manufactory which are *Cotten* both ways, have sent a pattern. It is a great deal lighter than a Cotton and the Colours look more lively.'[19] This was the new all-cotton material made possible by the act of 1774, and this rather confusing comment shows that the mixed fabrics had also been called cotton. Betsy Sheridan wrote with pleasure that the gown of Irish lawn which she was wearing in England had been much admired: 'It has been washed three times and appears now if anything better than when new .... It is always taken for a dutch chintz, but I take care to publish its country.'[20] Amongst Lady Grantham's wedding clothes in 1780 were 'one of the Irish Gold Linens, as a drest Polonaise ... and English Chintz and plain and striped Lutestring gowns, that have escaped my memory.'[21] The fashionable demand for these gowns for undress wear gave the industry as a whole a standard of quality and fashion, although a large proportion of its goods went into the markets of common wear.

The stuff manufactures were by this time suffering badly. In Lincolnshire fashionable people attended balls for the encouragement of the woollen manufactures for several years in succession in the 1780s and 1790s. All guests dressed in stuff of the same colour. Lady Banks wrote in 1791: 'I can't say much for the Manufacture, but it was certainly a charming good Meeting. Lady Brownlow is to be our Patroness next year.'[22] Norwich, the main centre of 'women's stuffs' and other worsted fabrics, turned to cotton and muslin manufacture to make good the loss of trade in stuffs: 'The plain Norwich cottons are very like the Manchester of which you once had a gown, which Molly now wears.'[23] Ann Plumptre wrote from Norwich of the success of the new manufacture there:

'The Manufactories have been in so flourishing a state that there has been full employment for the Poor all this Winter. I said Manufactories for upon the decay of the stuff Manufactory they have brought the Cotton Manufactory from Manchester thither, and there are some that carry on a considerable trade in it.'[24]

Even the Indian chintzes never seriously challenged the position of the more richly brocaded silks as the first fabrics of fashion, the fabrics of full-dress wear. The competition of the printed cottons had its effect on the cheaper silks and this was increasingly felt by the 1760s. By the 1780s the changing character of dress brought another fabric into use which was to lessen still further the demand for silks, this time for all but the silks of lightest weight and pattern. The fabric was another quality of linen or cotton, fine muslin or lawn, which was already used in the accessories of women's dress, and also in men's neckwear, but now became a fabric for the gowns themselves, inspired once more by Indian fabrics.

There was, at the beginning of the century, a small industry in Scotland, at Paisley, 'consisting chiefly of Bengals, in imitation of striped muslins' and by the middle of the century 'light goods of all kinds, such as plain, striped, spotted and figured clear lawns; embroidered, plain and spotted handkerchiefs, thread gauzes or catguts.' The same authority, referred to the setting-up of a silk Industry in Paisley in the 1760s, stating that 'Before this thread gauze had been in vogue, but a general mourning ensuing and Indian muslins being used for that purpose, this in great measure put a stop to the Paisley trade.'[25] This is confirmed by Talbot Williamson's advice to his brother on the mourning for George II in 1760: 'You desire 3 yards of gause. It is not the thing. Muslin is the wear and that is 10s a yard.'[26] The making of silk and fine lawn gauzes continued in Paisley; then in the 1780s cotton spinning and weaving was added to the local industries. The technical achievements in cotton spinning had made it possible to produce fine thread at a much cheaper rate and thin light gauzes were now woven in fine cotton rather than linen thread. Although there are only one or two possible examples of

Paisley's silk, linen, or early muslin gauzes surviving from the eighteenth century, the pattern books of the early years of the nineteenth century show a great variety of gauzes and figured muslins, the fashion fabrics of those years.

In England Samuel Oldknow, in his mills near Manchester, was also working on the production of muslins (Fig. 87). Advice on the London market came to him from Samuel Salte, a London warehouse man: 'Turn your weavers to muslins ... we now send you some patterns drawn (from) Different articles of Muslin come over as presents to the People of Fashion.' Oldknow worked hard on the quality of his muslins and Salte continued to advise him: 'The 4/4 and 6/4 spotted muslins will always do, well-executed; vary the spot, barley-corns, leaves and other little fancy objects, in short an infinite variety of small figured and sprigged muslins may yet be made.' Bowles and Birch customers, through Salte, in 1787 were critical and compared his work unfavourably with the Scotch muslins, 'the spotted 6/4 muslins. We have plenty from Scotland, why can't you as well do them as the Scotch people.'[27] Lady Louisa Stuart wrote from Lanarkshire in 1800: 'Tho all the best British muslins are made in this very county, I daresay the best are sold in London.'[28] For a short while the weavers of these patterned muslins and fine cambrics were in demand and enjoyed higher wages than those employed in the weaving of other cottons and linens. The spread of the fashion of wearing muslin gowns tempted many manufacturers to abandon their efforts to meet the tastes of people of fashion and settle for a middle market, for the muslins never had quite the range of wear of the printed cottons and linens.

Norwich, having taken to the cotton manufactory, did produce some high-quality muslins: 'I propose bringing you a very fine *Silver* Gown. It is a new Norwich manufactory. Everybody is ordering them: the whole gown comes to about 7 guineas and looks like a beautiful magnificent gold muslin.'[29] There was also a manufacture of muslin at Canterbury. Barbara Johnson has a small pattern of Canterbury muslin in her album, which is pale blue in colour and closely woven. Mrs Lybbe Powys bought muslin at Canterbury in 1798: 'Each of us bought a summer white Canterbury muslin of the famous Mr Calloway, as all the ladies, in compliment to his manufactory, intended to appear in them at the balls.'[30]

The heavier silks, the mixed silks and worsteds including the Irish poplin were completely unsuitable for the flowing lines of the new style; and their industries suffered through this change, gradual though it had been. The thin worsted stuffs could have achieved the new line, but except in the artificial efforts of the 'Stuff Balls', they remained only for winter undress of the gentry, with their cheaper qualities in common wear with the cottons and linens. It was soft clinging muslins which shaped the new style. Plain muslins were made costly by fine embroidery, mainly in white, or in gold and silver thread. Thin light

silks, in pale colours were used for slips beneath the transparent muslin gowns.

In common dress the disappearance of woollen fabrics, as the printed linens and cottons established themselves, was gradual. The quilted petticoat of black calimanco which Defoe referred to in the 1720s was still seen in the London streets in the 1780s, and the wearing of a stuff petticoat with a linen or cotton gown continued. Calimanco, a thinly woven worsted, often glazed, one of the Norwich stuffs, had been a popular fabric of common wear in women's gowns and petticoats and men's waistcoats. It was made plain, striped, and damasked and brocaded like silk. Defoe's phrase, 'the easy and gay dress of the callicoes', reveals the qualities of their widespread appeal. Some woollen stuffs had brightness of colour and pattern, but the printed cottons and linens had a new freedom and gaiety. Their floral patterns, though simpler, more repetitive in design and limited in colour than fashionable chintzes, still reflected the decorative taste of the time and held something of the exotic quality of their Indian source. They had in addition an important practical quality. They could be washed without damage so that they could constantly present a fresh appearance. Although, at first, one of Defoe's arguments against them was that they would increase the consumption by servants of soap—which was taxed (in Ann Cook's account no maid was allowed to wash a gown more frequently than once a quarter)—this was a quality which made them attractive to their wearers.[31]

Printed linen and cotton contributed a good deal to the cleanliness of common dress. They were not the first washable materials to have a place in outer dress. Plain fabrics like dimity, a twilled linen and cotton, later cotton only, was used for women's bodices or waistcoats, which either covered the stays or were worn in their place, beneath the woollen gowns of the beginning of the century, the 'kersey gown and a white dimity waistcoat' of Charles Johnson's *The Country Lasses*. Edward Kitchiner had patterned dimity in his shop, '30 yds of flowered and stript Dimity' in 1713, at 1s 1d a yard. The village girls of *The Life and Adventures of Sir Launcelot Greaves* in their Maytime dress wore 'clean short dimity petticoats' with their 'gawdy gowns of printed cotton.' Linen shifts, caps, handkerchiefs and aprons were worn by women, linen shirts and neck-cloths by men. French cambrics, which were prohibited by a series of acts in the 1740s and 1750s, and cambrics from Holland were the linens of fashion, but the less expensive Dutch and German linens and Irish and Scotch linen were used in common dress. The demand for linen for printing improved the quality and encouraged the flow of linen from Ireland and Scotland so that by the 1770s the proportion of foreign linen coming into the country had fallen. The wearing of clean linen was one of the features of English dress noted by foreign visitors and its wear extended, though lessening in quality and quantity, through all ranks, down to the two new shirts and one new

87 *Samuel Oldknow, muslin manufacturer, 1790–2 wearing the contrast of dark greenish blue coat and light buff-coloured waistcoat and breeches.*
*J. Wright of Derby*

88 *Inscribed 'A man in Wiltshire who was in the habit of mowing two acres of grass pr. day.' This drawing shows a well-made shirt, confirming the contemporary comments on the wearing of linen by common people. James Ward*

shift a year of Davies's labouring people of the 1790s. Gilbert White wrote in 1778: 'The use of linen changes of shirts or shifts, in the room of sordid and filthy woollen, long worn next to the skin, is a matter of neatness, comparatively modern.'[32] (Fig. 88). Overseers of the poor at the beginning of the century supplied two or three shirts or shifts to their pauper apprentices; it is possible that these undergarments could sometimes have been woollen, but Gilbert White, who was born in 1720, may have been thinking back as far as the older generation of his youth. In 1782 Moritz, when in London, wrote: 'I rarely see even a fellow with a wheelbarrow who has not a shirt on; and then too such an one, as shows it has been washed.'[33] A Russian traveller in London 1789-90 wrote of 'the unusual cleanliness and tidiness in the dress even of the simplest people.'[34] Francis Place, looking back from the 1820s to his childhood—he was born in 1771—had no doubt that the last quarter of the century and the early years of the nineteenth century had seen a striking improvement in cleanliness. He remembered the wives and daughters of the journeymen and shopkeepers of London in their leather stays and quilted camlet petticoats, 'worn day by day until they were rotten, and never washed. A great change was produced by improvements in the manufacture of cotton goods.'[35]

The marketing of textiles, of the woollen cloths and, to an even greater extent, of the printed linens and cottons was a factor of some practical importance in determining the dress of the common people. At the beginning of the century the principal manufacturers, those who—in Defoe's definition—make or cause to be made, goods for others to sell, sold their goods to wholesale dealers in London, and at the markets held in local centres. Celia Fiennes described the market for serges which she saw in Exeter in 1698, where piles of serges and woollen yarns for weaving them lay in long lines in the market hall. Samuel Curwen was in Exeter in 1776 at the time of a two-day fair for the sale of cloth: 'Kerseys, duroys, narrow cloths, shalloons, druggetts, serges, etc exposed both in the Inns and streets.' Celia Fiennes also noted the markets at Colchester where Bayes were bought to go to London; at Norwich with the 'Crapes, Callimanco and Damaskes, which is the whole business of the place ... fine and thin and glossy'; at Kendal for linsey woolseys and Kendal cottons, 'the Scotch use them for their plodds [plaids]', for this was woollen cloth, that is 'coating', not cotton; at Manchester, where the goods sold at this time were 'Linen Cloth, Cotten Tickings, Incles [Tapes]'.[36] Much of the cloth she saw would be exported, as it would throughout the century. For the home consumption a great deal went through the London wholesalers for redistribution to drapers' shops all over the country. Describing the cloth market at Leeds in the 1720s, Defoe said that the clothing manufactured in the West Riding, although also exported, was everywhere made use of in the home market, 'for the cloathing of the ordinary people who cannot go to the price of the fine medley cloths

made . . . in the western counties of England.'[37] The northern merchants
whose goods were the woollens of Yorkshire and later the printed linens
and cottons of Lancashire had another method of distribution, by
travelling merchants who carried goods by pack-horse to fairs and
markets in the principal towns, selling there to the country shopkeepers
and to the chapmen and pedlars who carried the goods into the villages
and hamlets. Later they travelled for orders, sending their goods by
waggon on the improved roads of the turnpike trusts.

Through the travelling merchants, the London wholesale dealers, and
similar dealers in the principal towns, the varied manufactures of
different districts were well distributed over the country. The country
drapers buying from London warehouses and local markets, sold again
to the pedlars, who were the final link in bringing goods into country
places, helping to create the market for the products of the expanding
textile industries. Their importance to the manufacturers was expressed
in 1785 in the opposition of the 'Manufacturers of Printed Silk, Linen
and Cotton handkerchiefs, callicoes, etc of the Town of Manchester' to
the bill to repeal the acts licensing hawkers:

> 'That many very great advantages have resulted from the said Body of
> Men to the Manufactures of the Town and Neighbourhood of
> Manchester as well as to the Manufactures in other Parts of this
> Kingdom, and the Quantity of Goods purchased by that Class of Dealers
> is much more considerable than may have been apprehended, and, from
> the Mode of their Sale which is generally from House to House in
> Country Villages and Districts remote from Towns where shopkeepers
> reside, great quantities of British Manufactures are sold which otherwise
> would not be disposed of.'[38]

The vigour of the new textile industries found its most profitable return
in supplying the needs of the middling market, expanding into the lower
reaches of this, rather than competing for the much smaller fashionable
market. They knew the value of all the traders who carried their goods
to every possible buyer. The importance of this method of distribution
to their customers was the part it played in bringing, with the goods, the
new fashion which the goods expressed, breaking down the isolation of
country places. By the end of the century the wearing of printed cottons,
and even white cambric muslin, had brought fashionable women's dress
and the dress of women of the common people closer than ever in fabric
and form. The pattern of selling also ensured that the same fabrics, the
same new items of dress, were carried all over the country; so that these
were available at the same moment in Norfolk or Dorset, and in both
places could be bought and worn wherever there was enough prosperity
for money to be spent on clothes.

# VIII

## *Dress and Society*

The creative influences which influenced dress during the century came from many different sources. People of fashion shaped and developed a personal appearance as a work of art, the most transient of all expressions, within the art of the time which in eighteenth-century England meant a European art, still strongly influenced by the classical culture of the Mediterranean though receiving influences from other parts of the world and making its own variations.

The style of dress for men and women which developed after 1710 and remained with minor variations into the 1750s was, in its clearly defined forms, with firm control both of its human element and surface decoration, in the spirit of the academic classicism which dominated architecture. The dress was, however, to the painter and sculptor unclassical in form, because classical dress itself was a drapery for the body, not a re-shaping of it. Their dilemma and their failure to solve it is revealed in the treatment of dress in many portraits of the time, although fortunately for our visual knowledge of the eighteenth-century appearance, other artists did accept contemporary dress. The new ideas which brought Gothick detail into architecture and revived the dress of Vandyke and Rubens for portrait-painting were expressed also in the actual clothes worn in fashionable masquerades. When Reynolds came to the problem, there was a new approach to classical antiquity, and contemporary dress was already losing its stiffness of form. His compromise, which became the model for a long series of portraits of women, was not only easily accepted, but as they were being painted in the 1760s to the 1780s, the changing dress became closer to the dress of the portraits. So strongly did this image impress itself that when Sophie von la Roche came to England in 1786 she was disappointed not to find English women 'like the originals of Reynold's pictures, nobly and simply attired with Greek coiffures.'[1] There is no way of assessing the influence of this image presented so often by Reynolds and his followers on an already changing style, but the style which emerged in the 1790s was clearly inspired by classical dress, although the movement towards it had another impulse, which again linked dress with art and literature. In

the neo-classicism of the second half of the century there was a romantic impulse, the attempt to discover and re-create a phase of the past: 'That neo-classicism constantly overlaps or fades into romanticism is a fact which it is scarcely necessary to underline.'[2] The literary classicism of the first half of the century already expressed this romantic approach as the poets wrote of country life and natural beauty in terms of the classical pastoral, turning away from the harsh realities of life to recapture a rural past that had never been. These romantic impulses created first the theatrical images of Arcadian princesses and peasants—there was still status in Arcadia—and later the more historically inspired Grecian styles of the end of the century.

Country life, however, had its own direct influence on dress and it was a strong one. For many, though not all, fashionable men and women, country life either in its more active pursuits of riding, hunting, shooting, fishing, walking, or in quiet enjoyment of the natural and man-made beauty of country and parkland, was preferred. The Marchioness Grey wrote of haymaking at Wrest in July 1745:

'I sit under John Dewel's oak to contemplate them, have a book in my pocket, but a cart loading with hay just upon the opposite corner of the canal engrosses my attention. Rest of morning occupation breaking brains over Worke, or relieving them with harpsichord. After dinner, billiards, harpsichord . . . or a bit of work, tea; and walking till night.'

She longed for her return to Wrest in early summer and regretted leaving it in the autumn. Her friend, Catherine Talbot, wrote to her as she was about to set out for London in 1744: 'How can you find it in your heart. . . . to go to so Antipastoral a place?'[3] Love of the country came in part from real experience and enjoyment of it, but it came also from literary response to it; with another image, of classical landscape and inhabitants, merging into the working landscape of the English countryside (Fig. 89). The real country life influenced women's dress by producing the plainer versions worn in the country, which were also worn for walking in town, and the riding habits worn not only for riding but for travelling between town and country. In dress of this kind the decorative element in fabric and form was restrained by the element of use. It was this plainer, practical version which passed most naturally to less fashionable social levels, and had far-reaching effect. The country and its way of life had even stronger influence on the dress of men, where in the same way the physical activities of the countryside demanded a plain version of the fashionable style, with the decorative element diminished and the function of dress, its practical element, emphasised. Some versions proclaimed an interest, a way of life, in which expression of status was ignored, as in the 'Newmarket dress'. The decorative detail such dress developed was often an over-development of the original practical detail, as in the multiplication of capes in Jack Chace's Newmarket frock, 'decorated with a great number of green, red or blue

*89 Summer—Sheep-shearing, c. 1780. The landowner and his family are visiting the shearers; on the right a man and a woman show the romantic idea of a shepherdess; the working shepherdess, without a gown, in tabbed stays and red petticoat, is offering a bowl to the visitors.*
*G. Robertson (detail)*

capes.' The farmer-like dress worn by some peers at the end of the century not only renounced the expression of social status, but identified the wearers with a practical, profitable activity, rather than an activity of leisure.

As these different ways of life modified the expression of status and its decorative art in the dress of the individual, so dress as a whole reflected the preoccupations of society. This movement away from formality and display in men's dress was strengthened by another influence, with political implications, the eighteenth-century idea of liberty. The young men who affected an aggressive negligence in common dress in the 1740s and 1750s expressed a casual rejection of established ways. In the second half of the century a stronger opposition arose from the intellectual convictions which led men to support the American colonies in their fight for independence and the French in their early stages of revolution. Many men of position expressed their revolutionary sympathies by adopting a careless attitude to dress and neglecting all but its essential formalities. Looking back to the early 1780s, Sir Nathaniel Wraxall saw

> 'Fox and his friends, who might be said to dictate to the town, affecting a style of neglect about their persons, and manifesting a contempt of all the usages hitherto established, first threw a sort of discredit on dress .... But though gradually undermined and insensibly perishing of an atrophy, dress never totally fell till the era of Jacobinism and of equality in 1793 and 1794.'[4]

This underlying idea of liberty found expression in another, very different dress, the dress of children. The change which was to create a distinctive dress for children, boys and girls, in the second half of the century, showed the influence of a new idea of childhood. The change has been attributed to the influence of Rousseau's *Emile*, published in 1762. But Rousseau himself had been much influenced by the writings of John Locke, the philosopher of the English Revolution of 1688. Locke's philosophy was based on the idea that man was born with the natural right of freedom, and when he published his *Thoughts on Education* he applied his ideas from the moment of birth, condemning the then widespread practice of cocooning a child in swaddling-clothes and bands, which robbed it of physical freedom. His views were already having their effect by the 1740s. Pamela, in Richardson's novel, reads Locke's book and Richardson devotes several chapters to her comments on it. That Locke's work is introduced into this context shows that his ideas were not only of political and intellectual significance, but were also a pervasive influence in eighteenth-century life. Pamela and her author follow Locke in strong opposition to the practice of swaddling. In this they were supported by the medical opinion of the time. Swaddling-bands were not included amongst the clothing for babies taken into the care of the Foundling Hospital; its medical advisors of the 1740s expressed themselves strongly against swaddling. In 1765 Grosley thought that the good shape, inseparable from the idea of beauty in England, was the result of 'the free and easy manner in which the bodies of children of the present generation have been formed and the little use made of swaddling cloaths or constraint of any sort.'[5] Twenty years later J. W. von Archenholz commented on the children, who were 'never bound up in swaddling-clothes but covered with a thin dress which gives perfect freedom to all their motions.'[6] At about the same time, in an issue of *The Lady's Magazine* in 1785, a doctor wrote that 'the barbarous custom of swaddling children like living mummies is now almost universally laid aside'; it had been laid aside long enough for him to think it necessary to describe the process which he thought many of his readers would never have seen.

The freedom from constraint accepted as natural for the infant extended into the period of childhood. The period between the age of three or four until the age of thirteen or fourteen acquired an identity of its own and its own style of dress. In the first half of the century girls wore for the brief period of infancy simple frocks of linen or muslin, fastening at the back and with a sash at the waist. At the age of three or four they put on a stiff, back-fastening bodice, boned and shaped like the stays of their mothers, with a separate skirt, the form of the stiff-bodied gown of earlier fashion, which gave them a fashionable adult shape until they changed to adult gowns when they were thirteen or fourteen. In everyday dress the frocks continued to be worn. From 1760s the frock and sash began to take over completely. The age for continuing to wear it, in best dress as well as everyday dress, gradually rose, until by the 1780s it was being worn by girls in their early teens in all dress (Fig. 90). Boys had worn frocks until they were breeched; they now acquired an intervening style and a new garment, a garment taken from occupational and common wear. Trousers were worn by sailors and fishermen and sometimes by countrymen, but they had never been an accepted garment for any kind of fashionable wear. They were worn now by boys. As an alternative there was a tight-fitting form, pantaloons, which during the 1780s, when they ended at any point between the knee and ankle, were more closely related to longer forms of breeches, but by the end of the century, like the trousers, these too were ankle-length. A jacket, not a coat, was worn with them, sometimes with a sash at the waist for younger boys. As the jacket grew shorter, rising at the waist as all waistlines were rising, the trousers were buttoned over and on to it. This made the skeleton suit, a distinctive dress for boys between the ages of three and seven or eight for the next forty years.

The significance of these new forms of dress for children is not only that they changed children's dress, but that adult changes were foreshadowed in them and were apparent here before clearly emerging in adult dress. The girls' dress, with its freer bodice and sash was the style which by the end of the 1780s was becoming adult fashion, carrying the same freedom into women's dress; once again women and girls were

dressed alike. Trousers did not remain a fashion for boys alone, but worked their way into men's dress, bringing to it after the end of the century a major change of form, from the coat, waistcoat and breeches of the eighteenth century to the coat, waistcoat and trousers of the nineteenth (Fig. 91).

Commercial and industrial activity, which was in its way also an expression of freedom, was an increasing preoccupation of eighteenth-century society. Its growing importance strengthened the element of use and practical activity in dress. The physical activities of country life had developed plain versions of fashionable dress. Daily application to financial, commercial and industrial activities had developed another, the dress of the merchant and manufacturer. The growing importance of these activities in eighteenth-century life brought a new status to the dress associated with them. This plainer style now expressed wealth, position and power through personal activity and achievement. It is at this point that a break appears between the dress of men and women, a division which is to become more apparent in the nineteenth century. Men's dress now expressed status through activity and achievement and relinquished most of its decorative element; women's still remained the expression of status by leisure achieved by the activity of others, and retained it. Social status was expressed within the new limitations of men's dress, but within the overall restraint of the style, in quality and small subtleties, not in the decorative splendour of the early eighteenth century, except in the increasingly archaic dress of the most formal ceremonial. The decorative element, though greatly diminished, did not at once and everywhere disappear; it remained for some time in the waistcoat, and continued to be expressed in the changing lines of dress as a whole, lines which it shared with women's dress. At the end of the century the same close-fitting line appeared in the clinging white muslins of one and the fine cloth which moulded body and limbs in the other, as the waistline of dress and the cut of coat and waistcoat rose to the same, high level (Fig. 87).

The commercial and industrial activities of the century had other effects on dress. The technical inventions which made possible the production of cheaper fabrics in large quantities, the type of fabrics produced and the marketing of them did not help to create fashion, but they were important practical influences in its spread. The distribution of fashion was made easier by the improvements which had been made by the second half of the century to main and other roads. The Rev. William Cole wrote in 1766 that the roads which linked Bletchley with the main road, Watling Street, at Fenny Stratford, 'were almost impassable when I first came to the Parish, and are now very good.'[7] Even at this time the carriage of goods between London and parts of the country was quicker than might be expected. In the 1730s some of the goods carried from London to the Purefoys in Buckinghamshire were three days on the road, but in the 1740s Mrs Eagles, a Buckingham

*90 Lady Palk with two of her children. Robert Palk was Governor of Madras and a supporter of Warren Hastings. His son was born c. 1766 which would make the boy shown here about three or four. He is wearing the wrapping gown which boys wore between the frock of infancy and their breeching at about this age. The girl, a few years older, now continues to wear the sashed white frock of infancy as a young girl's fashion.*
*N. Dance*

*91 Gentleman and Two Children, 1799. The gentleman has the raised waistline shown in the cut of coat and waistcoat: the boy wears the ankle-length pantaloons soon to take the place of the breeches of adult wear.*
*H. Edridge*

carrier, left the George Inn, Smithfield, at four o'clock on Tuesday morning and delivered goods at Shalstone, near Buckingham, on Wednesday evening; and Zachary Mead working from the same inn, left on Friday and arrived on Saturday.[8] When Lady Polwarth was staying at Staughton near Kimbolton, she sent her mother in London directions for getting a new cap to her, either by waggon which was slow, as it set out on Saturday and reached Staughton on Tuesday morning, or by the Kimbolton coach, which left London at six o'clock in the morning, twice a week and was at Staughton by five o'clock in the afternoon.[9]

Commercial activity had another influence, through its effect on the lives of those who had previously been more self-sufficient in producing their own clothing. Women who had spun to provide cloth for their families now worked for wages as, first in their own homes, then in factories, they produced fabrics which would be sold all over the country, which they themselves would buy, part of the new market for the mass-produced fabrics they were helping to make.

The end of the century saw the beginning of the journalism of fashion. The small pocket or memorandum books which were issued yearly from the middle of the century usually contained one or two small plates, showing examples of dress for the year. Barbara Johnson included several of these plates in her album. Nancy Woodforde had copies of *The Ladies' Pocket Book* which cost 1s. Notes on current fashions appeared from time to time in such journals as *The Gentleman's Magazine* and *The London Magazine,* but usually as a subject for comment. When *The Lady's Magazine* appeared in the 1770s it did not at first give space to fashion news as such. Notes on fashion began to appear after a few years, at first irregularly and then as an established monthly feature. At the end of the 1790s there were other journals published particularly for women; *The Lady's Monthly Museum* issued one or two coloured plates with fashion notes based on them each month. A series of plates, with descriptive notes, *The Fashions of London and Paris*, was also published from 1798; the notes in *The Lady's Magazine* often relate to these. These two series of coloured plates were more informative than the small plates of the pocket books, but they were pale shadows of plates published in France and of the finest English fashion publication of the time—probably of any time—fashion illustrations for the fashionable, the monthly issue of plates with commentary by Nicholas Heideloff, *The Gallery of Fashion*, published from 1794. It was not until the early years of the nineteenth century that fashion for its own sake became a subject for journalism and the business of spreading fashion by the printed word began.

Fashion news had been spread with surprising effectiveness throughout the country by a network of letters. Anyone who visited London or a place like Bath was expected to send news of fashions to relatives and friends at home; and not only news. Those who lived in

London or any convenient centre bought items of dress for friends and relatives in the country, and also carried out complicated commissions in dressmaking for them. The clothes themselves had a wide distribution through mercers, drapers, milliners, tailors and mantua-makers, who brought new fashions to their local centres. A mobile and fairly fashion-conscious gentry, having acquired their own clothes and knowledge of fashion, were the people of fashion for the less mobile, less well-informed ranks below them, their neighbours in country town, village and hamlet. They presented generally the simpler, less ephemeral versions of fashion, which were more easily understood, more practical to achieve. The actual clothes of their everyday wear often became dress wear for those in the ranks below. However great the differences in dress from the higher social levels to the lower, between the qualities which produce a minor work of art to the qualities of the working version, dress at the end of the eighteenth century presented a single style.

# Notes

## Introduction

1 Lady Newdigate-Newdegate, *The Cheverels of Cheverel Manor*, 1898, p.101
2 Lady Mary Wortley Montagu, *The Complete Letters*, Ed. Robert Halsband, 1965, III, p.35

## I Crown and Court

1 Mary Granville, Mrs Delany, *The Autobiography and Correspondence*, Ed. Lady Llanover, 1861–2, I, p. 138
2 *ibid.*, pp. 436, 437
For a full account of the fabrics of this wedding see N. Rothstein 'God Bless This Choye', *Costume* 11, 1977, pp. 56–72
3 Frances, Countess of Hartford and Henrietta Louisa, Countess of Pomfret, *Correspondence*, 1736–1741, 1805, I, p.225
4 Duchess of Northumberland, *The Diaries of a Duchess*, Ed. J. Greig, 1926, pp. 28, 31, 36
5 Mrs Delany, *op. cit.*, II, p. 28
6 Countess of Hartford, *loc.cit.*
7 Mrs Delany, *op.cit.*, II, p.297
8 Mrs Montagu, *Her Letters and Friendships*, Ed. R. Blunt, 1923, I, p.181
9 *ibid.*, p.83
10 Mrs Delany, *op.cit.*, II, p.147
11 *Verney Letters of the Eighteenth Century* from the MSS at Claydon House, Ed. Margaret Maria, Lady Verney, 1930, II, p.145
12 Mrs Delany, *op.cit.*, II, p.9
13 Countess of Hartford, *op.cit.*, I, p.36
14 Lady Jane Coke, *Letters to her friend Mrs Eyre*, Ed. Mrs A. Rathoborne, 1899, p.123
15 Mrs Montagu, *op.cit.*, I, p.96
16 Lady Mary Coke, *The Letters and Journals of Lady Mary Coke*, 1889–96, II, p.177
17 Mrs Delany, *op.cit.*, III, p.28
18 Mrs Montagu, *op.cit.*, I, p.218
19 Lady Louisa Stuart, *Gleanings from an Old Portfolio*, Correspondence between Lady Louisa Stuart and her sister Caroline, Countess of Portarlington . . ., Ed. Mrs G. Clark, 1895, II, p.28
20 Countess of Hartford, *op.cit.*, II, p.184
21 Mrs Delany, *op. cit.*, I, p. 198
22 Wrest Park Papers, Beds CRO L/30/9/3/40
23 Emily, Duchess of Leinster, *Correspondence*, Ed. B. Fitzgerald, Dublin, 1953, I, p. 309
24 Wrest Park Papers, L/30/9/3/41

25    *ibid.*, L/30/13/12/36

26    Sophie von la Roche, *Sophie in London, 1786, 1933, p.218*

27    Wrest Park Papers, L/31/137, 138

28    Mrs Delany, *op. cit.*, II, p.224

29    Wrest Park Papers, L/30/9/111/254, 173

30    Lady Louisa Stuart, *Selections from her Manuscripts*, Ed. J. A. Home,
        Edinburgh, 1899, p.187

31    Fanny Burney, *The Journals and Letters*, Ed. J. Hemlow, 1972–   , IV,
        p.292

32    Maria Josepha Holroyd, *The Girlhood of Maria Josepha Holroyd*, Ed. J. A.
        Adeane, 1896, p. 373

33    *The Spectator*, No. 145, 1711

34    Sarah Byng Osborn, *Letters*, 1930, p.8

35    Mrs Delany, *op. cit.*, II, pp. 28, 72, III, p.250

36    Wrest Park Papers, L/30/9/110/10

37    Mrs Delany, *op. cit.*, II, p.199

38    Wrest Park Papers, L/30/14/333/88, 100, 214

39    *ibid.*, L/30/9/97/98

40    Maria Josepha Holroyd, *op. cit.*, p. 31 ; Horace Walpole, *Correspondence*,
        Yale Edition XI, 1944, p.284 n.11, quoting St James Chronicle

41    Mary Hamilton . . . *Letters and Diaries*, Ed. E. & F. Anson, 1925, pp. 104,
        106

42    Samuel Curwen, *The Journal of Samuel Curwen, Loyalist*, Ed. A. Oliver,
        Salem, Massachusetts, 1972, II, pp. 769, 770

43    Lady Louisa Stuart, *Gleanings . . .* , pp. 117–18

44    The Rev. James Woodforde, *The Diary of a Country Parson*, Ed. J.
        Beresford, 1924–31, III, p. 128

45    Samuel Curwen, *op. cit.*, p. 769

46    Mary Hamilton, *op. cit.*, p. 51

47    Lady Mary Coke, *op. cit.*, III, p.68

48    Lichtenberg's *Visits to England*, Ed. M. L. Mare and W. H. Quarrell,
        Oxford, 1938, p.79

49    Mary Frampton, *Journal*, Ed. H. G. Mundy, 3rd ed. 1886, p. 117

50    Mrs Delany, *op. cit.*, I, p.146

51    Egmont Mss, *Diary of the first Earl of Egmont*, HMC, 1920, p. 448

52    Mrs Delany, *op. cit.*, III, p.34

53    Lady Jane Coke, *op. cit.*, p.95

54    Williamson Letters, Beds CRO, M/10/2/246/48

55    Lady Mary Coke, *op. cit.*, II, p. 296

56    Wrest Park Papers, L/30/11/123/22

57    *ibid.*, L/30/11/122/76 ; L/30/14/333/101 ; L/30/9/111/116 ; L/30/11/240/40 ;
        L/30/9/81/108

## II   People of Fashion

1    Mrs Delany, *op. cit.*, III, p. 591 ; *ibid.*, p.582

2    Lord Chesterfield, *Letters*, Ed. Lord Mahon, 1892, I, p. 250

3    Samuel Richardson, *History of Sir Charles Grandison*, 1902 ed., VI, p. 163

4    Lichtenberg, *op. cit.*, p. 33

5    Lady Jane Coke, *op. cit.*, p. 155

6  Wrest Park Papers, L/30/9/3/41; L/30/13/12/36

7  Lady Jane Coke, *op. cit.*, p. 83

8  The Hon. Mrs Edward Boscawen, *Admiral's Wife*, Ed. Cecil Aspinall–
   Oglander, 1940, p. 61

9  Wrest Park Papers, Letter 3240; 3212

10 Count Frederick Kielmansegge, *Diary of a Journey to England in the Years
   1761–1762*, 1902, p. 125

11 Mrs Papendiek, *Court and Private Life in the Time of Queen Charlotte*, Ed.
   Mrs V. D. Broughton, 1887, I, p. 218

12 E. Maxtone Grahame, *The Beautiful Mrs Graham and the Cathcart Circle*,
   1927, p. 94

13 Wrest Park Papers, L/30/11/240/13; L/30/16/16/19; L/30/9/111/173

14 Betsy Sheridan, *Journal*, Ed. W. Le Fanu, 1960, p. 59

15 Mrs Delany, *op. cit.*, 2nd series, 1862, I, p. 202

16 E. Maxtone Grahame, *op. cit.*, p. 92

17 John Hervey, 1st Earl of Bristol, *Diary . . .*, Wells, 1894, pp. 180–2

18 Samuel Richardson, *History of Sir Charles Grandison*, VI, p. 114

19 Lord Chesterfield, *Letters*, I, p. 335

20 The Rev. James Woodforde, *op. cit.*, II, p. 139

21 Wrest Park Papers, L/30/14/333/101, 214, 96, 185

22 The Hon. Mrs Edward Boscawen, *op. cit.*, p. 136

23 T. Smollett, *The Adventures of Peregrine Pickle*, 1751 (1964 ed.), p. 96

24 Horace Walpole, *Correspondence*, Yale, ed. IX, p. 338

25 *The Orrery Papers*, Ed. The Countess of Cork and Orrery, 1903, p. 44

26 *The Spectator*, No. 277

27 Henrietta, Countess of Suffolk, *Letters . . .*, 1824, I, p. 269

28 Wrest Park Papers, L/30/9/3/6, 7

29 *ibid.*, L/30/14/333/88; L/30/14/111/2

30 C. de Saussure, *A Foreign View of England in the Reigns of George I and
   George II*, 1902, p.113

31 M. Grosley, *A Tour to London . . .*, 1772, p. 87

32 F. de la Rochefoucauld, *A Frenchman in England 1784*, 1933, p. 22

33 Lady Jane Coke, *op. cit.*, pp. 36, 42, 83, 134

34 C. de Saussure, *op. cit.*, p. 203

35 Lady Mary Wortley Montagu, *The Complete Letters*, I, p. 439

36 Wrest Park Papers, L/30/11/122/71

37 Lady Hartford, *op. cit.*, III, p. 292

38 Madame du Bocage, *Letters Concerning England, Holland and Italy*, 1770,
   pp. 9, 28

39 Wrest Park Papers, L/30/11/122/303

40 *The Spectator*, No. 14, 1711

41 Lady Mary Coke, *op. cit.*, II, pp. 361–2

42 Wrest Park Papers, L/30/13/12/48

43 Lady Mary Coke, *op. cit.*, III, p. 82

44 The Noels and the Milbankes, *Their Letters for Twenty–Five Years, 1767–
   1792*, Ed. M. Elwin, 1967, p. 93

45 A. Heal, *London Tradesmen's Cards of the XVIII Century*, 1925, Pl. XXII

46 Wrest Park Papers, L/30/11/122/74; L/30/9/56/15; L/30/9/97/159

47 Betsy Sheridan, *op. cit.*, p. 166

48 Horace Walpole, *op. cit.*, XVII, p. 338

49 Wrest Park Papers, L/30/9a/2, p. 22

50 Samuel Richardson, *History of Sir Charles Grandison*, I, p. 167

51 Wrest Park Papers, L/30/9a/6/113; Lady Jane Coke, *op. cit.*, p. 123

52 Wrest Park Papers, L/30/9/60/71; L/30/9/97/98; L/30/9/111/254; L/30/14/333/171, 194

53 O. Goldsmith, *The Vicar of Wakefield*, 1766, EML ed., p. 85

54 *The Guardian*, No. 149 (John Gay), 1713

55 Wrest Park Papers, L/30/9/60/9

56 Mrs Delany, *op. cit.*, II, p. 513

57 Lady Mary Wortley Montagu, *op. cit.*, II, p. 21; Town Eclogues, 1716

58 Mrs Delany, *op. cit.*, II, p. 294

59 Lady Hartford, *op. cit.*, I, p. 225

60 Mrs Delany, *op. cit.*, III, p. 399

61 *ibid.*, I, p. 284

62 *The Spectator*, No. 145, 1711

63 Lady Hartford, *op. cit.*, III, p. 292

64 Wrest Park Papers, L/30/11/122/155

65 Horace Walpole, *op. cit.*, IX, p. 235

66 Lady Mary Coke, *op. cit.*, III, p. 116

67 Noels and Milbankes, *op. cit.*, p. 265

68 *ibid.*, p. 141

69 Wrest Park Papers, L/30/15/54/232

70 John Hervey, 1st Earl of Bristol, *op. cit.*, pp. 151, 153, 154, 155, 156

71 J. Swift, *Journal to Stella*, Ed. H. Williams, 1974, I, p. 105

72 Claver Morris, *Diary of a West Country Physician*, Ed. E. Hobhouse, Rochester, 1934, May 20, 1726

73 John Byng, *The Torrington Diaries*, Ed. C. B. Andrews, 1934, II, p. 49

74 Emily, Duchess of Leinster, *op. cit.*, I, p. 357

75 Mrs Delany, *op. cit.*, II, p. 139

76 The Hon. Mrs Edward Boscawen, *op. cit.*, p. 152

77 Lord Chesterfield, *Miscellaneous Works*, 1777, IV, p. 305

78 Horace Walpole, *op. cit.*, X, pp. 144, 146

79 C. de Saussure, *op. cit.*, p. 203

80 Madame du Bocage, *op. cit.*, pp. 9, 71

81 M. Grosley, *op. cit.*, p. 254

82 Lady Mary Coke, *op. cit.*, II, p. 20, III, p. 178

83 M. Grosley, *op. cit.*, p. 159

84 Wrest Park Papers, L/30/13/12/47

85 Betsy Sheridan, *op. cit.*, p. 59

86 M. Grosley, *op. cit.*, p. 254

87 Lady Hartford, *op. cit.*, II, p. 222

88 Wrest Park Papers, L/30/9/111/22; L/30/11/122/41

89 Mrs Montagu, *op. cit.*, I, pp. 339, 333

90 *The Guardian*, No. 149, 1713

91 Samuel Pepys, *Diary*, Ed. R. Latham and W. R. Matthews, 1970– , VII, p. 162, 12 June 1666

92 Z. C. von Uffenbach, *London in 1710*, Ed. W. H. Quarrell and Margaret Mare, 1934, p. 106

93 E. Maxtone Grahame, *op. cit.*, p. 94

94  Lady Mary Wortley Montagu, *op. cit.*, I, p. 313
95  Henrietta, Countess of Suffolk, *op. cit.*, II, p. 98
96  Wrest Park Papers, L/30/9/60/118
97  *ibid.*, L/30/11/122/106; L/30/9/60/82; L/30/13/12/47
98  Mrs Delany, *op. cit.*, I, pp. 588, 593
99  *ibid.*, III, 2nd series, p. 151; M. Hamilton, *op. cit.*, p. 222
100  C. de Saussure, *op. cit.*, pp. 113, 114–16
101  The Orrery Papers, *op. cit.*, p. 127
102  Wrest Park Papers, L/30/14/333/96
103  J. W. von Archenholz, *A Picture of England*, 1789, II, p. 115
104  P. Kalm, *Account of his Visit to England in 1748*, Ed. J. Lucas, 1892, p. 52
105  Samuel Curwen, *op. cit.*, II, p. 887
106  C. P. Moritz, *Travels of Carl Philipp Moritz in England in 1782*, 1924 (rep. of 1795 trans.), p. 53
107  Samuel Curwen, *op. cit.*, II, p. 930
108  Betsy Sheridan, *op. cit.*, p. 119
109  Sir Nathaniel William Wraxall, *The Historical and Posthumous Memoirs*, Ed. H. B. Wheatley, 1844, II, pp. 269, 2
110  Lord Chesterfield, *Letters*, I, pp. 249–50
111  J. Macky, *A Journey Through England*, 5th ed. 1732, I, pp. 163–4
112  F. de la Rochefoucauld, *op. cit.*, p. 28
113  Samuel Curwen, *op. cit.*, II, p. 770
114  Mrs Delany, *op. cit.*, I, p. 69; III, pp. 261, 298
115  Betsy Sheridan, *op. cit.*, p. 142
116  *The Wentworth Papers*, 1705–1739, 1883, p. 124
117  Mrs Delany, *op. cit.*, II, p. 478; I, pp. 96, 100
118  Wrest Park Papers, L/30/11/122/195; L/30/13/9/28; L/30/9/81/12; L/30/11/240/8
119  The Hon. Mrs Edward Boscawen, *op. cit.*, p. 48
120  Wrest Park Papers, L/30/9/17/167
121  Mrs Delany, *op. cit.*, 2nd series, II, p. 572
122  *The Jerningham Letters*, Ed. E. Castle, 1896, I, p. 23
123  *The Wentworth Papers, op. cit.*, p. 304
124  Wrest Park Papers, L/30/11/122/297

## III   The Gentry

1  *The Spectator* No. 129, 1711
2  Nicholas Blundell, *The Great Diurnal of Nicholas Blundell* of Little Crosby, Lancashire, Lancs. and Ches. Rec. Soc., 1968, I, 1702–1711, pp. 314–16, 111, 248; *Blundell's Diary and Letter Book*, 1702–1720, Ed. M. Blundell, Liverpool, 1952, pp. 180, 167, 179, 256
3  The Rev. Wm. Cole, *The Blecheley Diary of the Rev. William Cole*, Ed. F. G. Stokes, 1931, p. 44
4  *The Purefoy Letters*, 1735–1753, Ed. G. Eland, 1931, *passim*
5  S. Richardson, *Clarissa*, 1747–8, EML ed. 1962, IV, pp. 497, 466; II, p. 289; I, pp. 207, 376; II, p. 525; III, pp. 310, 445
6  F. Burney, *Journals and Letters*, Ed. J. Hemlow, Oxford, 1972, II, p. 129

7   The Williamson Letters, Beds CRO, M/10/2/128; M/10/2/246/84;
        M/10/2/162; M/10/4/72; M/10/4/84; M/10/4/116; M/10/2/246/113;
        M/10/2/129; M/10/2/246/122

8   *John Salusbury of Leighton Buzzard, 1757–9* in J. Godber ed. *Some
        Bedfordshire Diaries*, Beds. Hist. Rec. Soc. XL, 1960, pp. 46–94

9   The Williamson Letters, *op. cit.*, M/10/4/53, 14

10  F. de la Rochefoucauld, *op. cit.*, pp. 56–7, 162

11  J. Austen, *Letters to her Sister Cassandra and Others*, Ed. R. W. Chapman,
        1932, 2nd ed. 1952, p. 11: *Northanger Abbey*, Oxford ed., 1933, p. 45

12  T219. 1973

13  The Rev. James Woodforde, *The Diary of a Country Parson*, 1758–1802,
        Ed. J. Beresford, 1924–31, 5 vols. *passim*: Woodforde Papers and
        Diaries, Ed. D. H. Woodforde, 1932, *Diary of Nancy Woodforde*, 1792,
        *passim*

14  C. de Saussure, *op. cit.*, p. 232

15  *The Purefoy Letters*, *op. cit.*, II, pp. 216, 217, 323

16  The Williamson Letters, *op. cit.*, M/2/246/92, 93; M/10/4/67, 87, 76, 54

17  J. Woodforde, *op. cit.*, III, pp. 25, 26, 28, 94, 96, V, p. 415

18  Dudley Ryder, *Diary 1715–6*, Ed. W. Matthews, 1934, pp. 18–19

19  Lord Chesterfield, *Letters* V (Essays), p. 285

20  D. Ryder, *op. cit.*, pp. 131, 66, 356

21  Mrs Delany, *op. cit.*, I, p. 556

22  C. de Saussure, *op. cit.*, p. 203

23  Mrs Delany, *op. cit.*, II, p. 147

24  Catherine Hutton, *Reminiscences of a Gentlewoman of the Last Century*,
        Ed. Mrs C. H. Beale, 1891, pp. 30, 117, 33

25  D. Defoe, *The Complete English Tradesman*, 1726, I, pp. 245, 34

26  R. Steele, *The Funeral*, II, 1

27  D. Defoe, *op. cit.*, I, p. 77

28  Francis Coventry, *Pompey the Little*, 1752, Oxford ed. 1974, p. 184

29  The Williamson Letters, *op. cit.*, M/10/2/126

30  C. de Saussure, *op. cit.*, p. 323

31  J. W. von Archenholz, *A Picture of England*, 1789, II, p. 115

32  C. P. Moritz, *op. cit.*, p. 83

33  Arthur Young, *Autobiography of Arthur Young*, Ed. M. Betham–Edwards,
        1898, p. 60

34  M. Grosley, *op. cit.*, p. 154

35  C. P. Moritz, *op. cit.*, pp. 49–50

36  F. A. Wendeborn, *A View of England towards the Close of the Eighteenth
        Century*, 1786, Eng. ed. 1791, I, pp. 193, 224

37  Samuel Curwen, *op. cit.*, passim

38  Sylas Neville, *Diary 1767–1788*, Ed. B. Cozens–Hardy, Oxford, 1950,
        p. 38

39  Mrs Montagu, *op. cit.*, II, p. 16

40  J. Woodforde, *op. cit.*, II, p. 273

41  Wrest Park Papers, *op. cit.*, L/30/9/97/192

42  J. Macky, *op. cit.*, II, p. 238

43  Mrs Montagu, *op. cit.*, II, p. 102

44  C. Hutton, *op. cit.*, pp. 36, 21

45  Samuel Curwen, *op. cit.*, I, p. 366, II, p. 628

46  William Hutton, *Life of William Hutton and the History of the Hutton Family*, (1816), Ed. L. Jewitt, 1872, pp. 164, 300
47  C. Hutton, *op. cit.*, pp. 29, 31
48  Lady Sarah Lennox, *The Life and Letters of*, 1745–1826, 1901, p. 145
49  Lady Mary Coke, *op. cit.*, II, p. 61
50  M. Hamilton, *op. cit.*, p. 48
51  J. Macky, *op. cit.*, I, pp. 117–18, 140
52  *The Guardian*, No. 149, 1713
53  T. Smollett, *op. cit.*, p. 43
54  Celia Fiennes, *The Journeys of Celia Fiennes*, Ed. C. Morris, 1947, p. 19
55  T. Smollett, *op. cit.*, p. 44
56  F. Burney, *Evelina*, 1778, Oxford ed. 1968, p. 393
57  The Noels and the Milbankes, *op. cit.*, p. 35
58  Mrs Montagu, *op. cit.*, II, p. 81
59  B. Sheridan, *op. cit.*, p. 187
60  C. Anstey, *The New Bath Guide*, 1766, 1970 ed., p. 24
61  Lady Newdigate–Newdegate, *op. cit.*, pp. 16, 36
62  Wrest Park Papers, *op. cit.*, L/30/11/122/121, 301
63  The Noels and Milbankes, *op. cit.*, p. 204
64  Samuel Curwen, *op. cit.*, I, p. 208
65  Lady Jane Coke, *op. cit.*, p. 54
66  Wrest Park Papers, *op. cit.*, L/30/9/56/91
67  Lady Newdigate–Newdegate, *op. cit.*, p. 202
68  The Orrery Papers, *op. cit.*, p. 86
69  T. Smollett, *op. cit.*, p. 40

## IV   Servants

1   F. de la Rochefoucauld, *op. cit.*, p. 25
2   G. S. Thomson, *The Russells in Bloomsbury, 1669–1771*, 1940, p. 238
3   Beds CRO, PO 13, pp. 68–71
4   S. Richardson, *Clarissa*, *op. cit.*, III, p. 103
5   *Verney Letters*, *op. cit.*, I, p. 173
6   G. S. Thomson, *op. cit.*, pp. 237, 263
7   F. Burney, *The Early Diary of Frances Burney*, 1768–1778, Ed. A. R. Ellis, 1889, II, p. 139
8   *Verney Letters*, *op.cit.*, I, p. 34
9   Sir Walter Calverley, *The Notebook of Sir Walter Calverley*, Surtees Society, 1886, pp. 102–3
10  N. Blundell, *Great Diurnal, op. cit.*, App. B, pp. 314–16; *Diary and Letter Book*, *op. cit.*, p. 102
11  *The Purefoy Letters, op. cit.*, I, pp. 134, 137, 147; II, pp. 302, 307, 310, 309
12  W. Cole, *op. cit.*, pp. 70–1
13  J. Woodforde, *op. cit.*, II, p. 212; IV, p. 29; V, p. 249
14  J. Macdonald, *Memoirs of an Eighteenth-Century Footman*, Ed. J. Beresford, 1927, pp. 180, 71.
15  J. Smollett, *Humphrey Clinker*, *op. cit.*, p. 103
16  J. Woodforde, *op. cit.*, II, p. 212
17  J. Baker, *The Diary of John Baker*, Ed. P. C. Yorke, 1931, p. 378

18   N. Blundell, *Diary and Letter Book, op. cit.*, p. 102
19   *Ipswich Journal*, 1759
20   J. Macdonald, *op. cit.*, pp. 93, 163
21   J. Smollett, *Humphrey Clinker, op. cit.*, p. 3
22   Beds CRO, BS 2049
23   J. Macdonald, *op. cit.*, p. 96
24   J. Smollett, *Humphrey Clinker, op. cit.*, p. 417
25   M. J. Holroyd, *op. cit.*, p. 331
26   Count Frederick Kielmansegge, *op. cit.*, p.53
27   D. Defoe, *Everybody's Business, Nobody's Business*, 1725, pp. 2–3, 17
28   *London Magazine*, 1783, pp. 128–9
29   *Lady's Magazine*, 1785, p. 126
30    C. de Saussure, *op. cit.*, p. 203
31   M. Grosley, *op. cit.*, p. 74
32   J. W. Archenholz, *op. cit.*, II, p. 118
33   S. Richardson, *Sir Charles Grandison, op. cit.*, I, p. 265
34   Mrs Delany, *op. cit.*, I (2nd series), p. 138
35   The Noels and the Milbankes, *op. cit.*, p. 410
36   Mrs Lybbe Powys, *Passages from the Diaries*, 1756–1800, 1899, p.4
37   J. Woodforde, *op. cit.*, II, p. 72; V, p. 304; III, p. 143; IV, p. 249
38   R. S. Fitton and A. P. Wadsworth, *The Strutts and the Arkwrights*, 1758–1830, 1959, pp. 149, 162
39    A. Cook, *Ann Cook and Friend*, 1940, pp. 42–3
40   J. Hervey, *Letterbooks*, 1894, III, pp. 272–3
41   G. S. Thomson, *Letters of a Grandmother*, 1732–5, 1943, p. 85; Lady Mary Wortley Montagu, *op. cit.*, III, p. 294
42   Wrest Park Papers, L/30/9/111/242
43   Mrs Delany, *op. cit.*, III (2nd series), p. 483
44   J. Smollett, *Humphrey Clinker, op. cit.*, p. 422
45   Beds CRO, BS 2049
46   J. Woodforde, *op. cit.*, V, p. 107
47   J. Smollett, *Humphrey Clinker, op. cit.*, p. 47
48   R. B. Sheridan, *The Rivals*, 1775, I, ii
49   H. Fielding, *Tom Jones*, EML ed., I, p. 117; J. Smollett, *Humphrey Clinker, op. cit.*, p. 47
50   S. Richardson, *Clarissa, op. cit.*, III, p. 310; IV, p. 423
51   S. Richardson, *Pamela*, EML ed., I, pp. 8, 13, 32, 41, 42, 64, 65, 270
52   Beds CRO, X 216/13
53   J. Woodforde, *op. cit.*, II, p. 156
54   S. von la Roche, *op. cit.*, p. 89
55   J. Woodforde, *op. cit.*, III, p. 30

## V   The Common People

1   T. Baker, *Tunbridge Wells or the Yeomen of Kent*, 1713, I, i
2   T. Smollett, *The Life and Adventures of Sir Launcelot Greaves*, 1762, Oxford ed. 1973, p. 23
3   Lady Newdigate–Newdegate, *op. cit.*, p. 11
4   J. Woodforde, *op. cit.*, IV, p. 298
5   *The Jerningham Letters, op. cit.*, I, p. 203

6   W. Marshall, *The Rural Economy of Norfolk*, 1795, I, pp. 37, 39
7   P. Kalm, *op. cit.*, pp. 248, 326
8   Mrs Delany, *op. cit.*, II (2nd series), p. 310
9   John Byng, *op. cit.*, II, p. 98
10  S. Pepys, *op. cit.*, VIII, p. 382
11  J. Swift, *op. cit.*, I, p. 272
12  D. Ryder, *op. cit.*, p. 310
13  J. Macky, *op. cit.*, I, p. 120
14  P. Kalm, *op. cit.*, p. 337
15  Wrest Park Papers, *op. cit.*, L/30/9a/2, p. 13; L/30/9a/6, p. 155
16  S. von la Roche, *op. cit.*, p. 89
17  Mrs Cowley, *The Belle's Stratagem*, II, i
18  C. P. Moritz, *op. cit.*, p. 159
19  J. W. von Archenholz, *op. cit.*, II, p. 136
20  Sir J. Hawkins, *The Life of Samuel Johnson*, 1781, Ed. B. H. Davis, 1962,
        p. 113
21  Madame du Bocage, *op. cit.*, I, p. 61
22  C. P. Moritz, *op. cit.*, p. 59
23  S. Hutchinson, *Letters*, Ed. K. Coburn, 1954, p. 33
24  Samuel Bamford, *Tawk o' Searth Lankeshur*, 1850, p.7
25  M. Mitford, *Our Village*, 1947 ed., pp. 34, 83
26  The *Workman's Guide* by a Lady, (1840), p. 164
27  S. Hutchinson, *op. cit.*, p. 72
28  J. McEvoy, *Statistical Survey of the County of Tyrone*, Dublin, 1802,
        p. 153, quoted in A. T. Lucas, 'The Hooded Cloak in Ireland . . .'
        *Journ. Cork. Hist. and Arch. Soc.*, LVI (1951), pp. 104–119
29  P. Kalm, *op. cit.*, p. 13
30  B. de Monconys, *Voyage d'Angleterre* . . . Lyons, 1666; Pepys, *op. cit.*, I,
        p. 27
31  H. Walpole, *op. cit.*, XVII, p. 435
32  D. Defoe, *The Complete English Tradesman*, *op. cit.*, p. 265–6
33  Beds CRO, ABP/W 1734/1736
34  S. Druitt, The Will of Jane Youngs of Burley in the County of
        Southampton, *Costume* 11, 1977, pp. 113–17
35  H. de Misson, *Memoirs and Observations on his Travels in England*, 1685,
        (1719)
36  B. L. de Muralt, *Lettres sur les Anglois et les François*, 2nd ed. 1727, p. 11
37  C. de Saussure, *op. cit.*, p. 219
38  Beds CRO, X171/208
39  M. Grosley, *op. cit.*, p. 17
40  Hon. John Byng, *op. cit.*, I, p. 217
41  C. P. Moritz, *op. cit.*, p. 138
42  P. Kalm, *op. cit.*, p. 52
43  Beds CRO, X52/103
44  Thomas Turner, *The Diary of Thomas Turner of East Hoathly* (1754–65),
        Ed. F. M. Turner, 1925, p. 7
45  D. Defoe, *The Complete English Tradesman*, op. cit., pp. 263–4
46  M. Grosley, *op. cit.*, p. 89
47  J. H. Jesse, *George Selwyn and His Contemporaries*, 1882, IV, p. 311
48  *The Tatler*, No. 85

49   J. Woodforde, *op. cit.*, IV, p. 249
50   M. Mitford, *op. cit.*, p. 127
51   J. Macdonald, *op. cit.*, p. 71
52   Wrest Park Papers, *op. cit.*, L/30/9/111/49
53   The Purefoy Letters, *op. cit.*, II, p. 318
54   E. M. Forster, *Marianne Thornton*, 1956, p. 49
55   T. Pennant, *A Journey from London to the Isle of Wight*, 1801
56   W. Cobbett, *Rural Rides*, 1830, 1958 ed., p. 95
57   R. Owen, *The Life of Robert Owen*, 1857, p. 19
58   F. Burney, *The Early Diary*, I, p. 239
59   G. Eliot, *Adam Bede*, Blackwood ed. (n.d.), p. 36
60   S. Bamford, *Autobiography* (1788–1872), Ed. W. Chaloner, 1967, I, p. 5
61   Sir Frederick Eden, *The State of the Poor*, 1797, I, pp. 554–8
62   S. Bamford, *Tawk o' Searth Lankeshur*, *op. cit.*, pp. 7, 10
63   Chetham's Library, MS 31989
64   J. Collier, *Works*, Rochdale, 1894, p. 299
65   S. Bamford, *Tawk o' Searth Lankeshur*, *op. cit.*, pp. 7–8
66   P. Kalm, *op. cit.*, p. 244
67   R. Pococke, *Travels through England during 1750, 1751 and Later Years*, 1888, I, p. 44
68   Wrest Park Papers, L/30/9/111/51
69   J. Macky, *op. cit.*, II, p. 155
70   Wrest Park Papers, L/30/9/111/51, 229
71   C. Hutton, *op. cit.*, p. 52
72   W. H. Pyne, *op. cit.*, pl. 5
73   C. Hutton, *op. cit.*, p. 125
74   S. Neville, *op. cit.*, p. 281
75   W. Cowper, *Correspondence*, 1904, I, p. 211
76   A. Young, Annals of Agriculture, 1801, XXXVII, p. 448 (Harrold, Bedfordshire)
77   Sir Frederick Eden, *op. cit.*, pp. 557–8
78   A. Young, *Farmer's Tour Through the East of England*, 1771, I, p. 446
79   D. Davies, *The Case of the Labourers in Husbandry*, 1795, p. 15
80   Beds CRO, ABP/W 1723/78
81   Beds CRO, P 64/14
82   F. G. Emmison, 'Relief of the Poor at Eaton Socon 1706–1834', *Beds. Hist. Rec. Soc.*, Vol. XV, 1933, p. 69

## VI   Buying and Making Clothes

1   Lady Mary Wortley Montagu, *op. cit.*, II, pp. 19, 21, 53
2   Henrietta, Countess of Suffolk, *op. cit.*, I, pp. 80, 84
3   Wrest Park Papers, *op. cit.*, L/30/14/333/97, 105
4   Lady Mary Coke, *op. cit.*, II, p. 51; IV, p. 340
5   D. Defoe, *The Complete English Tradesman*, *op. cit.*, pp. 235–7
6   C. de Saussure, *op. cit.*, pp. 74, 79
7   The Williamson Letters, *op. cit.*, M/10/4/82
8   S. von la Roche, *op. cit.*, pp. 141, 87, 262
9   John Hervey, 1st Earl of Bristol, *op. cit.*, pp. 151, 155, 149, 108; Wrest Park Papers, *op. cit.*, L/31/138, 140

10  Lady Mary Coke, *op. cit.*, IV, p. 180; I, p. 54

11  Wrest Park Papers, *op. cit.*, L/30/9/3/25

12  *The Verney Letters, op. cit.*, II, p. 127

13  Wrest Park Papers, *op. cit.*, L/30/50/17

14  *ibid.*, L/30/9/3/40; L/30/11/122/72

15  *ibid.*, L/31/141

16  *ibid.*, L/30/9/3/112–13

17  Lady Mary Coke, *op. cit.*, I, pp. 114–19

18  Wrest Park Papers, *op. cit.*, L/30/9/97/90; L/30/11/122/72; L/30/11/240/6; L/30/9/81/11

19  J. L. Clifford, *Hester Lynch Piozzi* (Mrs Thrale), 1941, p. 153 (1952 ed.)

20  Lady Louisa Stuart, *op. cit.*, II, p. 118

21  Wrest Park Papers, *op. cit.*, L/30/9/60/48

22  Maria Josepha Holroyd, *op. cit.*, p. 26

23  Emily, Duchess of Leinster, *op. cit.*, I, p. 355

24  J. Collyer, *The Parents and Guardians Directory and the Youth's Guide*, 1761

25  Mrs Delany, *op. cit.*, II, p. 224

26  J. Boswell, *The Ominous Years*, 1774–6 (1963), p. 141

27  I. de G. Sieveking, *Memoir of Sir Horace Mann*, 1912, p. 37

28  John Hobson, *The Journal of Mr John Hobson*, Surtees Society, LXV, 1877, p. 280

29  Mrs Delany, *op. cit.*, II, p. 25

30  R. Campbell, *The London Tradesman*, 1747, p. 190

31  John Hervey, 1st Earl of Bristol, *op. cit.*, p. 153

32  The Hon. Mrs. Edward Boscawen, *op. cit.*, p. 48

33  Wrest Park Papers, *op. cit.*, Letter 13702

34  *The Verney Letters, op. cit.*, I, p. 173; II, p. 61

35  *The Purefoy Letters, op. cit.*, II, pp. 295, 296, 298

36  Nicholas Blundell, *The Great Diurnal, op. cit.*, II, p. 156

37  John Baker, *The Diary of John Baker*, Ed. P. C. Yorke, 1931, pp. 449, 476

38  Francis Place, *The Autobiography of Francis Place*, Ed. M. Thale, 1972, pp. 74, 80, 125

39  The Noels and the Milbankes, *op. cit.*, pp. 267–70

40  Trade Card, Museum of London, Z1704/15 (1783)

41  James Lackington, *Memoirs . . .* , 1792, p. 208

42  Samuel Curwen, *op. cit.*, II, p. 865; I, p. 78; II, p. 656

43  The Rev. Wm. Cole, *op. cit.*, p. 28

44  A. Heal, *London Tradesmen's Cards of the XVIII Century*, 1968 ed., Pls. LXXIII, LXXIV

45  R. Campbell, *op. cit.*, p. 204

46  C. Morris, *Diary of a West Country Physician*, 1659–1726, Ed. E. Hobhouse, Rochester, 1934, Nov. 1710

47  Wrest Park Papers, *op. cit.*, L/30/12/34/15

48  The Williamson Letters, *op. cit.*, M/10/4/39, 13, 52

49  A. Heal, *op. cit.*, pl. LXXII

50  J. L. Clifford, *op. cit.*, p. 156

51  Emily, Duchess of Leinster, *op. cit.*, II, p. 75; Lady Sarah Lennox, *op. cit.*, I, p. 119

52  Wrest Park Papers, *op. cit.*, L/30/9/60/48

53  T. Smollett, *Humphrey Clinker, op. cit.*, p. 111

54   M. Hamilton, *op. cit.*, p. 261
55   M. Frampton, *op. cit.*, p. 3
56   Wrest Park Papers, *op. cit.*, L/30/9/111/35; L/30/13/12
57   Maria Josepha Holroyd, *op. cit.*, p. 13
58   S. von la Roche, *op. cit.*, p. 83
59   C. Morris, *op. cit.*, 1718, December
60   John Hervey, 1st Earl of Bristol, *op. cit.*, pp. 108, 182
61   R. Owen, *The Life of Robert Owen*, 1857, pp. 13, 21, 22, 18
62   N. Blundell, *The Great Diurnal*, *op. cit.*, pp. 34, 77, 94, 178, 202, 273, 257, 169
63   *The Purefoy Letters*, *op. cit.*, II, pp. 316, 319, 303
64   The Rev. Wm. Cole, *op. cit.*, pp. 8, 94
65   The Rev. J. Woodforde, *op. cit.*, passim; Nancy Woodforde. *op. cit.*, *passim*
66   J. Boswell, *In Extremis*, 1776–8, 1971, p. 351
67   The Hon. John Byng, *op. cit.*, p. 154
68   *Browns and Chester*, Portrait of a Shop. 1780–1946, 1947, p. 24
69   P. Clabburn, 'A Provincial Milliner's Shop in 1785' *Costume*, 11, 1977, pp. 100–111
70   T.S. Willan, *An Eighteenth–Century Shopkeeper, Abraham Dent, of Kirkby Stephen*, 1729–1803, Manchester, 1970, *passim*
71   R. Owen, *op. cit.*, pp. 8–9
72   Beds CRO, P Bw P/W 1713/2
73   N. Blundell, *The Great Diurnal*, *op. cit.*, p. 242
74   T. Marchant, *The Marchant Diary*, Sussex Arch. Collections, Vol. 25, 1873, p. 184
75   D. Defoe, *A Tour Through the Whole Island of Great Britain*, 1724–6, EML ed., II, p. 337
76   Journals of the House of Commons, XL, p. 1018
77   C. Smith, *The Old Manor House*, 1969 ed., p. 58
78   J. Austen, *op. cit.*, p. 32
79   S. Richardson, *Pamela*, *op. cit.*, I, p. 33
80   The Rev. J. Woodforde, *op. cit.*, passim
81   Journals of the House of Commons, XL, p. 1038
82   James Brome, *Travels Over England, Scotland and Wales*, 1707, 2nd ed., p. 55
83   Wrest Park Papers, *op. cit.*, L/30/9a/5, p. 104
84   J. Gay, The Shepherd's Week, 1714, 11.73–8
85   Samuel Curwen, *op. cit.*, I, p. 118
86   T. Smollett, *Roderick Random*, 1748, EML ed., p. 318
87   S. Richardson, *Clarissa*, *op. cit.*, III, p. 304
88   Lady Mary Wortley Montagu, *op. cit.*, II, p. 457
89   F.A.Wendeborn, *op. cit.*, p. 115
90   Sir Frederick Eden, *op. cit.*, I, p. 554
91   David Davies, *op. cit.*, p. 175
92   Lady Louisa Stuart, *op. cit.*, I, p. 169
93   Wrest Park Papers, *op. cit.*, L/30/9/56/15
94   *ibid.*, L/30/9/56/17–18; L/30/11/339/100
95   Maria Josepha Holroyd, *op. cit.*, pp. 15, 24
96   F. Burney, *Journals and Letters*, *op. cit.*, IV, 1973, p. 14

97 Mrs Delany, *op. cit.*, III, 2nd series, p. 507; I, pp. 159, 618
98 Wrest Park Papers, *op. cit.*, L/30/11/122/236
99 H. Walpole, *op. cit.*, XXXII, 1965, pp. 219–220
100 S. Richardson, *Pamela, op. cit.*, I, p. 11
101 Mrs Papendiek, *op. cit.*, II, pp. 48, 82
102 The Williamson Letters, *op. cit.*, M/10/4/34, 42
103 Nancy Woodforde, *op. cit., passim*
104 C. Hutton, *op. cit.*, pp. 54, 213
105 Maria Holroyd, *op. cit.*, pp. 259, 273
106 J. Austen, *op. cit.*, pp. 10, 56
107 Mrs Delany, *op. cit.*, I, p. 124
108 Wrest Park Papers, *op. cit.*, L/30/13/12/36
109 Mrs Papendiek, *op. cit.*, I, pp. 146, 169, 229, 248, 292, 295; II, pp. 147, 293
110 Dudley Ryder, *op. cit.*, p. 51
111 N. Blundell, *The Great Diurnal*, I, p. 77
112 J. Austen, *op. cit.*, pp. 44, 49, 45, 138
113 Wrest Park Papers, *op. cit.*, Letter 3142

## VII  Fabrics and Wearers

1 J. Austen, *op. cit.*, pp. 35, 99
2 N. B. Harte, State Control of Dress and Social Change, in Coleman, D. C. and John A. H. Eds., *Trade, Government and Economy in Pre–Industrial England*, 1976, pp. 132–65
3 D. Defoe, *The Complete English Tradesman, op. cit.*, pp. 263, 260
4 N. Blundell, *The Great Diurnal, op. cit.*, II, pp. 6, 36 and n. 83, p. 59
5 P. Kalm, *op. cit.*, p. 248
6 Emily, Duchess of Leinster, *op. cit.*, I, p. 167
7 H. Walpole, *op. cit.*, XXXIII, p. 64; XXXI, p. 98, p. 98, n.2
8 Lady Mary Coke, *op. cit.*, II, p. 288
9 Wrest Park Papers, L/30/9/111/5
10 S. Richardson, *Clarissa, op. cit.*, II, p. 346
11 9–10 Will. 3, c.9; 11–12 Will. 3, c.11
12 Wm. Hervey, *Journals*, 1755–1814, Bury St Edmunds, 1906, VII, p. 214; A. Young, *Six Months Tour through the North of England*, 1770, Letter 1, 1768
13 The Rev. Wm. Cole, *op. cit.*, pp. 242, 223, 9
14 A.P. Wadsworth and J. de L. Mann, *The Cotton Trade and Industrial Lancashire*, Manchester, 1931, p. 133, quoting HL. MSS VII, 250
15 D. Defoe, *An Humble Proposal to the People of England*, 1729, p. 50
16 Journals of the House of Commons XL, p. 835
17 M. Edwards, *Growth of the British Cotton Trade*, 1780–1815, Manchester, 1967, p. 30, quoting *Manchester Mercury*, 14 November 1786
18 cf. Chap. III pp. 76–9
19 The Williamson Letters, *op. cit.*, M/10/4/53, 34
20 Betsy Sheridan, *op. cit.*, p. 59
21 Wrest Park Papers, *op. cit.*, L/30/24/18
22 *Dear Miss Heber*, Ed. F. Bamford, 1936, p. 112
23 Lady Jerningham, *op. cit.*, I, p. 37

24   Wrest Park Papers, *op. cit.*, L/30/9/74

25   J. Hunter, 'The Paisley Textile Industry, 1695–1830,' in *Costume* 10, 1976, pp. 1–15, quoting W. Semple, *History of Renfrewshire*, 1782

26   The Williamson Letters, *op. cit.*, M/10/2/246

27   G. Unwin, *Samuel Oldknow and the Arkwrights*, Manchester, 1924, p. 60; John Rylands Lib. Eng. Ms 751, June 1786, June 1787

28   Lady Louisa Stuart, *op. cit.*, III, p. 9

29   Lady Jerningham, *op. cit.*, I, p. 37

30   Mrs Lybbe Powys, *op. cit.*, p. 315

31   D. Defoe, *Everybody's Business Nobody's Business*, 1725, p. 13; Ann Cook, *op. cit.*, p. 43

32   Gilbert White, *The Natural History of Selborne*, 1788, EML ed., p. 189

33   C. P. Moritz, *op. cit.*, p. 31

34   N. M. Karamzin, *Letters of a Russian Traveller*, 1789–90, 1957, p. 266

35   F. Place, *op. cit.*, p. 51

36   C. Fiennes, *op. cit.*, pp. 245, 142, 149, 191, 224; S. Curwen, *op. cit.*, I, p. 281

37   D. Defoe, *Tour through the Whole Island of Great Britain*, 1724–6, EML ed. I, p. 207

38   Journals of the House of Commons, XL, p. 1001

## VIII   Dress and Society

1   S. von la Roche, *op. cit.*, p. 179

2   J. Summerson, *Architecture in Britain*, 1530–1830, 1953, p. 247

3   Wrest Park Papers, *op. cit.*, L/30/9a/1, p. 48; Letter 3333

4   Sir Nathaniel Wraxall, *op. cit.*, p. 99

5   M. Grosley, *op. cit.*, p. 255

6   J. W. von Archenholz, *op. cit.*, II, p. 135

7   The Rev. Wm. Cole, *op. cit.*, p. 4

8   *The Purefoy Letters*, *op. cit.*, I, Introd. p. xxvii

9   Wrest Park Papers, *op. cit.*, L/30/9/60/71

# Glossary

Terms which appear in quotations or text and are not described in their
context or discussed in the text

*Alamode, allamode* a thin silk of plain weave originally lustred and usually black

*Alapeen, alopeen* a wool and silk, plain weave

*Baby* a doll

*Baize, bays* woollen fabric, plain weave

*Balloon hat*(W) hat with large, balloon–like crown of silk over wire or cane
framework, 1783–6

*Barmoodas (Bermudas) hats* (W) hats of plaited fibre imported from Bermuda

*Bath lace* bobbin lace made in Devonshire and sold in Bath

*Berger hat* (W) straw hat with low crown and brim of varying width during
the century

*Bodies* see *Stays*

*Bombazine* a fabric of silk and worsted, usually black or grey and used for
mourning

*Bosom friend* (W) shaped tippet, often of fur, to cover the bodice, worn at the
end of the century

*Calamanco, callimanco* worsted fabric, satin weave with glazed surface

*Cape* turn–down collar of any size

*Capuchin* (W) short, hooded cloak

*Cardinal*(W) hooded cloak, three–quarter to full length, often, though not
always, scarlet

*Carmelite* purplish brown

*Caul* (W) crown of a cap or headdress

*Cellbridge hat* from the Irish industry at Cellbridge

*Chapeau bras* (M) hat made to carry under the arm with a low crown and the
brim cocked flat on to it.

*Chenille, shaneel* silk thread with a pile making it look like a furred caterpillar
(Fr. chenille)

*Cherry–derry* a fabric with silk warp and cotton weft

*Clouded* (satin) warp–printed

*Coat* (W) usually a petticoat

*Crape* 1) a silk and worsted fabric (Norwich crape) used for mourning 2) silk
woven from hard–spun yarn giving a crimped surface

*Damask* fabric with woven pattern reversible by interchange of warp and weft

*Denmark satin* worsted fabric which may here be the same as *double stuff*
recorded as the fabric of black breeches in the same wardrobe two years
before; double often means extra warp threads in the fabric

*Dimity, dimothy* strong fabric with linen warp and cotton weft woven in twill
and weaves derived from twill; Indian dimity was all cotton

*Domino* a long, full cloak with loose sleeves and sometimes a hood, worn at
masquerades

*Dresden work* fine white embroidery in openwork patterns which gave it the
delicacy of lace

*Drugget* strong closely woven woollen fabric

*Florant, florinet* a worsted fabric used here for breeches with this variation in the name in the two entries for them

*Floss* untwisted silk

*Flowered, flourished* embroidered, although flowered also meant with a floral pattern

*Fly* (M) here used for frock

*Fustian* the general term for many types of fabric made with linen warp and cotton weft

*Gaudy gown* (W) may simply mean a festive gown, not necessarily a showy one

*Gauze* open weave fabric with twisted warp threads holding the weft

*Handkerchief* (W) usually the square or triangle of fabric worn over the neck and shoulders

*Headclothes* (W) surviving as a term for cap from the more complex caps which had been made up of separate pieces of fabric

*Incles* linen tapes or narrow bindings

*Irish stuff* poplin, a fabric with silk warp and worsted weft

*Isabella* yellowish grey

*Japan* lacquer

*Jennet, jeanette* a fine variety of jeans, a cotton and linen twill

*Jesuit* (W) a gown or jacket buttoning high in the neck

*Jockey boots* (M) boots ending below the knee usually with contrasting tops

*Joseph* (W) a riding jacket, green in most references

*Kevenhuller, Khevenhuller hat* (M) a large hat with a high peaked cock in front

*Kissing strings* (W) the side pieces of a cap extending to meet and fasten under the chin

*Lappets* (W) streamers, longer than kissing strings, either extending from the cap or attached to it, hanging down at the front or behind or pinned up

*Linsey, linsey–woolsey* a linen and woollen fabric

*Lustring, lutestring* silk in plain weave with a lustrous finish, plain, striped or figured; one of the most popular of eighteenth–century fabrics, especially for summer wear

*Manchester* a term given to a range of linen and cotton fabrics; from the middle of the century often synonymous with cotton, i.e. Manchester velvet was cotton velvet

*Mantell (Mantle) hood* (W) a hooded cloak

*Marcella, marseilles* quilted linen or cotton

*Mob* (W) a plain cap with gathered crown and frill, varying in shape and size with changing hair styles

*Mode* see *Alamode*

*Nankeen* plain closely woven cotton, usually pale brown or buff colour

*Padua serge* twilled worsted

*Paduasoy* a heavy silk of plain weave, often figured

*Persian* a thin light silk

*Pic–nic bonnet* (W) named from the fashion for Pic–nic Societies in 1802 in which groups of people met for supper each bringing a share of the entertainment

*Polish dress* (W) 'Some of the ladies wear a Polish dress which is made tight to the waist; ''tis commonly of satin trimmed with fur and silver or gold' (Lady Mary Coke in Vienna, 1772)

*Polonaise* (W) 1) a short gown with centre back and side seams with pleats at the seams opening out into the skirt 2) a gown with looped-up skirt

*Pompadour* purple

*Pompon* (W) a small ornament of lace, ribbon, feathers, jewels worn on the head with or without a cap

*Primings* used here in the sense of facings

*Prunella* twilled worsted

*Robings* (W) revers extending from the neck down the bodice opening of a gown

*Round gown* (W) a gown with no centre front opening in the skirt

*Russet* coarse woollen fabric of homespun wool, usually brown or grey

*Shag* worsted fabric made like velvet with a long pile

*Shalloon* twilled worsted

*Skeleton cap* (W) a cap without fabric foundation of flowers, jewels, feathers etc. wired to shape

*Sleeve knot* bow of ribbon worn on the sleeve, usually where the ruffle tapered to a narrow frill for the bend of the elbow

*Souflee* probably a general, ephemeral term used to describe some transparent fabric used for the puffed up neckwear of the 1780s

*Stays* (W) 1) stiff foundation for the bodice of the gown 2) bands holding the bodice fronts in place over the stomacher

*Stomacher* (W) triangular panel filling the front opening of the bodice of the gown, often a decorative feature

*Stormont* (W) a gown of the 1780s named after Lady Stormont; according to the Lady's Magazine of 1781, worn with a sash

*Stuff* used as a general term for any fabric; more specifically for the light worsted fabrics of women's gowns

*Suit* (W) 1) dress of matching gown and petticoat 2) matching cap, handkerchief, tucker and ruffles

*Surtout* overcoat

*Swanskin* fabric of worsted warp and wool weft

*Tabby* a fabric in plain weave, frequently used for silk in this weave

*Tambour* chain–stitch embroidery worked with a hook; called after the drum–like frame on which the fabric was stretched

*Taminy, tammy* a rather coarse twilled worsted

*Tiffany* fine open weave silk

*Tippet* a short cape or shoulder covering

*Top–knot* knot of ribbon worn on top of the head or cap

*Trollopee* a loose form of sack

*Tucker* the frilled band of linen, muslin or lace edging the neck opening of a gown

*Vermilion, vomilion* in this reference appears to be an alternative to dimity

*Vicuna* fabric made from the wool of the South American vicuna

*Weepers* (M) white linen or muslin cuffs added to the coat for mourning wear

*Wildebore* a worsted fabric here worn for mourning

# Bibliography

A selection of useful works in addition to those referred to in the text and notes; a list of articles which discuss in greater detail subjects dealt with in the text; and publications by museums of relevant material in their collections.

ADBURGHAM, A., *Women in Print*, Writing Women and Women's Magazines from the Restoration to the Accession of Victoria, Allen & Unwin, 1972

ARNOLD, J., *Patterns of Fashion I* (1660–1860), Wace, 1964, Macmillan, 1972
*Handbook of Costume*, Macmillan, 1973

BELL, Q., *On Human Finery*, Hogarth Press, 1948, 1976

BOUCHER, F., *A History of Costume in the West*, Thames and Hudson, 1967

BRADFIELD, N., *Costume in Detail*, 1730–1930, Harrap, 1968

COLEMAN, D. C., *Courtaulds*, An Economic and Social History, I, Oxford University Press, 1969

CUNNINGTON, C. W. and P., *Handbook of English Costume in the Eighteenth Century*, Faber 1957
*The History of Underclothes*, M. Joseph, 1951

CUNNINGTON, P., *Costume of Household Servants* from the Middle Ages to 1900, A. & C. Black, 1972

CUNNINGTON, P. and BUCK, A., *Children's Costume in England*, from the Fourteenth to the End of the Nineteenth Century, A. & C. Black, 1965

CUNNINGTON, P. and LUCAS, C., *Costume for Births, Marriages and Deaths*, A. & C. Black, 1978
*Charity Costumes*, A. & C. Black, 1978
*Occupational Costume in England from the 11th century to 1914*, A. & C. Black, 1967

CUNNINGTON, P. and MANSFIELD, A., *English Costume for Sports and Outdoor Recreations* from the Sixteenth to the Nineteenth Centuries, A. & C. Black, 1969

DAVENPORT, M., *The Book of Costume*, Crown Publishers, New York, 1948

DAVIS, D., *A History of Shopping*, Routledge and K. Paul, 1966

EDWARDS, M., *The Growth of the British Cotton Trade*, 1780–1815, Manchester University Press, 1967

EDWARDS, R., *Early Conversation Pictures* from the Middle Ages to about 1730, Country Life, 1954

EVELYN, M. and J., *Mundus Muliebris*, or the Ladies Dressing-Room Unlock'd, 1690, ed. J. L. Nevinson, The Costume Society, 1977

GARLICK, K., *Sir Thomas Lawrence*, Routledge and Kegan Paul, 1954

GEORGE, M. D., *London Life in the Eighteenth Century*, Kegan Paul, 1935, Penguin Books, 1965
*Hogarth to Cruikshank*, Social Change in Graphical Satire, Lane, 1967

HECHT, J. J., *The Domestic Servant Class in Eighteenth Century England*, Routledge and Kegan Paul, 1956

HUGHES, E., *North Country Life in the Eighteenth Century*, Oxford University Press, 1965

IRWIN, J. and BRETT, K. B., *Origins of Chintz*, HMSO, 1970

KERSLAKE, J., *Early Georgian Portraits in the National Portrait Gallery, 1714–60*, HMSO, 1978

LAVER, J., *Taste and Fashion* from the French Revolution to the present day, Harrap, 1937

LENS, B., *The Exact Dress of the Head, 1725–6* ed. J. L. Nevinson, *The Costume Society*, 1970

MARSHALL, D., *The English Domestic Servant in History*, Historical Association, 1949

MILLAR, O., *Pictures in the Royal Collection*: Tudor, Stuart and Early Georgian Portraits, Phaidon, 1963

MINGAY, G. E. *English Landed Society in the Eighteenth Century*, Routledge and K. Paul, 1963

MONTGOMERY, F. M. *Printed Textiles*, Thames and Hudson, 1970

MOORE, D. L., *Fashion through Fashion Plates, 1770–1970*, Ward Lock, 1971

NICOLSON, B., *Joseph Wright of Derby*, Routledge and K. Paul, 1968

OAKES, A. and HILL, M. H., *Rural Costume*, its Origin and Development in Western Europe and the British Isles, Batsford, 1970

OPPÉ, A. P., *The Drawings of Paul and Thomas Sandby* at Windsor Castle, Phaidon, 1948

PASTON, G., *Social Caricature in the Eighteenth Century*, Methuen, 1905

PAVIERE, S. H., *The Devis Family of Painters*, F. Lewis, 1950

PIKE, E. R., (ed) *Human Documents of Adam Smith's Time*, Allen and Unwin, 1974

PINCHBECK, I., *Women Workers and the Industrial Revolution*, Routledge, 1930, 1974

PRAZ, M., *Conversation Pieces*, A Survey of the Informal Portrait Group in Europe and America, Methuen, 1971

RAINES, R., *Marcellus Laroon*, Routledge and K. Paul, 1967

SITWELL, S., *Conversation Pieces*, Batsford, 1936
*Narrative Pictures*, Batsford, 1937

SQUIRE, G., *Dress, Art and Society*, 1560–1970, Studio Vista, 1974

TAYLOR, B., *George Stubbs*, Phaidon, 1975

THORNTON, P., *Baroque and Rococo Silks*, Faber, 1965

WADSWORTH, A. P. and MANN, J. de L., *The Cotton Trade and Industrial Lancashire*, Manchester University Press, 1931

WATERHOUSE, E., *Gainsborough*, E. Hulton, 1958
*Reynolds*, Phaidon, 1973

WAUGH, N., *Corsets and Crinolines*, Batsford, 1954
*The Cut of Men's Clothes*, 1600–1900, Faber, 1964
*The Cut of Women's Clothes*, 1600–1930, Faber, 1968

WEBSTER, M., *Francis Wheatley*, Routledge and K. Paul, 1970

WESTERFIELD, R. B., *Middlemen in English Business*, Yale, 1915, 1968

WILDEBLOODE, J. and BRINSON, P., *The Polite World*, a Guide to English Manners and Deportment from the thirteenth to the nineteenth century, Oxford University Press, 1965

WILLIAMS, R., *The Country and the City*, Chatto and Windus, 1973

# Articles in Journals

ARNOLD, J., 'A Pink Silk Domino, 1760–70', *Costume*, Journal of the Costume Society, No. 3, 1969; 'A Mantua, 1708–9', *Costume*, No. 4, 1970; 'A Silver Embroidered Court Mantua and Petticoat, c. 1740', *Costume*, No. 6, 1972; 'A Mantua, 1760–5', *Costume*, No. 7, 1973

BUCK, A., 'The Countryman's Smock', *Folk Life*, Journal of the Society for Folk Life Studies, Vol. 1, 1963; 'Variations in Englishwomen's Dress in the Eighteenth Century', *Folk Life*, Vol. 9, 1971; 'The Costume of Jane Austen and her Characters', *The So–called Age of Elegance*, Costume Society, 1970; 'The Dress of Domestic Servants in the Eighteenth Century', *Strata of Society*, Costume Society, 1974

CLABBURN, P., 'Parson Woodforde's View of Fashion', *Costume*, No. 5, 1971

DAVIS, R., 'English Foreign Trade, 1700–1774', *Econ. Hist. Rev.* 2nd ser., XV, 1962

GINSBURG, M., 'The Tailoring and Dressmaking Trades, 1700–1850', *Costume*, No. 6, 1972

INDER, P. M., 'Eighteenth Century Hats in Exeter Museum', *Costume*, No. 7, 1973

MACTAGGART, P. and R. A., 'Some Aspects of the Use of Non–Fashionable Stays', *Strata of Society*, Costume Society, 1974

MANSFIELD, A., 'Dyeing and Cleaning Clothes in the Late Eighteenth and Early Nineteenth Centuries', *Costume*, No. 2, 1968

MARLY, D. de, 'The Vocabulary of the Female Headdress, 1678–1713', *Waffen- und Kostümkunde*, Munich, 1975

MARSHALL, D., 'Domestic Servants of the Eighteenth Century', *Economica*, 1929

MURRAY, A. W., 'From Breeches to Sherryvallies.', *Waffen- und Kostümkunde*, 1974

PAYNE, F., 'Welsh Peasant Costume', *Folk Life*, Vol. 2, 1964

ROBINSON, E., 'Eighteenth Century Commerce and Fashion; Matthew Boulton's Marketing Techniques', *Econ. Hist. Rev.* 2nd ser., XVI, 1963

ROTHSTEIN, N. and THORNTON, P., 'The Importance of the Huguenots in the London Silk Industry', *Proc. Hug. Soc.*, Vol. XX, No. 1, 1960

SWAIN, M., 'Men's Nightgowns of the Eighteenth Century', *Waffen- und Kostümkunde*, 1972; 'Nightgown into Dressing Gown', *Costume*, No. 6, 1972

TARRANT, N., 'Lord Sheffield's Banyan', *Costume*, No. 11, 1977

VIGEON, E., 'Clogs or Wooden Soled Shoes', *Costume*, No. 11, 1977

# Museum Publications

**Museum of London**

Halls, Z., 'Women's Costumes, 1600–1750'; 'Women's Costumes, 1750–1800'; 'Men's Costumes 1560–1750'; 'Men's Costumes, 1750–1800', HMSO, 1969–73

**National Portrait Gallery**

Arnold J., 'Perukes and Periwigs: a survey, *c.* 1660–1740', HMSO, 1970

**Bristol Museum and Art Gallery**

Blaise Castle House, Bennett, H. and Witt, C., 'Eighteenth Century Women's Costume at Blaise Castle House' (n.d.)

**Chertsey Museum**

Rowley, C., 'Costume in Chertsey Museum, 1700–1800', 1976

**Manchester City Art Galleries**

Gallery of English Costume, Buck, A., 'Women's Costume: The Eighteenth Century', 1954

**Worcestershire County Museum**

Bullard, D., 'Catalogue of the Costume Collection, Pt. 1, 1645–1790', 1966

**Worthing Museum**

Bullard, D., 'Catalogue of the Costume Collection, Pt. 1, Eighteenth Century', 1964

# Index

Aberystwyth 150

Abington, Mrs 25–6

Aken, J. Van 123

Alterations to clothes 26, 80, 115, 170, 183–5

Amelia, Princess (d. Geo. II) 16, 23, 44, 49, 82

American War of Independence 57, 152, 204

Ampthill, Beds 132, 185

Angelis, P. 123

Anne, Princess (d. Geo. II) 13, 76, 82

Anson, Ly 18, 26, 33, 159, 160, 181

Antonie, Rich., John 114

Apprentices 155

Apron (M) 91, 138, 149
 Freemason's a. 96

Apron (W) 22, 27, 38, 43–4, 48–9, 65, 111, 115, 118, 119, 133, 144–6, 148, 154, 155, 163, 176, 178, 181, 182; Fig. 17
 mourning a. 60, 61, 85, 133

Archenholz, J. W. von 92, 128, 205

Assemblies, balls, masquerades 25–7, 33 37–40, 44, 76, 78, 89, 96–7, 101, 121, 182

Augusta, Princess of Wales 15, 84, Fig. 1

Austen, J. 76, 86, 177, 184, 186


Baker, J. 164

Bamford, S. 130, 131, 144, 148–9

Banyan, see Nightgown

Bath 27, 43, 67, 79, 80, 96, 99–101, 184, 208

Bathing (M) drawers, waistcoat 100

Bathing (W) gown, hat, jacket, petticoat 100

Bedford, Duke of 21, 103, 105
 Duchess of 25, 34

Bedford 74
 Races 76, 182

Bedfordshire 24, 72, 74–6, 82, 85, 92, 114, 134–5, 155, 174, 179, 185, 191

Bequests of clothes, 'castings' 108–111, 112–8, 132–3, 135, 154–5, 185

Berkshire 131, 136, 154, 180, 187, 188

Bicester 67, 170

Bigg, W. R. 127, 131, Col. pl. 3, Fig. 80

Biggleswade 174, 187

Birmingham 98–9, 136, 183

Bletchley, Bucks 65, 106, 171, 191, 207

Blundell, John 134–5, 138, 179

Blundell, Nicholas 65, 106, 108, 147, 164, 169, 170, 176, 184, 188
 Fanny 65, 170
 Mally 65, 170
 Mrs B. 65, 170, 188

Bocage, Mme du 36, 48, 130, 150

Boots (M) 56, 57, 59, 69, 76, 81, 96, 134, 135
 jockey b. 58

Boscawen, Hon. Mrs Ed. 27, 32–3, 47, 62, 164

Bosom friend 80

Boswell, J. 163, 172

Bracegirdle, Mrs 132

Brackley, Northants 67, 69, 170

Breeches 20, 21, 28, 31–2, 67, 76, 80, 81, 82, 92, 95–6, 134, 135, 136, 138, 146,

147, 149, 154, 164, 166, 178, 184, 187, 189, 207
breeches-makers 164–5, 171
leather br. 56, 58, 76, 95, 134, 135, 138, 147, 148, 149, 164–5, 170
Bristol, 1st Earl of 29–30, 45–6, 65, 113, 158, 164, 169
Ly B. 113
Brummell, G. 59
Buckingham 67, 68, 69, 170, 207
Buckinghamshire 65, 67, 70, 76, 106, 163, 170, 191, 207
Buckles 16, 23, 28, 31, 58, 62, 65, 67, 118, 135, 138, 148, 176, 184
Burnaby, W. 90, 190
Burney, Fanny 19–20, 72, 100, 105, 143, 181
Bury St Edmunds 34, 76, 169
Bustles 28
Buxton 101
Byng, Admiral 32–3
Hon. John 46, 122, 135, 172

Campbell, R. 163, 167
Canes, walking sticks 55, 91, 100, 101
cudgel 58
Canterbury 195
Caps (M), *see* nightcaps
Caps (W) headclothes, headdresses 14, 19–20, 22, 34–5, 38–9, 74, 79, 97, 109, 115, 116, 121, 128, 130, 144, 148, 150–1, 154, 155, 161, 162, 172, 173, 176, 182
butterfly, skeleton c. 15, 101
handkerchief 148
mob c. 72, 121, 144, 148
mourning 61–2, 85
nightcap 72, 158, 168
Cardington, Beds 92, 185
Carlisle 192
Caroline, Princess (d. Geo. II) 23, 76, 82
Caroline, Queen 13, 16, 23, 33, 82, 89, 122
Carriers 207, 208
Carter, Mrs E. 60
Cassock 81
Castle Rising, Norfolk 124
Cater, Mrs 76, 85, 182, 193
Fanny C. 76, 182
John C. 167
Sophia C. 76, 182
Centlivre, Mrs S. 106, 179
Charlotte, Princess Royal 181
Charlotte, Queen 14, 15, 19, 22, 24, 28, 181
Cheshire 130, 136
Chester 97, 172–3
Chesterfield, Lord 25, 31, 47, 57, 88
Children 63, 154, 158, 176, 180, 204–7
Chipping Norton 27, 67, 170

Christening, royal 15
Classical influence 11, 27, 40, 201, 203
Cleaning and dyeing 70, 113, 197–8
Cleanliness 90, 92, 103, 121, 131, 197–8
Clergymen 91, *see also* Cole, Williamson, Woodforde
Cloak (M) 170, 184
domino 37
Cloak (W) 54, 80, 82, 100, 111, 115, 130–1, 133, 150–1, 154, 159, 163, 166, 183
cardinal 75, 173
domino 37
red 38, 121, 130–1, 150
riding hood 130, 132, 155, 163, 166
rocket 133
Coat (M) 13, 20–1, 23, 28, 31, 45, 55, 59, 62, 67, 72, 76, 80–1, 82, 89, 90, 94, 95, 96, 98, 134, 135, 138, 146–7, 149, 154, 163, 164, 166, 170, 171, 185, 187, 207
frock 23, 32–3, 34, 45, 55–9, 62, 81, 89, 92, 107, 108, 134, 140, 170, 203
Coat (W), *see* petticoat
Coat, greatcoat (M) 47, 56, 95–6, 134, 135, 166
coachman 103
surtout 63, 75
Coat, greatcoat (W) 55, 85, 99, 100, 101, 166
pelisse 80
Cobbett, W. 142
Coke, Lady Jane 16, 23, 26, 34, 38, 40–1, 43, 101
Coke, Lady Mary 16, 37, 44, 48, 99, 156, 158, 161, 162, 190
Colchester 76, 169, 198
Cole, Rev. W. 65, 106–7, 166, 171, 191, 207
Colman, G. 90
Cook, Mrs Ann 113, 115, 118, 197
Coronation 13
Cosmetics, toilet equipment 32, 173
false teeth 190
habit brush 171
perfume 167, 171
rouge 35, 36
shaving soap 171
Court 13–24, 34, 61–2, 88–9
Coventry, F. 58, 91
Cowley, Mrs 37
Crosby, Lancs 65, 106
Cumberland 146–7, 149
Curwen, S. 22, 56, 59, 95–6, 98, 101, 166, 179, 198

Davies, David 154, 180, 198
Defoe, D. 89–90, 91, 109, 110, 136, 176, 192, 197, 198
Delany, Mrs 15–6, 18, 19, 20, 23, 25, 37,

40, 42, 43, 47, 54, 60, 63, 89, 114, 122,
162, 163, 181, 183
Derby 76, 98, 101
Derbyshire 23, 152, 178
Devizes 136, 187
Devonshire 188, 191
Duchess of 105
Duke of 105
Doublet (W) 52
Drapers, linen and woollen
country 98, 169, 170, 171, 173–4,
174–6, 185, 187, 192
London 68–70, 88, 158, 164, 170, 193
Drawers (M) 95
Dressmakers, mantua-makers, milliners
19, 98, 101, 115, 160–2, 172–3, 180,
182, 184, 185, 210
country 80, 172, 173, 184
London 22, 33, 36, 53, 61, 75, 79, 80,
85, 160, 161, 162, 172
seamstress 166
Dublin 60, 180

Eaton Socon, Beds 155
Eden, Sir Fredk. 146–7, 154, 180, 188
Edinburgh 28, 62, 131
Effingham, Lord 56
Eliot, George 144
Epsom 52, 99, 100, 149
Eversholt, Beds 135
Exeter 96, 198
Museum 127

Fans 60, 65, 79, 118, 133
mourning 23
Farmers, farming 50, 56, 106, 120–2,
124, 134–5, 138
Farquhar, G. 65, 106
Fashion dolls 33–4
Fashion plates 208
Feathers 19–20, 22, 34, 35, 39, 57, 79,
114, 172, 181
Fermanagh, Lord 164
Lady 105, 164
Fielding, H. 65, 91
Fiennes, Celia 100, 198
Fox, Lady Caroline (Ly. Holland) 18,
47, 162, 190
Fox, C. J. 57, 204
Frampton, M. 168
France 53, 156–7, 189–90
influence of, 27, 33–6
Revolution 33, 204
Frederick, Prince of Wales 15, 16, 23,
82, 98
Frock, round fr., smock fr. (M) 140–2
children 205
Fur 13, 14, 17, 20, 70, 80, 114

Gaddesden, Herts 121

Galloshes (M) 69
Garters (M) 136, 187
Gay, J. 30, 52, 132, 179
George I 13, 23, 82
George II 13, 23, 82, 122
George III 14, 21, 22, 23
George, Prince of Wales 21, 59, Fig. 31
Girdle (W) 60, 65
Glasgow 131, 192–3
Gloves (M) 23, 96, 134, 136, 163, 171,
176, 187
mourning 23
Gloves (W) 65, 118, 163, 172, 173, 176,
183
habit gl. 79
mourning 23, 60, 85
Gowns (M), *see also* Nightgown
civic 88
clerical 81
Gowns (W) gown and petticoat, *passim*
named types, bedgown, 112, 144–6,
147, 148, 166, Figs 55, 76
Brunswick 77
chemise 44
hooded 47, Fig. 21
Jesuit 61
mantua 14–5, 17, 19, 26, 41, 60, 65,
133, 156, Fig. 2
negligée 34, 43, 72–4, 77–8, 120
nightgown 22, 23, 36, 38, 41–3, 48–9,
53, 60, 61, 65, 72, 75, 77, 85, 101, 111,
116, 118, 156, 160
polonaise 28, 182, 193, Fig. 7
half p. 53
quilted, wadded 47, Fig. 21
robe à la turque 28
rocket 148, *see also* cloak
round g. 72, 78
sack 19, 23, 26–7, 28, 33, 34, 36, 40–1,
43, 48, 53, 74–5, 77, 85, 115, 183, 184
stiff-bodied g. 13–4, 33, 146, 160, 205
Stormont 77
trained 13–4, 17, 18, 19, 26
washing 23, 148
worked 69, 76, 80, 181, 182
wrapping 40, 70, 74, 132, 160, 166, 192
Grantham, Lord 34, 164
Lady G., *see* Lady Mary Grey
Grey, Lady Amabel (Lady Polwarth)
18, 24, 26, 37, 38, 40, 49, 52–3, 60–1,
101, 159, 161, 162, 168–9, 181, 183,
208
Grey, Lady Jemima (Lady
Ashburnham) 19, 158, 160
Grey, Lady Mary (Lady Grantham) 24,
38, 61–2, 101, 159, 161, 193
Grey, Marchioness 18, 24, 36, 38, 43,
50, 60–1, 62, 63, 101, 124–6, 159,
160–1, 179, 181, 203
Grosley, M. 48, 49, 94, 204–5

Haberdashers, warehouses
  country 171, 172, 173
  London 37, 70, 163, 166, 195
Hairdressing, hairdressers, barbers *see
  also* Wigs
Hairdressing (M) 56, 57, 58, 75, 89, 91,
  138, 143, 166–7, 171
Hairdressing (W) 13, 34, 34–6, 37, 38,
  49, 54, 72, 76, 79, 88, 105, 109, 121,
  144, 150, 168–9, 171, 201
  hairdressers 68, 76, 166–9, 171
  hair powder and pomatum 30, 35, 57,
    69, 75, 92, 105, 143, 167, 168, 171,
    176
  combs 167, 171, 176, 179
  hair tax 81
Hamilton, M. 22, 54, 99, 168
Handkerchiefs (M) 96
  neck h. 138–9, 140, 154, 176, 178, Figs
    71, 72, 75
Handkerchiefs (W) 172, 176, 181, 182,
  200
  head h. 148, 150–1
  mourning 61, 85
  neck h. 16, 43, 44, 65, 99, 111, 118,
    130, 133, 143, 144, 146, 147, 154, 155
  pocket h. 155
  Vandyke h. 38
Hartford, Lady 14, 15, 16, 17, 36, 43, 50
Hats (M) 21–2, 31, 34, 37, 57, 58, 69, 81,
  89, 92, 134, 136, 138, 147, 148, 149,
  154, 171
  chip, straw 21
  Khevenhullar 58
Hats (W) and bonnets 22, 38, 40, 48–9,
  52, 53, 70, 79, 80, 96, 98–9, 111, 114,
  115, 120, 121, 122–8, 131, 147, 148,
  150–1, 154, 155, 166, 171, 172, 182
  balloon 39, 79, 173
  berger 39
  Camperdown 79
  chip, straw, 'Barmoodas' 38, 40, 65,
    70, 116, 118, 121, 122–7, 133, 154,
    155, 173
  felt, beaver 72, 123, 151
  gipsy 126, 148
  mourning 85
  picnic 79
  riding cap 52, 54
  riding h. 52, 98–9, 171
  Rubens 39
  Spanish 39
Heathcote, Lady 38, 101, 113–4, 180
Heideloff, N. 208
Hertfordshire 121, 122, 124, 130, 132,
  188
Hillersden, E. 154
Hogarth, W. 124, 144
Holderness, Lady 190
Hollar, W. 123

Holme, R. 140
Holroyd, L. 20
  M. J. 181, 183
  S. 109, 169
Hoods (W) 48, 65, 70, 115, 120, 123,
  133, 154–5, 159, 163, 173
  capuchin 70
  mantel h. 70
  mourning h. 23, 60
Hoop, hoop petticoat 10, 17, 19, 27–8,
  36, 37, 38, 43, 49, 65, 70, 72, 89, 109,
  159, 161, 163
Howard, John 92, 138
Huguenots 189
Husborne Crawley (Beds) 72, 75
Hutton, C. 89, 98–9, 150–1, 182
  W. 98

Ibbetson, J. C. 150, Figs 78, 79
India 189–90, 191, 192
  E. Indies 46
Ireland 192, 193

Jacket (M) 76, 149, 154
  boys 205
Jacket (W) 38, 52–3, 80, 105, 150, 151
Jerningham, Lady 121
Jewellery 13, 14, 15, 16, 17, 25, 37, 58,
  65, 89, 116, 133, 158, 176, 190
  mourning j. 61–2, 85, 114
Johnson, Barbara 76–9, 186, 189, 193,
  195, 208
Johnson, Charles 122, 197
Journalism 11–12, 208

Kalm, P. 56, 103, 121, 124, 130, 131,
  132, 135, 149, 188
Kielmansegge, Count 109
Kirkby Stephen, Westmorland 173
Kissing strings 120

Lackington, J. 166
Lancashire 65, 106, 130, 131, 136, 148,
  176, 192
Lansdowne, Lady 33, 156
La Roche, S. von 19, 118, 126, 158, 169
Lawyers 88, 91
Leather 56, 58, 69, 70, 76, 95, 96, 108,
  109, 116, 132, 133, 134, 136, 138, 147,
  149, 164–5, 170, 176, 189
Leeds 198
Leicester 136
  Races 138
Leighton Buzzard, Beds 75–6, 82
Lincoln 172
Lincolnshire 154
Livery 105–9
Locke, John 204
London, *passim*, shopping in L. 157–66
Louisa, Princess (s. Geo. III) 24

Macaronis 58, 100
Macclesfield, Cheshire 136
Macdonald, John 107, 108, 140
Macky, J. 58, 97, 124, 150
Malvern Wells 131
Manchester 98, 136, 170, 172, 193, 194, 195, 198, 200
Margate 101
Marie Antoinette 36, 44–5
Markets, fairs 124–6, 178–9
Mary, Princess (d. Geo. II) 14, 15, 42
Meppershall, Beds 134, 185
Mercers 18, 20, 90, 157–61, 171, 210
   Allanson 159
   Brownsmith 171
   Carr 18, 159, 160
   Hinchcliffe 158
   John 20
   King 159, 161
   Smith 171
   Swann 18, 159
   Vansommer 159, 161
   Vickers 158
Milbanke, Judith 37, 44
Millbrook, Beds 72, 75
Mitford, Mary Russell 131, 139
Mittens 85, 118, 177
Mobberley, Cheshire 130
Montagu, Mrs Elizabeth 15, 16, 50, 52, 96–7, 100
Montagu, George 48
Montagu, Lady Mary Wortley 11, 35, 41–2, 52, 113, 156, 179
Moritz, C. P. 56, 92, 94, 127, 130, 135
Morning gown (M), *see* nightgown
Morris, Dr. C. 46, 167
   Mrs M. 169
Mourning 16, 22–4, 31, 60–3, 70, 76, 77, 82–5, 98, 121, 133, 155, 185, 194
   servants 63, 108, 112, 114

Nash, Beau 43
Nebot, B. 123
Neckcloths, cravats, stocks 58, 82, 96, 134, 138, 177, 197
   mourning 23
   'neckings' 134
Netherlands 176, 189, 191
Newdigate, Lady 11, 101, 121
Newmarket 52, 58
Nightcaps (M) 46–7, 68, 82, 96, 134
   travelling cap 82
Nightgowns (M) 45–6, 68, 81–2, 88, 99, 163, 166, 177, Figs 20, 47
Nightgowns (W), *see* gowns
Noel, Elizabeth 100
   Judith, *see* Milbanke
   Mary 111
Nonconformity 92, 98, 138
Norfolk 79, 82, 121, 124, 185

Norfolk, Duke of 56
North, Lord 57
Northampton 136
Northamptonshire 180, 191
Norwich 79–81, 96, 121, 136, 159, 171–2, 173, 174, 185, 187, 194, 195
Nottingham 96, 98, 174

Occupations
   carter 140
   coachmen, grooms 58, 76, 103, 106, 140
   costermongers 139
   cowmen 140
   donkeywoman 131
   falconer 135
   fisherwomen 143
   footmen 107, 108, 120, 123, 140
   milkmaids 127
   servants, gen. 103–119
   shepherds 140
   shopkeepers 89, 138, 143
Oldknow, S. 195, Fig. 87
Olney, Bucks 76
Ormskirk, Lancs 170
Orrery, Earl of 33, 56
Ossory, Lady 75, 181
Owen, Robert 143, 169–70, 174
Oxford 27, 80–1, 135, 171
Oxfordshire 130, 135, 151, 185

Paisley 194–5
Papendiek, Mrs 182, 183–4
Parasols, umbrellas 100, 101, 171
   umbrella and walking stick 101
Paris 19, 33–6, 50, 63, 65, 156–7, 161, 162, 169
Pattens 100–1, 109, 121, 131–2
Pennant, T. 141
Pepys, S. 52, 122, 149
   Mrs P. 132
Petticoats, part of dress, *passim*
   quilted p. 43, 65, 70, 72, 116, 118, 119, 133, 159, 163, 166, 197, 198
   under p. 70, 118, 132, 147
Physicians 91
Place, F. 164–5, 198
Plymouth 96
Pompadour, Mme de 34
Portland, Duke of 20, 37
   Duchess of 37, 181
Poulton, W. 135
Poyntz, Miss (Lady Spencer) 15, 43
Preston, Elizabeth 185
Purefoy, Elizabeth 67–70, 74, 106, 108, 207
   Henry 65–7, 106, 140, 164, 207
Purses 133, 183
Pyne, W. H. 146, 150

Queensberry, Duchess of 15, 52

Ready-made clothes 146, 166, 173, 176, 185
Reynolds, Sir J. 40, 201
Richardson, S. 25, 70, 111, 115, 177, 181, 204
Riding habits (W) 22, 52–4, 65, 75, 77, 79, 98–9, 160, 165–6, 171, 203, Figs 26, 27
  habit shirt 79
  r. greatcoat 99
  joseph 40
  r. skirt 54
Riverstone, Lord 156
Robinson, Fredk. 21, 24, 31–2, 34, 39, 56, 156
Rochefoucauld, F. de la 34, 59, 103
Romney, G. 11
Rousseau, J.-J. 204
Rubens, Sir P. 37, 39–40, 201

Salusbury, John 75–6, 82, 171
Sandby, P. 146
Sash (M) 68
Sash (W) 28, 44
Sash (C) 205
Saussure, C. de 34, 48, 55, 88–9, 158
Scarborough 101
Scotland 131, 136, 176–7, 192, 194–5
Second-hand clothes 108–114, 146, 154, 166, 179–80, 185
Shalstone, Bucks 65, 106, 208
Shawl, scarf-shawl, mourning scarf 60, 114, 119, 150, 178
  plaid 131
Sheridan, Betsy 28, 38, 56, 60, 100, 193
Shifts (W) 42, 65, 118, 133, 146, 147, 154, 155, 177, 197–8
Shirts (M) 72, 82, 90–1, 92, 95–6, 134, 136, 138, 147, 154, 166, 176, 183, 187, 197–8
Shoes (M) 76, 81, 90, 92, 96, 134, 136, 138, 148, 154, 171
  shoes and clogs 96
  clogs 149
  mourning s. 23
  nailed shoes 149
  wooden slippers 81
Shoes (W) 60, 65, 76, 109, 116, 118, 120, 122, 146, 148, 154, 155, 171–2
  clogs 65, 109, 132
  mourning s. 23, 85
Shoemakers 76, 89, 171
Sleeves (M) sep. 95
Smith, Charlotte 126, 177
Smock, *see* Frock (M)
Smollett, T. 33, 92, 100, 102, 114, 120, 168
Smuggling 190

Somerset 79–80, 136
Spa 99, 101
Spain 34, 156
Spatterdashes 69
Sport, outdoor recreations 55, 59, 65, 67, 203
  bathing 99–101
  fishing 59, 75, 81
  gardening 44, 81
  hunting and coursing 59, 67, 81
  racing 58, 76
  riding 52–4, 55, 56, 58, 67, 69, 75, 98, 101, 138
  shooting 55, 58, 75, 76
  walking 48–50, 55, 59, 75, 79, 98, 100–1
Spurs 56, 69, 134, 135
Stays (W) 10, 36, 41, 121, 122, 143, 146, 147, 154, 155, 160, 170, 171, 176, 198, 205
  staymakers 170, 171
Stays (bands) 14, 15, 16
Steele, R. 64
Stockings (M) 31, 58, 69, 81, 92, 96, 134, 136, 138, 146, 147, 149, 154, 174, 176, 177, 179, 184
Stockings (W) 65, 109, 116, 118, 120, 146, 147, 148, 151, 154, 155, 163, 173, 174, 176, 177
Stomacher (W) 14, 15, 18, 26, 34, 75, 85, 120
Stormont, Lord 29
  Lady 52
Stourbridge fair 124, 178–9
Strutt, Elizabeth 112
Stuart, Lady Louisa 19, 180, 195
Stubbs, G. 127, 144, Figs 62, 63
Suit (M) 21, 28–9, 31, 32, 62, 64, 67, 80, 82, 88, 91, 92, 94, 95, 98, 107, 134–5, 137, 140, 154, 155, 156, 164, 170, 179, 188
  skeleton s. (boy's) 205
Suit (W) 71, 77, 115, 133, 155, 170, 185
Sumptuary laws 186–7
Swaddling bands, clothes 158, 204–5
Swift, J. 46, 122
Sword 21, 55, 58, 82, 88
  mourning s. 23, 62, 89

Tailoring, tailors 34, 52, 62, 67, 160, 163–6, 169–70, 171, 210, Fig. 82
Talbot, Catherine 185, 186, 203
Textiles
  Cotton, calico, muslin, *passim*
  chintz, printed cotton 45, 68, 70, 77, 81, 113, 118, 120, 130, 150, 172, 189, 191–2, 193
  Dutch ch. 193
  Indian ch. 99, 189–192, 194
  corduroy 165

dimity, Indian 77
muslin, Canterbury 78, 195
m. India 28, 101
nankeen 52, 171
velveret, velveteen, Manchester
    velvet 75, 81, 107, 178, 189
marseilles quilting, marcella 96, 178
Cotton industry 191–2, 194–5
Linen, *passim*
cambric 35, 65, 82, 116, 118, 197
canvas 100, 140, 183
Doulace 176
drill 140
gauze 38, 61, 82, 111, 183
Ghenting 176
harden 173
Holland, Garlick Holland 65, 91, 116,
    176
Irish l. 95, 132, 134, 183, 193, 197
Osnaburgh 176
printed linen 72, 77, 118, 147, 173,
    176, 192, 193
Scotch l. 118, 176, 197
Linen industry 192, 194–5, 197
Hemp, Suffolk 183
Silk, silk satin, *passim*
alamode, mode 60, 70, 131
bombazine 23, 60, 77, 82, 85, 159,
    174
brocade 15, 18, 20, 28, 74, 89, 189,
    194
clouded satin 78
crape 36
damask 16, 20, 28, 43, 45–6, 65, 70,
    74, 77, 80, 118, 133, 158, 184
ducape 78
flowered s. (woven or emb.) 18, 28,
    43, 77, 159
gauze, tiffany g. tiffany 20, 28, 61, 158,
    184
lustring, lutestring 16, 20, 36, 60, 70,
    72, 77, 80, 158, 193
figured l. 77
mantua silk 118
paduasoy 20, 77–8, 115, 158
painted s. 180–1, 190
persian 44, 158
Spitalfields 132
tabby 42, 60, 77
watered t. 77
flowered t. 159
taffeta, taffety 77, 126
tissue, gold or silver 13, 14, 15–6, 19,
    23–4, 29, 89
velvet 14, 20,'21, 28, 95, 99
'widow's' s. 61
Silk industry 189, 194
Wool, cloth, worsted, *passim*
baize 95, 174
Bath coating 81, 166

calamanca, callimanco 85, 88, 116,
    132–3, 136, 138, 159, 174, 187, 197,
    198
camlet 52, 77, 121, 159, 164, 170, 174, 198
cantaloon 174
damask 45, 133, 174, 198
Denmark satin 96
drugget 136, 174, 187, 188, 198
duffle 131
duroy 198
flannel 47, 95, 118, 132, 143, 146, 147,
    149, 150, 174, 178
florant, florinet 95, 96
homespun 116, 118
Kendal cotton 198
kersey 122, 188, 197, 198
moleskin 96, 166
plush 107, 134
prunella 75
russet 116
serge 106, 174, 188, 198
shag, shagreen 96, 135, 166, 174, 188
shalloon 136, 174, 187, 198
stuff 38, 77, 88, 112, 143, 147, 148,
    154, 174, 185,186, 195
double st. 95
flowered st. 77
printed st. 193
swanskin 132
tammy, taminy 119, 133
vicuna 31, 156
wildebore 85
Mixed fabrics
alapeen 68
burdett 174
cherry-derry 118
crape, Norwich crape, mourning
    crape 23, 61, 82, 118, 159, 174, 185,
    198
dimity, dimothy 68, 79, 120, 122, 197
figured d. 176
fustian 76, 77, 134, 140, 149, 174, 189
jennet 178
linsey-woolsey 109, 116, 127, 144,
    154, 198
poplin 21, 23, 31, 60, 77, 174
Embroidery 15–6, 20, 21, 22, 28, 29,
    31, 32, 33, 34, 43, 44, 69, 80, 89, 113,
    114, 161, 181–2, 295, Figs 17, 85
Dresden work 114
professional embroiderers 20, 162
Lace 19, 35, 61, 65, 72, 89, 99, 113,
    114, 118, 133, 157, 158, 161, 162, 163,
    174, 176, 177, 190, 191
Bath lace 28
blond 36, 74, 75, 111, 114
silver lace 160–1
netting 182
lace (gold and silver binding) 33, 52,
    67, 89, 105, 106, 107, 109, 116, 135, 170

Lacemakers, lace merchants, lace shops 19, 67, 152, 162–3, 170, 191
  Ribbon 35, 49, 61, 85, 120, 122, 126, 127, 149, 157, 161, 171, 172, 173, 179
  Trimmings 10, 15, 18–9, 26, 28, 34, 67, 74–5, 78, 99, 158, 160–2, 163, 173, 181
Thrale, Mrs 162, 168
Tilborgh, G. van 123
Tippet 34, 36, 70, 80, 114, 173, 181
  ermine t. 70
  feather t. 114, 181
  fur t. 80
Travelling salesmen, Scotchmen 176–8, 200
Trousers, pantaloons 21, 205–7
Tucker 19, 116, 182
Tunbridge Wells 53, 99, 101, 102, 124

Uniform 57
  Windsor u. 21, Col. pl. 2

Vandyke, Sir A. 11, 38, 39, 40, 201
Verney, John 105
  Sir Ralph 105, 164
Veil 121
Victoria and Albert Museum 77

Wainwright, H. 132–3
Waistcoats (M) 20, 21, 23, 24, 31–2, 34, 56, 57, 58, 67, 72, 76, 80, 81, 82, 85, 89, 95, 96, 107, 108, 134, 135, 136, 138, 146, 147, 149, 154, 164, 166, 171, 181, 182, 185, 187, 197, 207
  quilted 56, 96
  sleeved 31, 149
  under-w. 47, 82, 95
  w. fronts 45, 178, Figs 9, 36
Waistcoats (W) 38, 42, 52, 79, 99, 122, 197, Fig. 15
Wales 149–151, 154, 188
Walpole, H. 38, 48, 132, 163, 181, 190
Warwickshire 136
Watch 88
Wedding clothes 13–4, 15, 19, 28, 39, 40, 42–3, 71, 72–4, 111, 118, 151, 161–2

Weepers 23, 63
Wendeborn, F. A. 94, 180
Westmorland 173
Weston Longeville, Norfolk 79–82, 85, 171–2
Whip 56, 58
White, Gilbert 198
Wigs (M) 20, 21, 29–30, 46, 55, 64, 68–9, 75, 90, 96, 134, 135, 138, 166–7, 171
  bag w. 37, 89, 92
  bob w. 30, 56, 58
  two-curl bob 81, 143
  campaign w. 29–30, 65
  cut w. 108
  long or full-bottomed 29, 64, 90, 91, 109
  smug 90
  tie, tying 29–30, 56
Wigs (W) 52, 168
Willan, T. S. 173
Williamson, Rev. Edmond 72–5, 91
  Christian ('Tidy', Mrs Russel) 72–5, 82, 84, 91, 132, 158
  Mary (née Tipping) 72–5, 84–5, 167, 182, 193
  Talbot 23, 72–5, 82, 189, 194
Wills 113–4, 115, 118, 132–3, 135
Wiltshire 136, 152
Woodforde, Rev. James 22, 31, 79–82, 85, 96, 103, 107, 108, 112, 119, 121, 135, 138–9, 171–2, 177–8, 184, 189, 190
  Nancy 79–82, 85, 112, 118, 119, 171–2, 173, 182, 184, 185, 208
Wraxall, Sir N. W. 56–7, 204

York 96–7
Yorke, Agneta 38
  Sir Joseph 21, 36
  Mary 24, 50, 113, 140, 150
  Miss 19
Yorkshire 105, 136, 140, 146, 149, 150, 163, 174, 187, 188, 200
Young, Arthur 92, 154
Youngs, Jane 133